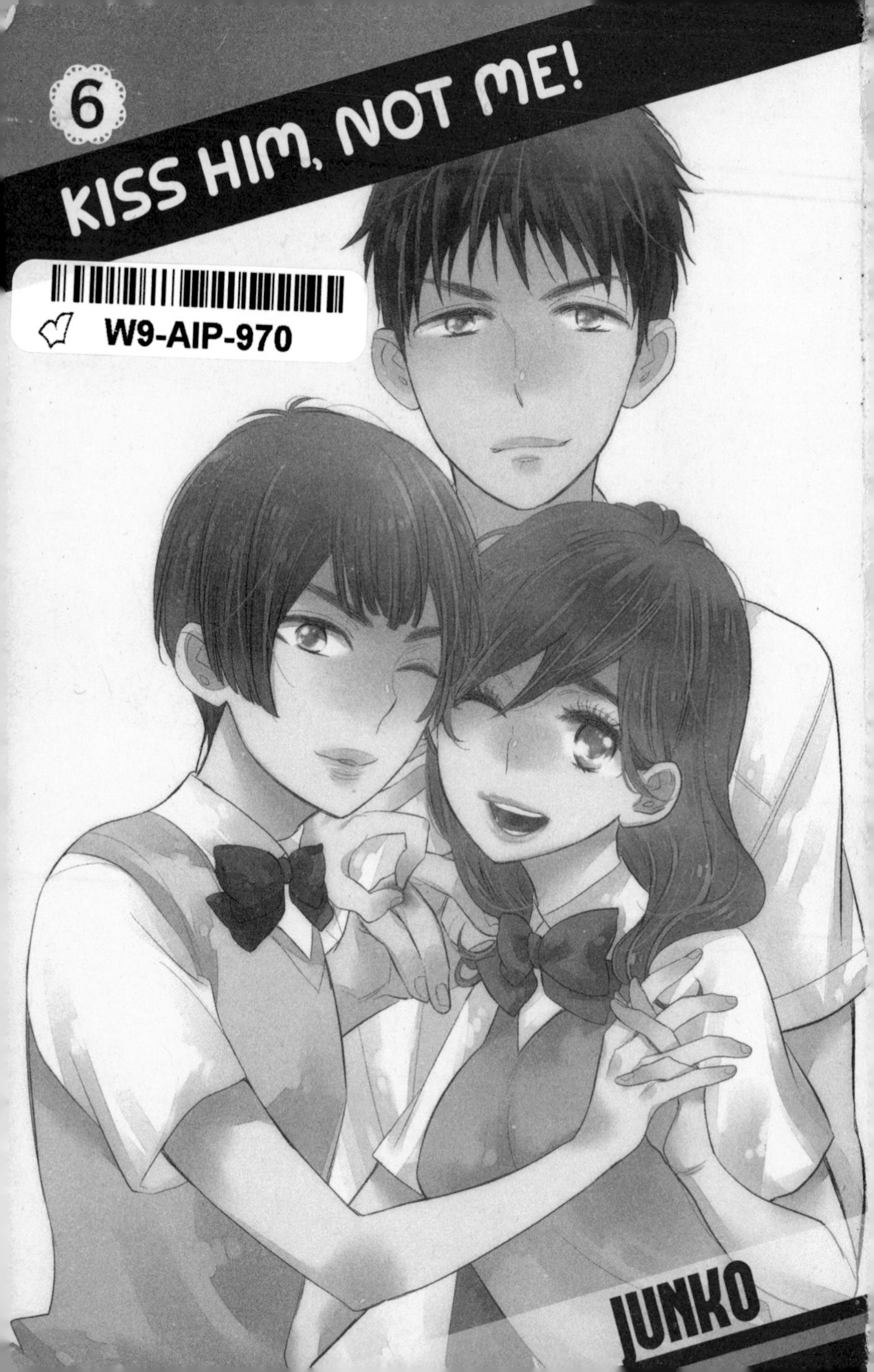
6
KISS HIM, NOT ME!
JUNKO

CONTENTS

STORY

THE VERY FIRST HISTORY CLUB PRESIDENT, MUTSUMI-SENPAI'S BROTHER, KAZUMA, COMES TO KAE'S SCHOOL AS A STUDENT TEACHER. KAZUMA'S PERSONALITY IS THE TOTAL OPPOSITE OF HIS LITTLE BROTHER, AND HE AGGRESSIVELY MAKES PASSES AT KAE.

MUTSUMI-SENPAI APPROACHES KAZUMA AND FIRMLY TELLS HIM TO "STAY AWAY FROM KAE," BUT HE FALLS VICTIM TO A MERCILESS COUNTER-ATTACK.

IN THE END, THE TWO BROTHERS SETTLE THE MATTER WITH A CARD GAME, AND MUTSUMI-SENPAI SOUNDLY WINS! HAVING REALIZED HIS FEELINGS, WILL MUTSUMI-SENPAI FINALLY MAKE A MOVE ON KAE...?!

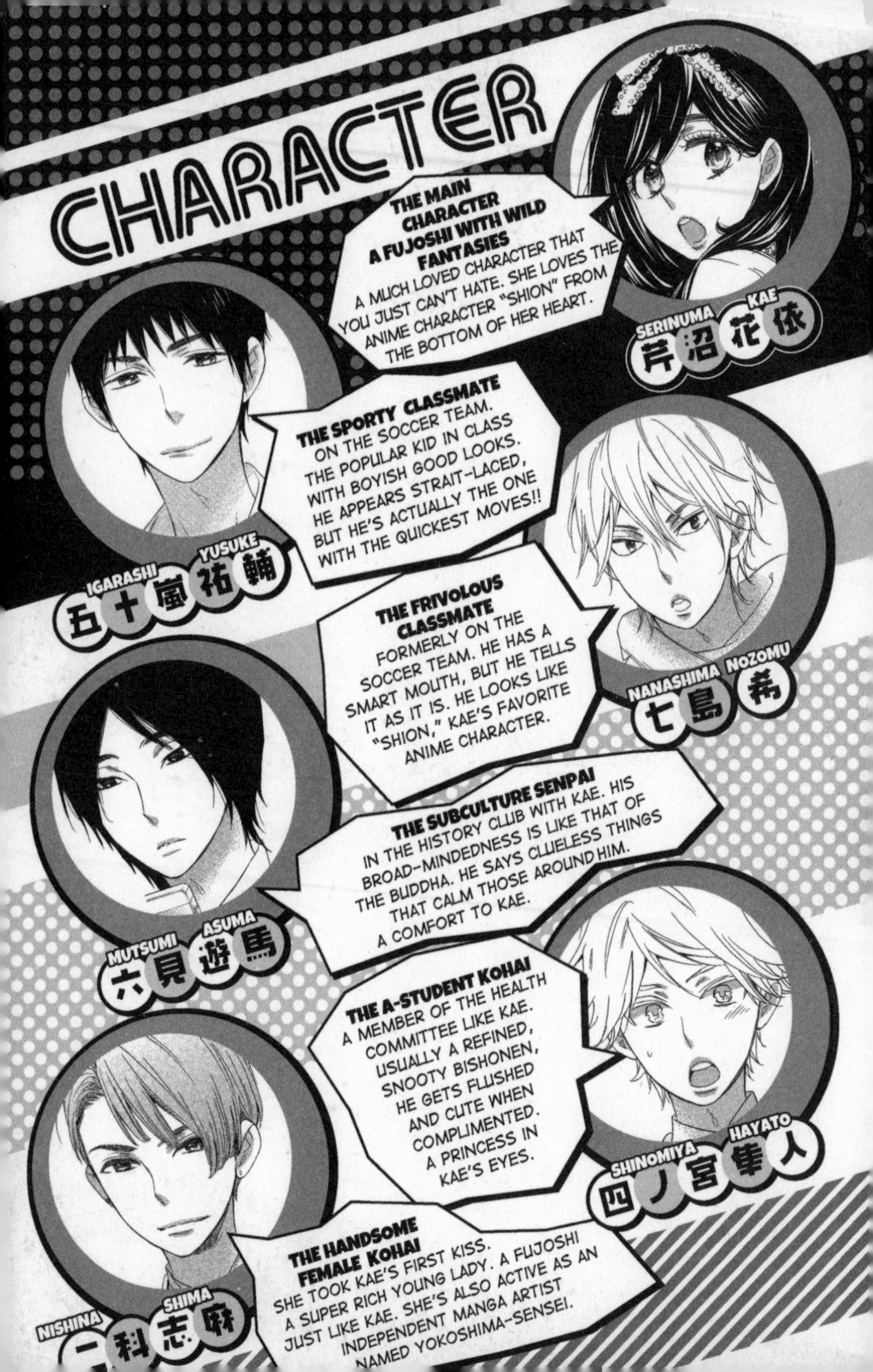
CHARACTER
THE MAIN CHARACTER A FUJOSHI WITH WILD FANTASIES
A MUCH LOVED CHARACTER THAT YOU JUST CAN'T HATE. SHE LOVES THE ANIME CHARACTER "SHION" FROM THE BOTTOM OF HER HEART.
SERINUMA KAE
芹沼花依
THE SPORTY CLASSMATE
ON THE SOCCER TEAM. THE POPULAR KID IN CLASS WITH BOYISH GOOD LOOKS. HE APPEARS STRAIT-LACED, BUT HE'S ACTUALLY THE ONE WITH THE QUICKEST MOVES!!
IGARASHI YUSUKE
五十嵐祐輔
THE FRIVOLOUS CLASSMATE
FORMERLY ON THE SOCCER TEAM. HE HAS A SMART MOUTH, BUT HE TELLS IT AS IT IS. HE LOOKS LIKE "SHION," KAE'S FAVORITE ANIME CHARACTER.
NANASHIMA NOZOMU
七島希
THE SUBCULTURE SENPAI
IN THE HISTORY CLUB WITH KAE. HIS BROAD-MINDEDNESS IS LIKE THAT OF THE BUDDHA. HE SAYS CLUELESS THINGS THAT CALM THOSE AROUND HIM. A COMFORT TO KAE.
MUTSUMI ASUMA
六見遊馬
THE A-STUDENT KOHAI
A MEMBER OF THE HEALTH COMMITTEE LIKE KAE. USUALLY A REFINED, SNOOTY BISHONEN, HE GETS FLUSHED AND CUTE WHEN COMPLIMENTED. A PRINCESS IN KAE'S EYES.
SHINOMIYA HAYATO
四ノ宮隼人
THE HANDSOME FEMALE KOHAI
SHE TOOK KAE'S FIRST KISS. A SUPER RICH YOUNG LADY. A FUJOSHI JUST LIKE KAE. SHE'S ALSO ACTIVE AS AN INDEPENDENT MANGA ARTIST NAMED YOKOSHIMA-SENSEI.
NISHINA SHIMA
二科志麻

KiSS HiM, NOT ME!

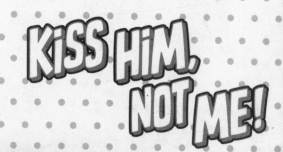

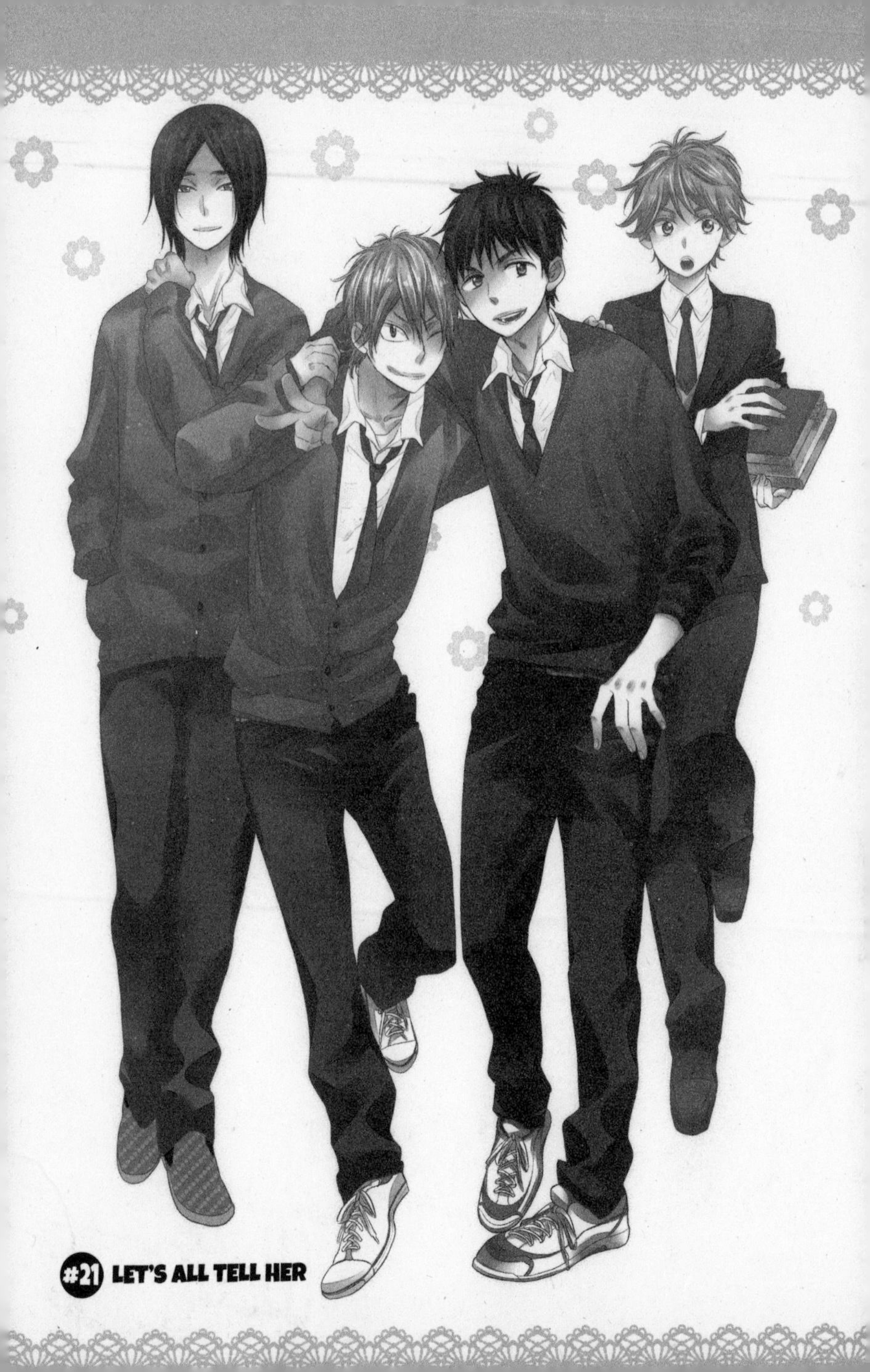

#21 LET'S ALL TELL HER

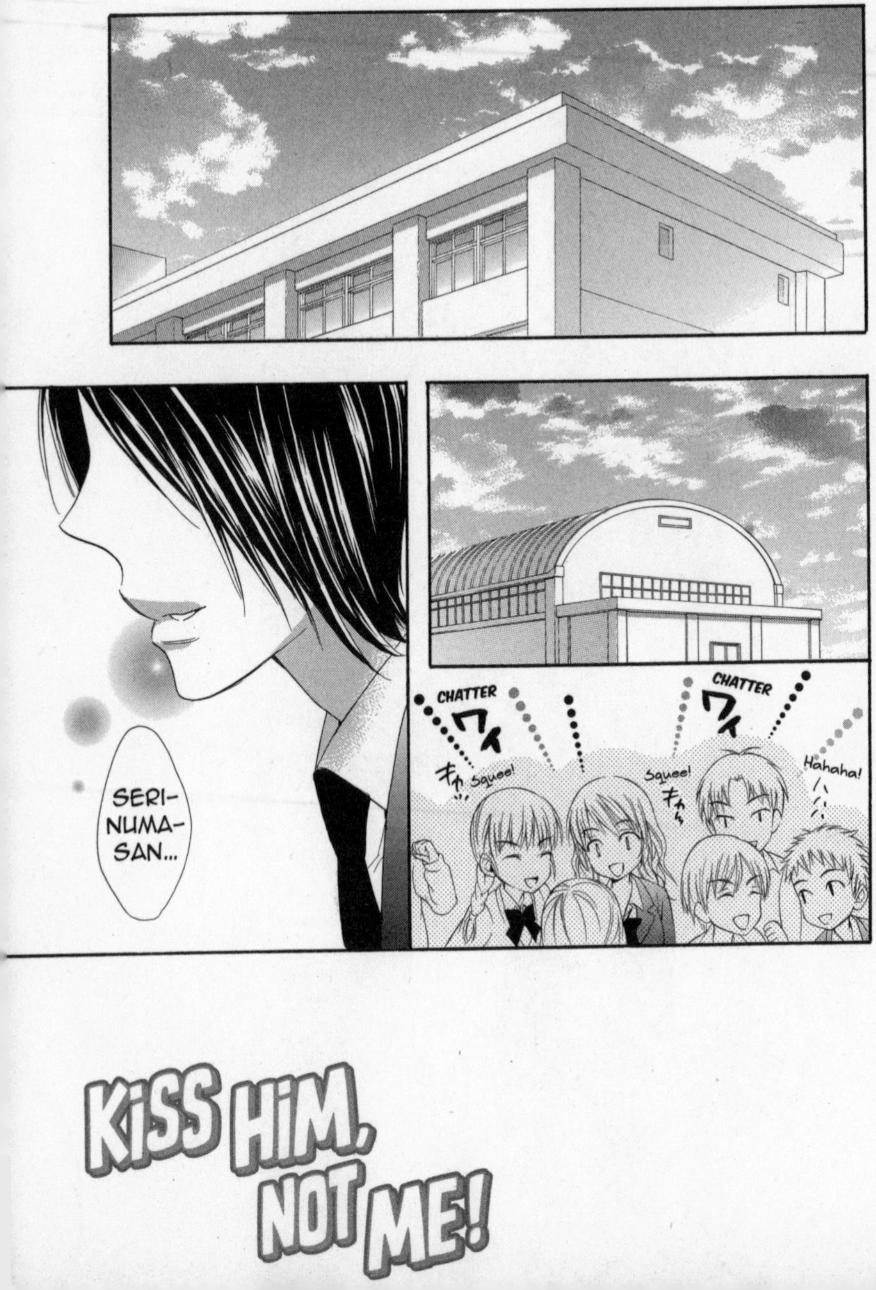
CHATTER
ワイ
Hahaha!
ハハハ
Squee!
キャ
CHATTER
ワイ
Squee!
キャ
SERI-NUMA-SAN...

KiSS HiM, NOT ME!

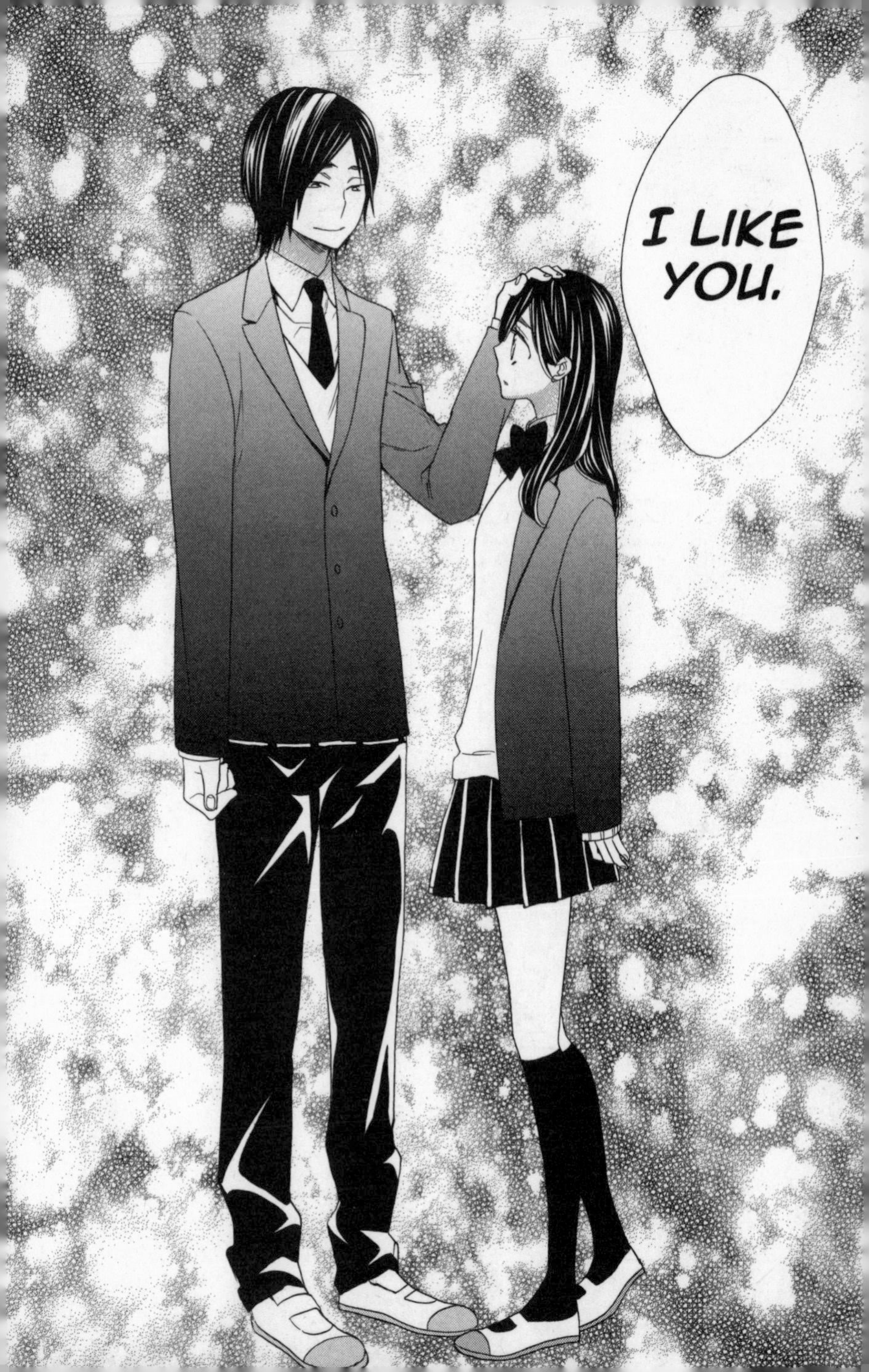
I LIKE YOU.

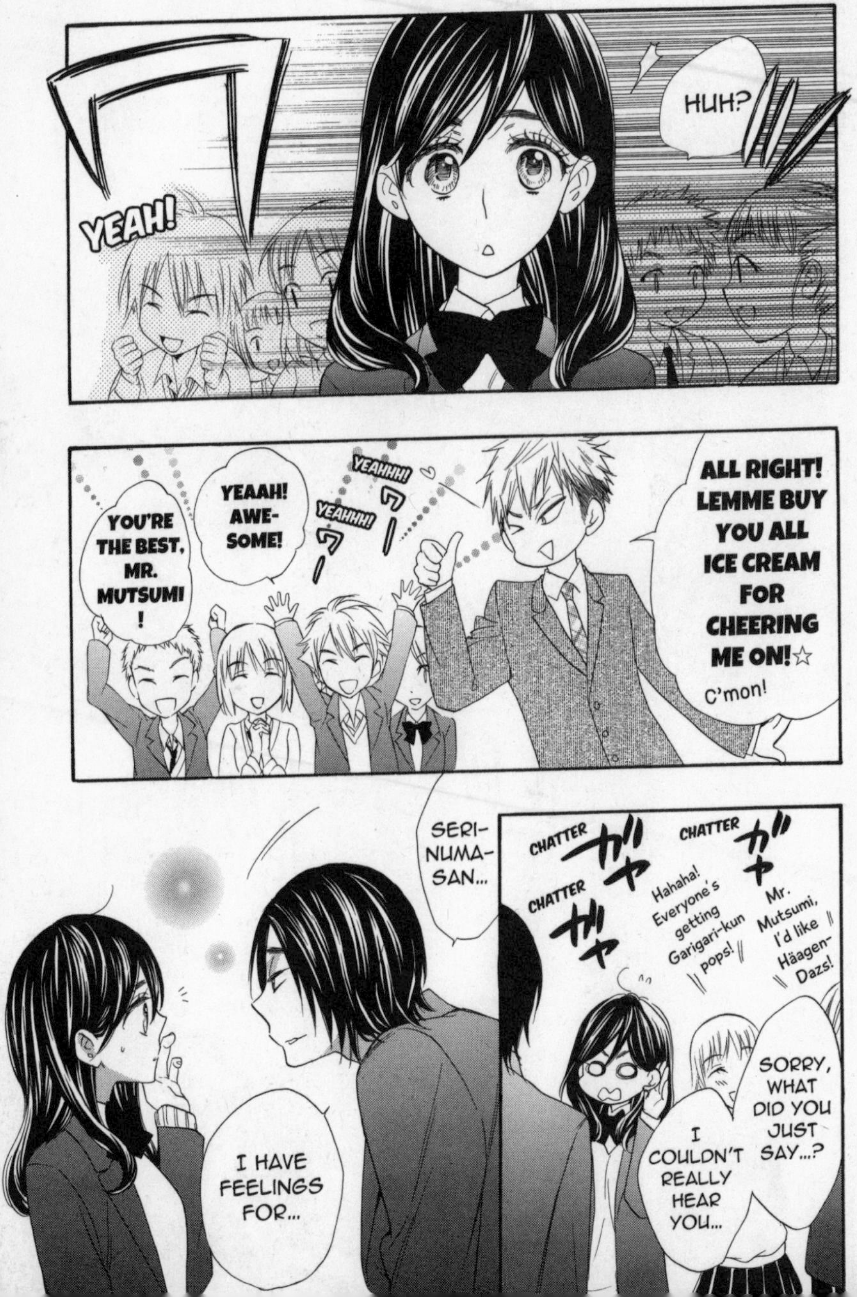
HUH?
YEAH!
ALL RIGHT! LEMME BUY YOU ALL ICE CREAM FOR CHEERING ME ON!☆
C'mon!
YEAHHH! ワー
YEAHHH! ワー
YEAAH! AWE-SOME!
YOU'RE THE BEST, MR. MUTSUMI!
CHATTER ガヤ
CHATTER ガヤ
CHATTER ガヤ
Mr. Mutsumi, I'd like Häagen-Dazs!
Hahaha! Everyone's getting Garigari-kun pops!
SORRY, WHAT DID YOU JUST SAY...?
I COULDN'T REALLY HEAR YOU...
SERI-NUMA-SAN...
I HAVE FEELINGS FOR...

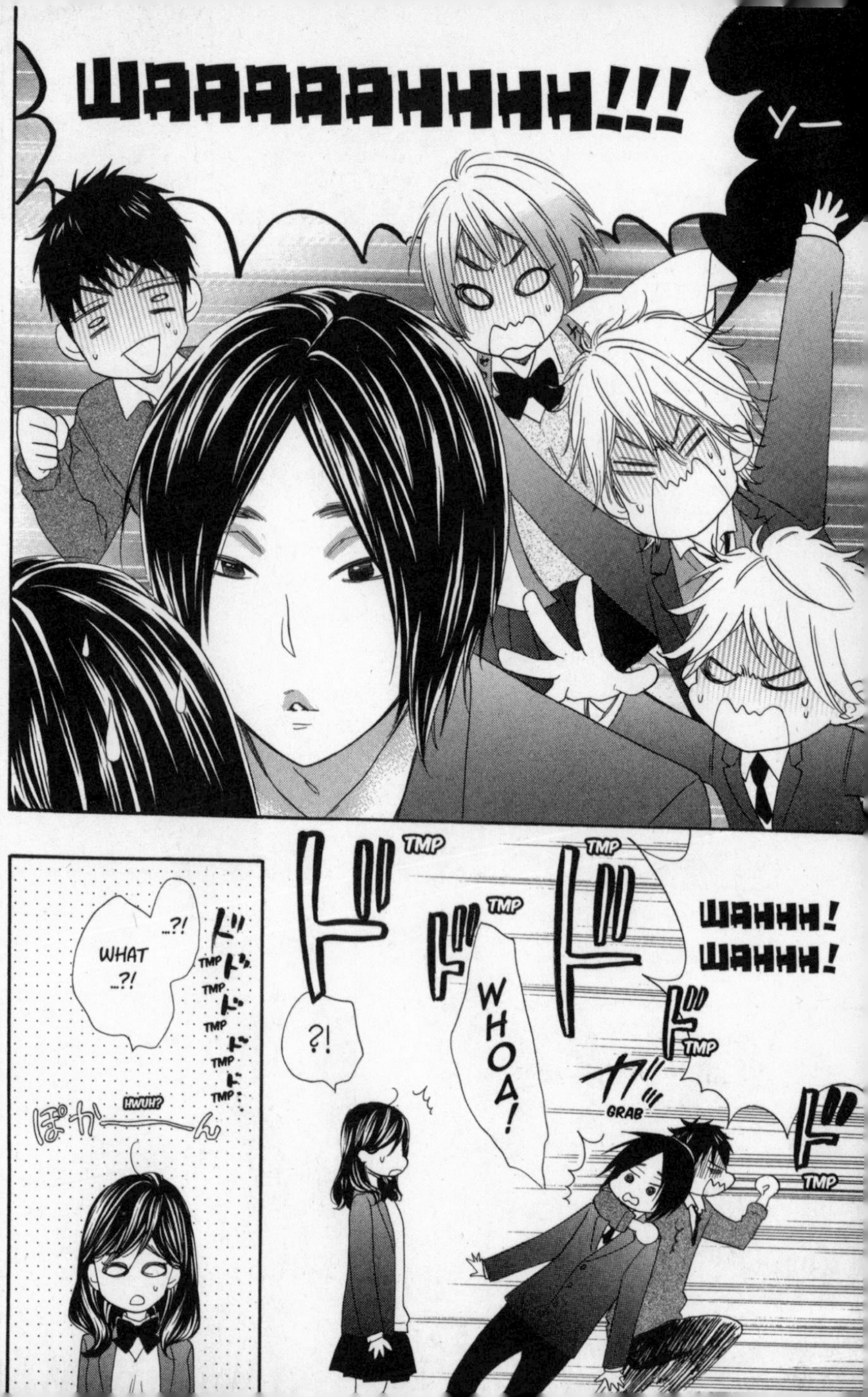
Y—
WAAAAAAHHHHH!!!
TMP
TMP
WAHHH! WAHHH!
TMP
WHOA!
?!
TMP
GRAB
TMP
...?! WHAT ...?!
TMP
TMP
TMP
TMP
TMP
HWUH?
ぽか〜ん

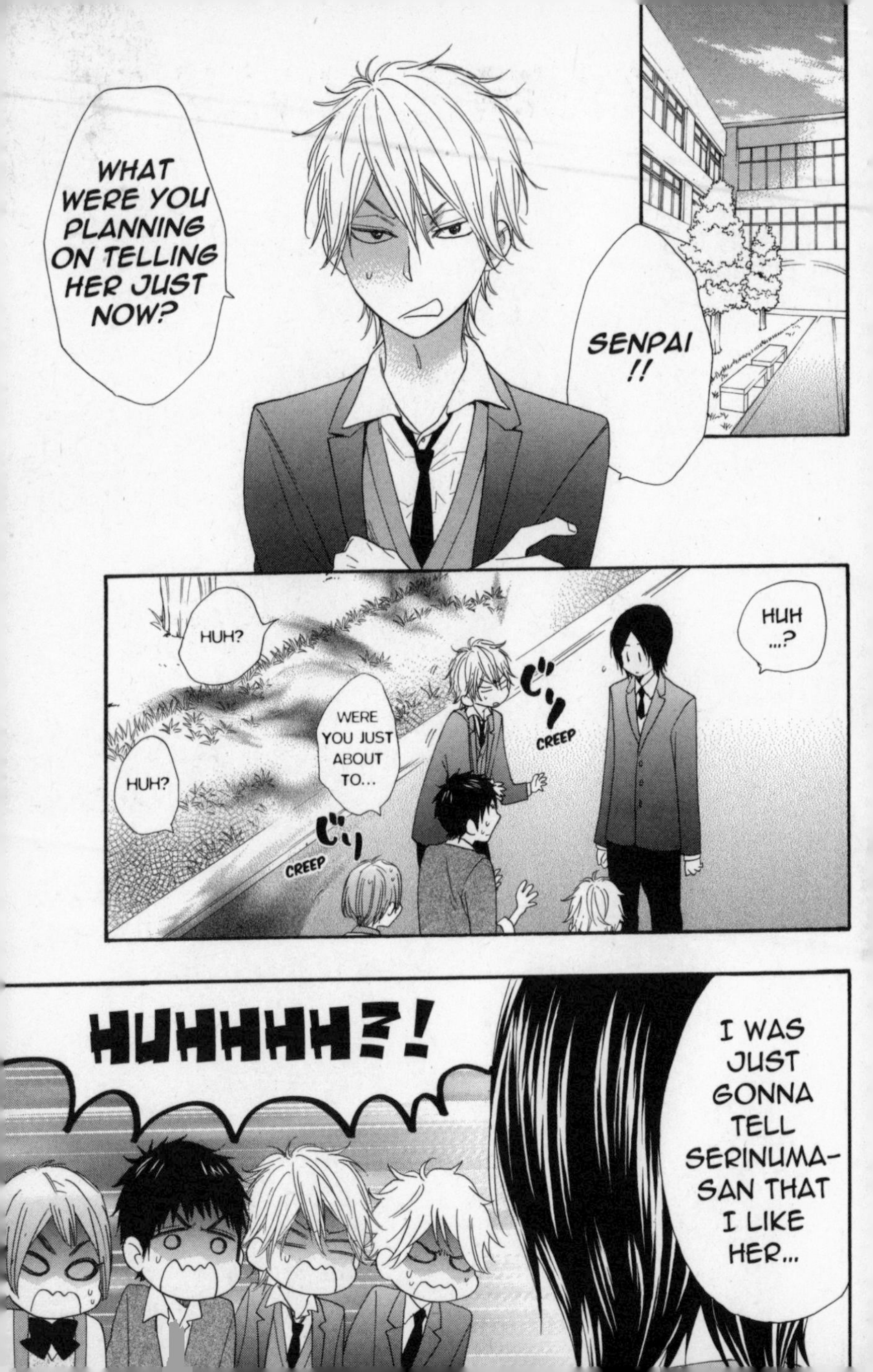
SENPAI !!
WHAT WERE YOU PLANNING ON TELLING HER JUST NOW?
HUH ...?
CREEP
WERE YOU JUST ABOUT TO...
HUH?
HUH?
CREEP
I WAS JUST GONNA TELL SERINUMA-SAN THAT I LIKE HER...
HUHHHH?!

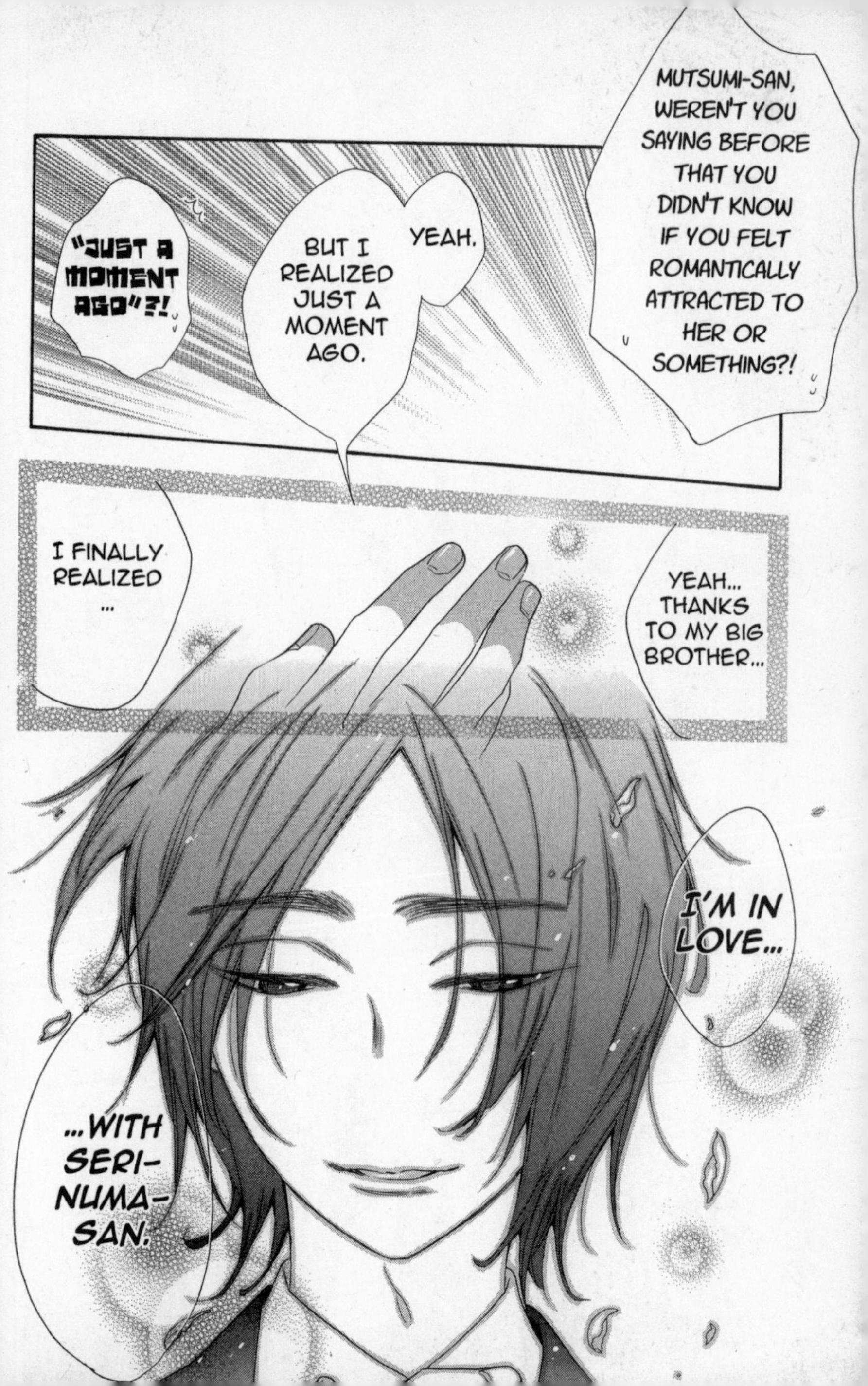
MUTSUMI-SAN, WEREN'T YOU SAYING BEFORE THAT YOU DIDN'T KNOW IF YOU FELT ROMANTICALLY ATTRACTED TO HER OR SOMETHING?!
YEAH.
BUT I REALIZED JUST A MOMENT AGO.
"JUST A MOMENT AGO"?!
YEAH... THANKS TO MY BIG BROTHER...
I FINALLY REALIZED ...
I'M IN LOVE...
...WITH SERI-NUMA-SAN.

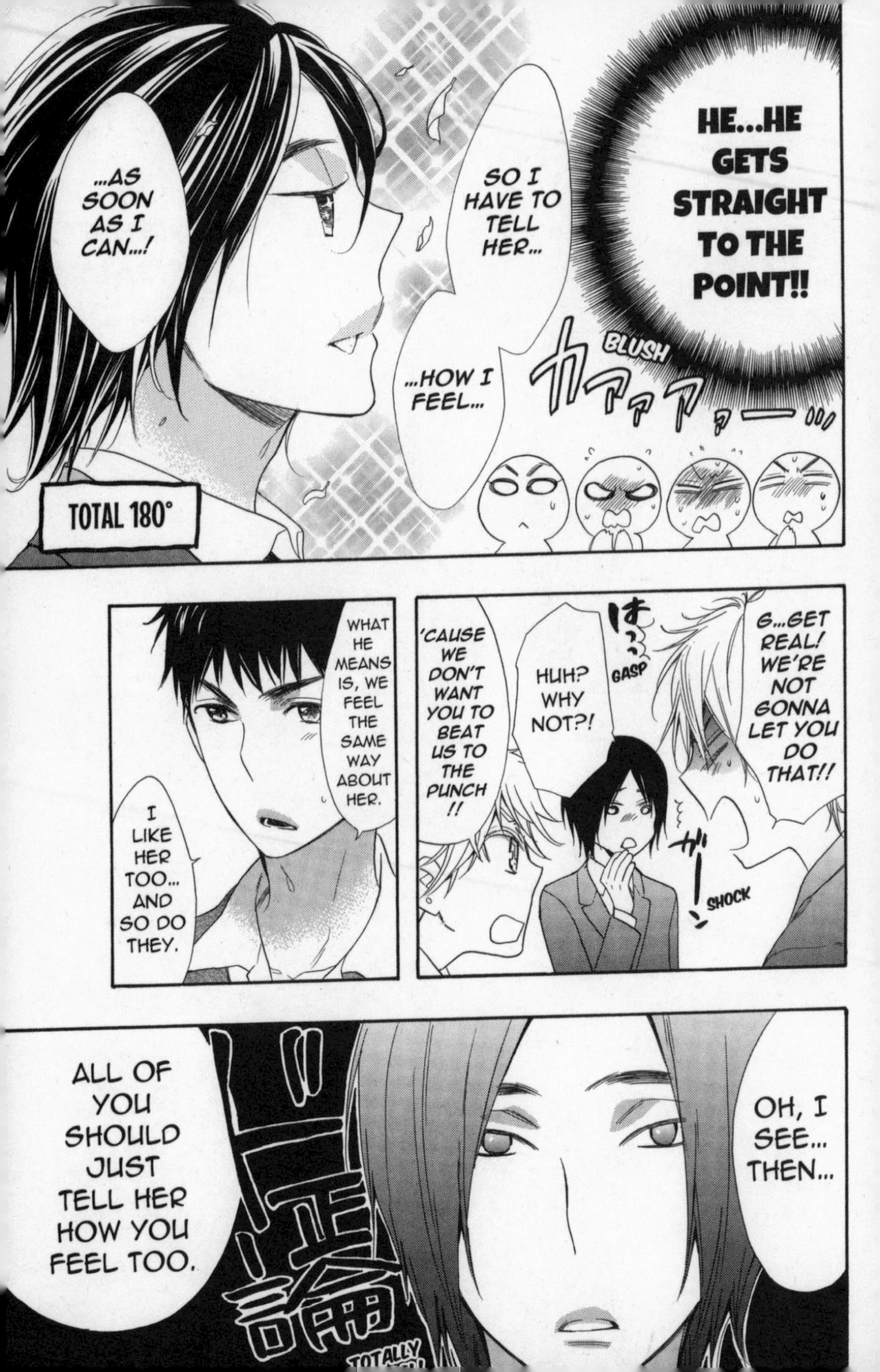
HE...HE GETS STRAIGHT TO THE POINT!!
BLUSH
SO I HAVE TO TELL HER...
...HOW I FEEL...
...AS SOON AS I CAN...!
TOTAL 180°
G...GET REAL! WE'RE NOT GONNA LET YOU DO THAT!!
SHOCK
GASP
HUH? WHY NOT?!
'CAUSE WE DON'T WANT YOU TO BEAT US TO THE PUNCH!!
WHAT HE MEANS IS, WE FEEL THE SAME WAY ABOUT HER.
I LIKE HER TOO... AND SO DO THEY.
OH, I SEE... THEN...
ALL OF YOU SHOULD JUST TELL HER HOW YOU FEEL TOO.
TOTALLY

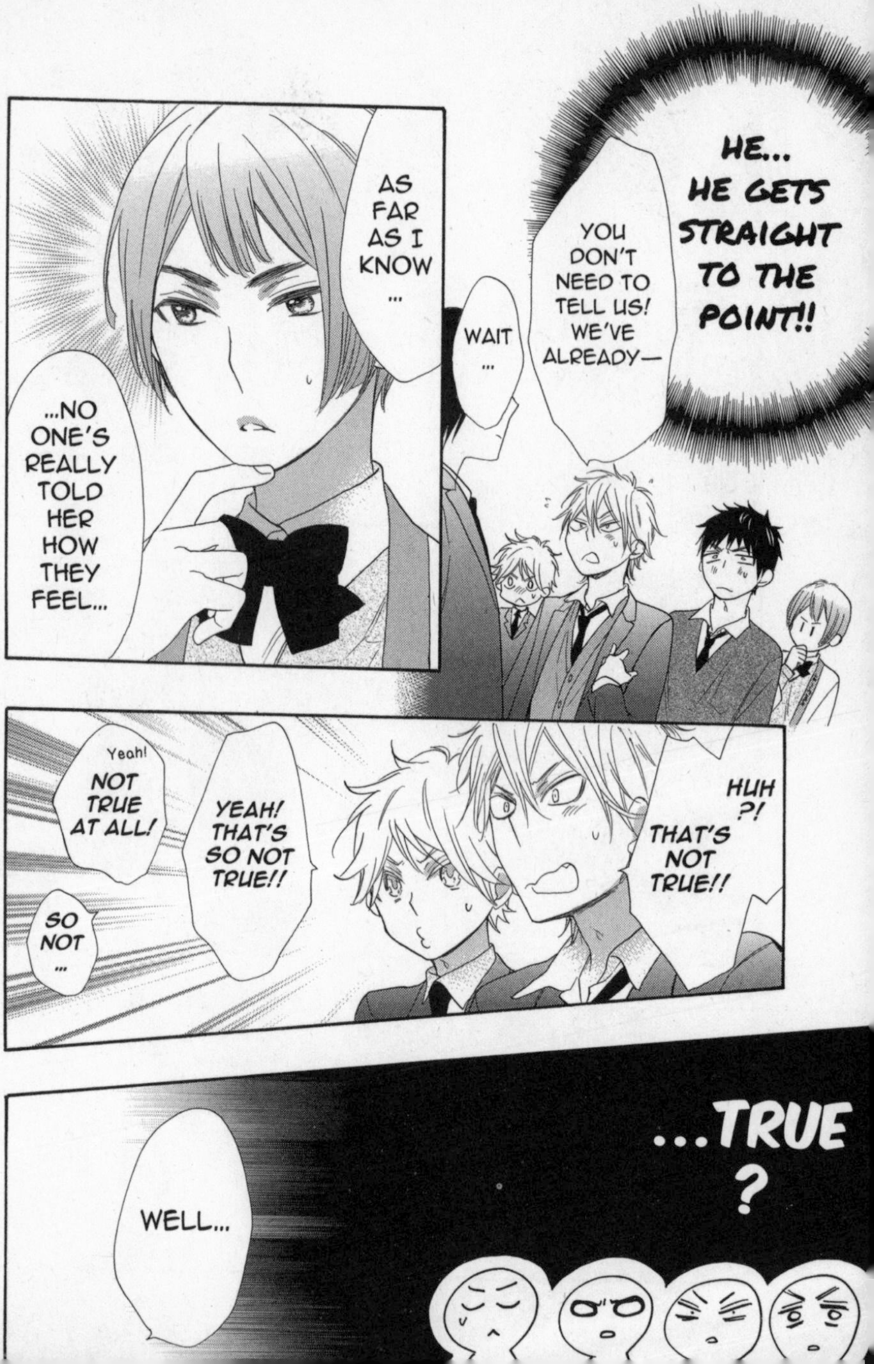
HE... HE GETS STRAIGHT TO THE POINT!!
YOU DON'T NEED TO TELL US! WE'VE ALREADY—
WAIT...
AS FAR AS I KNOW...
...NO ONE'S REALLY TOLD HER HOW THEY FEEL...
HUH?! THAT'S NOT TRUE!!
YEAH! THAT'S SO NOT TRUE!!
Yeah! NOT TRUE AT ALL!
SO NOT...
...TRUE?
WELL...

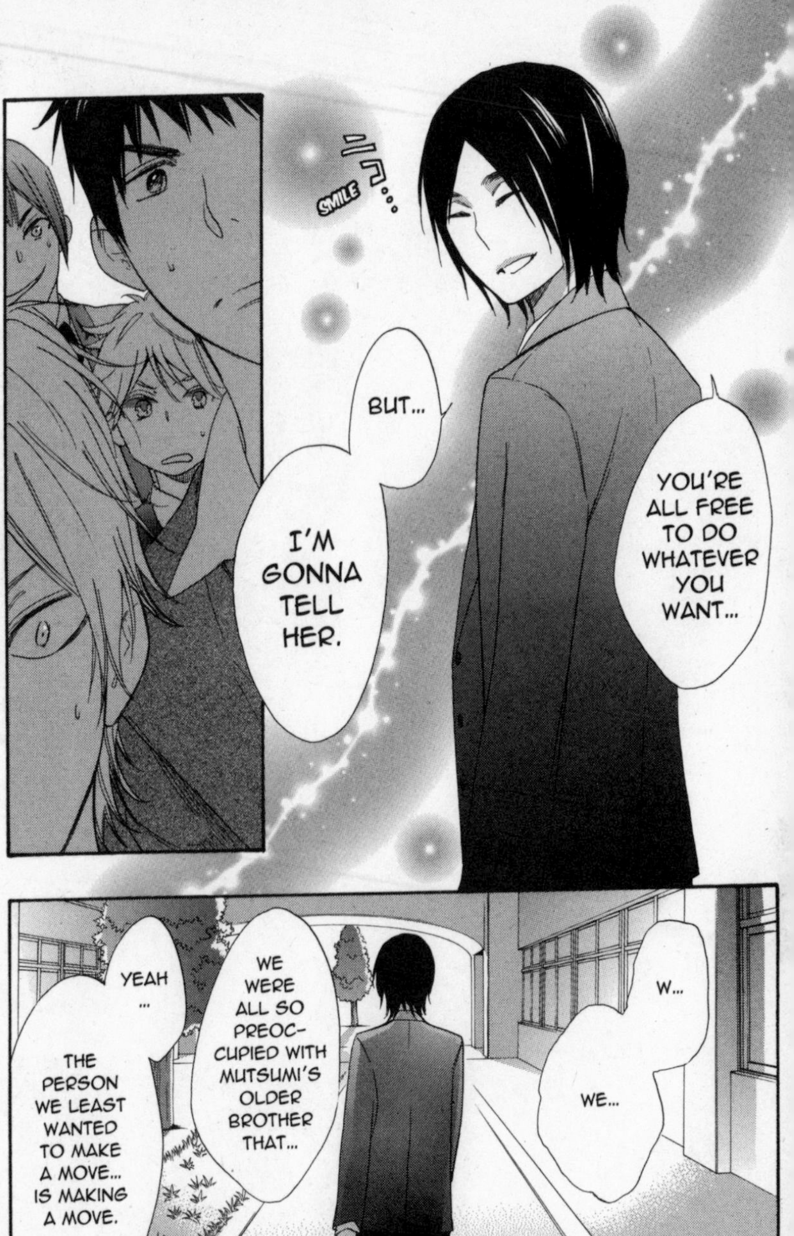
ニコ
SMILE
YOU'RE ALL FREE TO DO WHATEVER YOU WANT...
BUT...
I'M GONNA TELL HER.
W...
WE...
WE WERE ALL SO PREOCCUPIED WITH MUTSUMI'S OLDER BROTHER THAT...
YEAH ...
THE PERSON WE LEAST WANTED TO MAKE A MOVE... IS MAKING A MOVE.

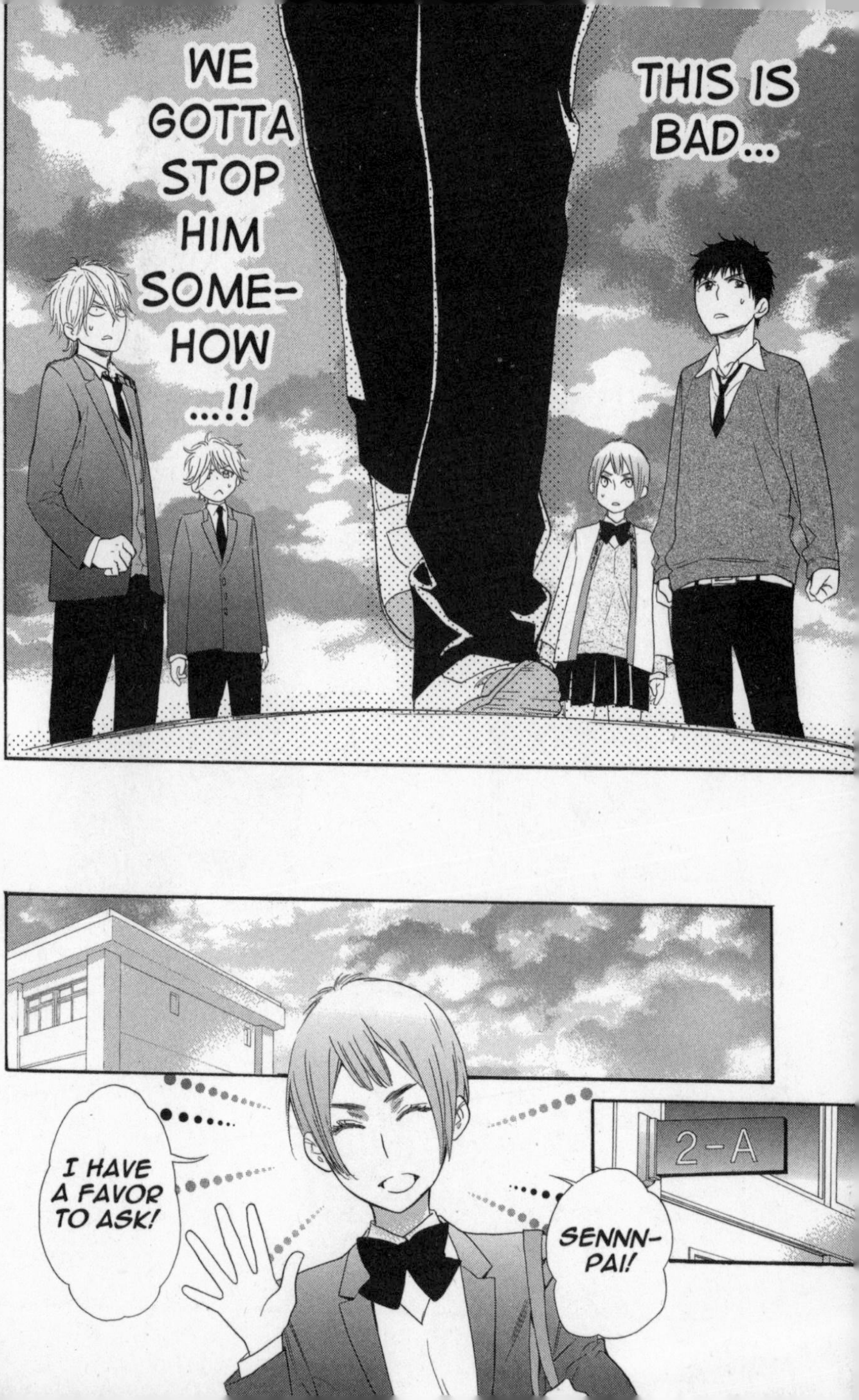
THIS IS BAD...
WE GOTTA STOP HIM SOME-HOW ...!!
2-A
SENNN-PAI!
I HAVE A FAVOR TO ASK!

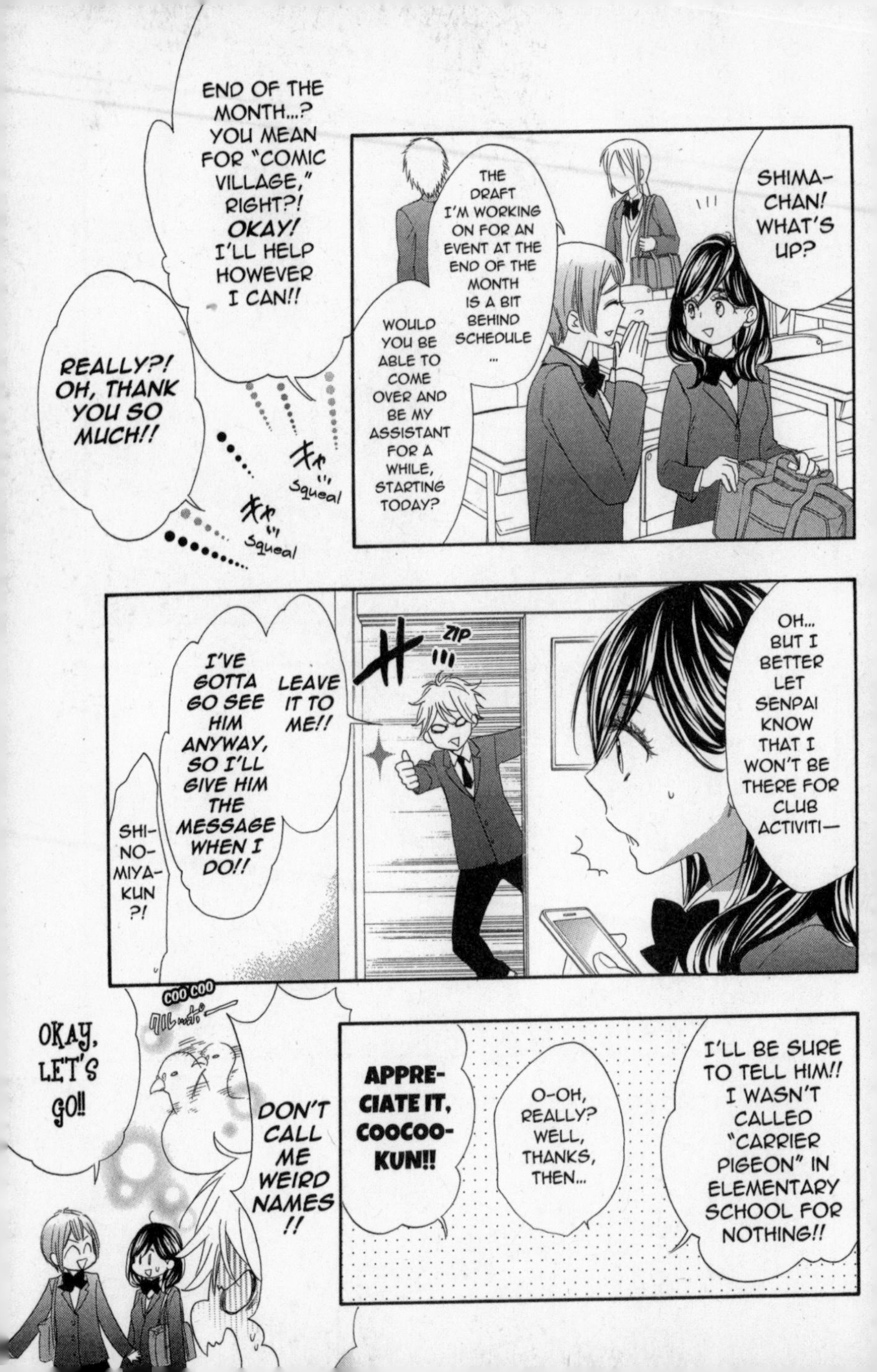
SHIMA-CHAN! WHAT'S UP?
THE DRAFT I'M WORKING ON FOR AN EVENT AT THE END OF THE MONTH IS A BIT BEHIND SCHEDULE ...
WOULD YOU BE ABLE TO COME OVER AND BE MY ASSISTANT FOR A WHILE, STARTING TODAY?
END OF THE MONTH...? YOU MEAN FOR "COMIC VILLAGE," RIGHT?! OKAY! I'LL HELP HOWEVER I CAN!!
REALLY?! OH, THANK YOU SO MUCH!!
キャ Squeal
キャ Squeal
OH... BUT I BETTER LET SENPAI KNOW THAT I WON'T BE THERE FOR CLUB ACTIVITI—
ZIP
LEAVE IT TO ME!!
I'VE GOTTA GO SEE HIM ANYWAY, SO I'LL GIVE HIM THE MESSAGE WHEN I DO!!
SHI-NO-MIYA-KUN?!
I'LL BE SURE TO TELL HIM!! I WASN'T CALLED "CARRIER PIGEON" IN ELEMENTARY SCHOOL FOR NOTHING!!
O-OH, REALLY? WELL, THANKS, THEN...
APPRE-CIATE IT, COOCOO-KUN!!
DON'T CALL ME WEIRD NAMES!!
COO COO
OKAY, LET'S GO!!

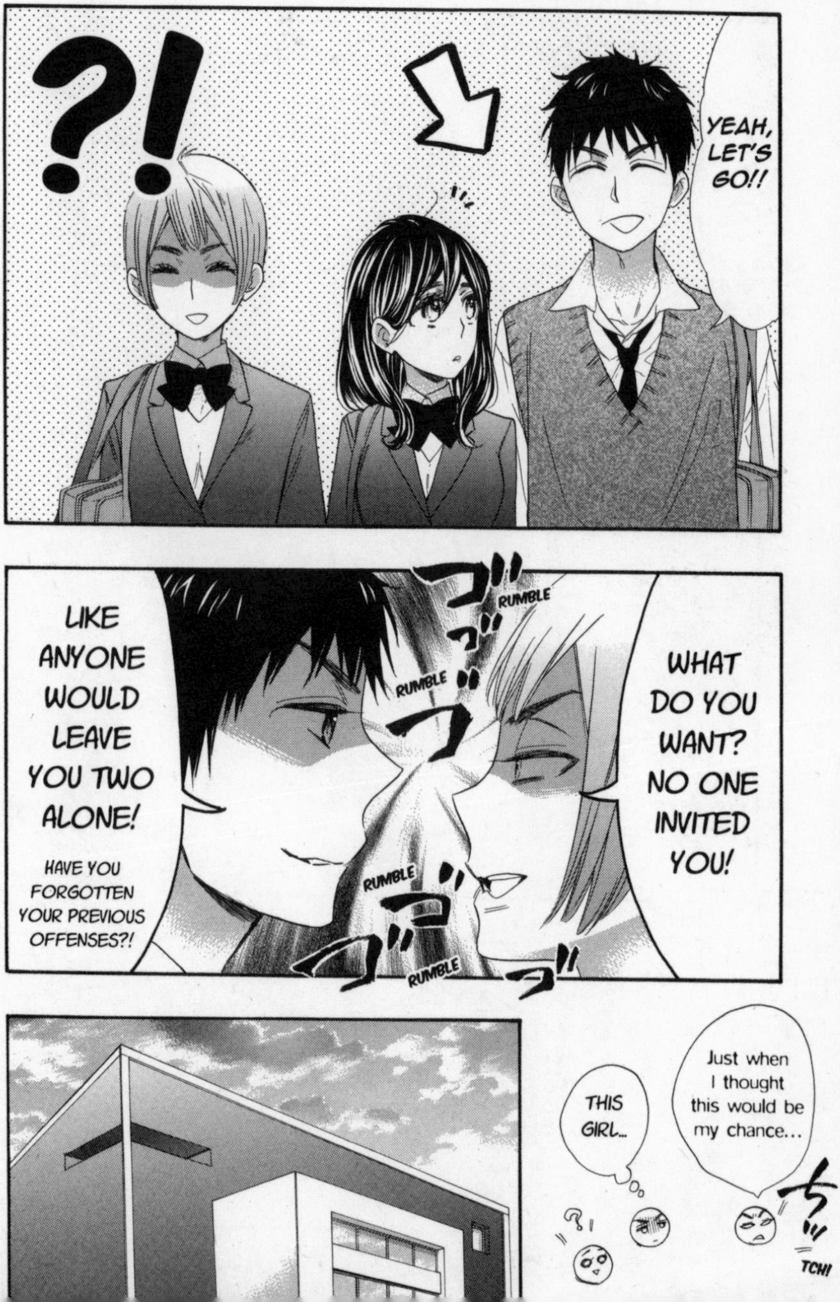
YEAH, LET'S GO!!
?!
WHAT DO YOU WANT? NO ONE INVITED YOU!
RUMBLE
RUMBLE
LIKE ANYONE WOULD LEAVE YOU TWO ALONE!
HAVE YOU FORGOTTEN YOUR PREVIOUS OFFENSES?!
RUMBLE
RUMBLE
Just when I thought this would be my chance...
TCH!
THIS GIRL...

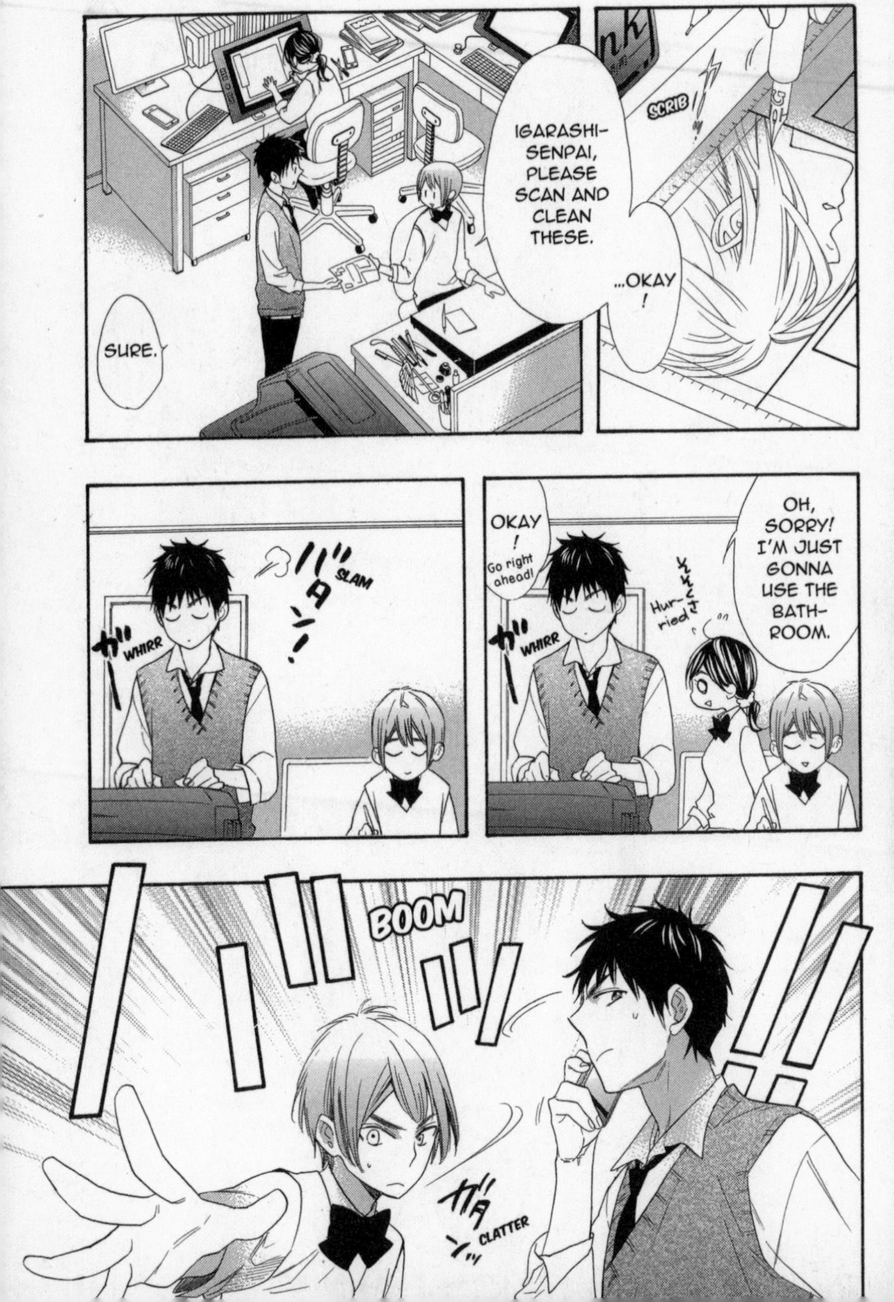
SCRIB
IGARASHI-SENPAI, PLEASE SCAN AND CLEAN THESE.
...OKAY!
SURE.
OH, SORRY! I'M JUST GONNA USE THE BATHROOM.
Hur-ried
OKAY! Go right ahead!
WHIRR
SLAM
WHIRR
BOOM
CLATTER

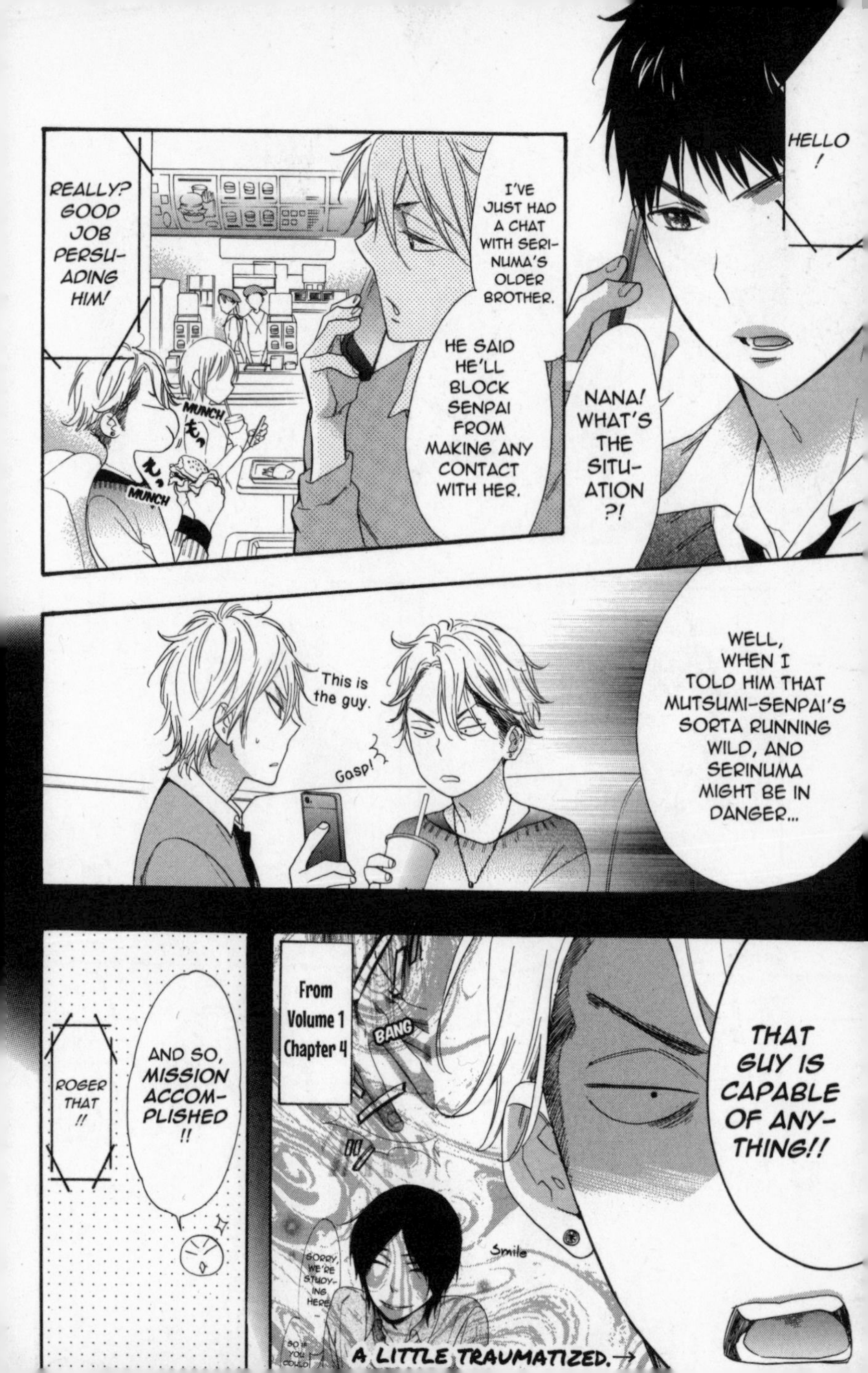
HELLO!
NANA! WHAT'S THE SITUATION?!
I'VE JUST HAD A CHAT WITH SERINUMA'S OLDER BROTHER.
HE SAID HE'LL BLOCK SENPAI FROM MAKING ANY CONTACT WITH HER.
REALLY? GOOD JOB PERSUADING HIM!
MUNCH
MUNCH
WELL, WHEN I TOLD HIM THAT MUTSUMI-SENPAI'S SORTA RUNNING WILD, AND SERINUMA MIGHT BE IN DANGER...
This is the guy.
Gasp!
THAT GUY IS CAPABLE OF ANYTHING!!
From Volume 1 Chapter 4
BANG
Smile
SORRY, WE'RE STUDYING HERE... SO IF YOU COULD
A LITTLE TRAUMATIZED.→
AND SO, MISSION ACCOMPLISHED!!
ROGER THAT!!

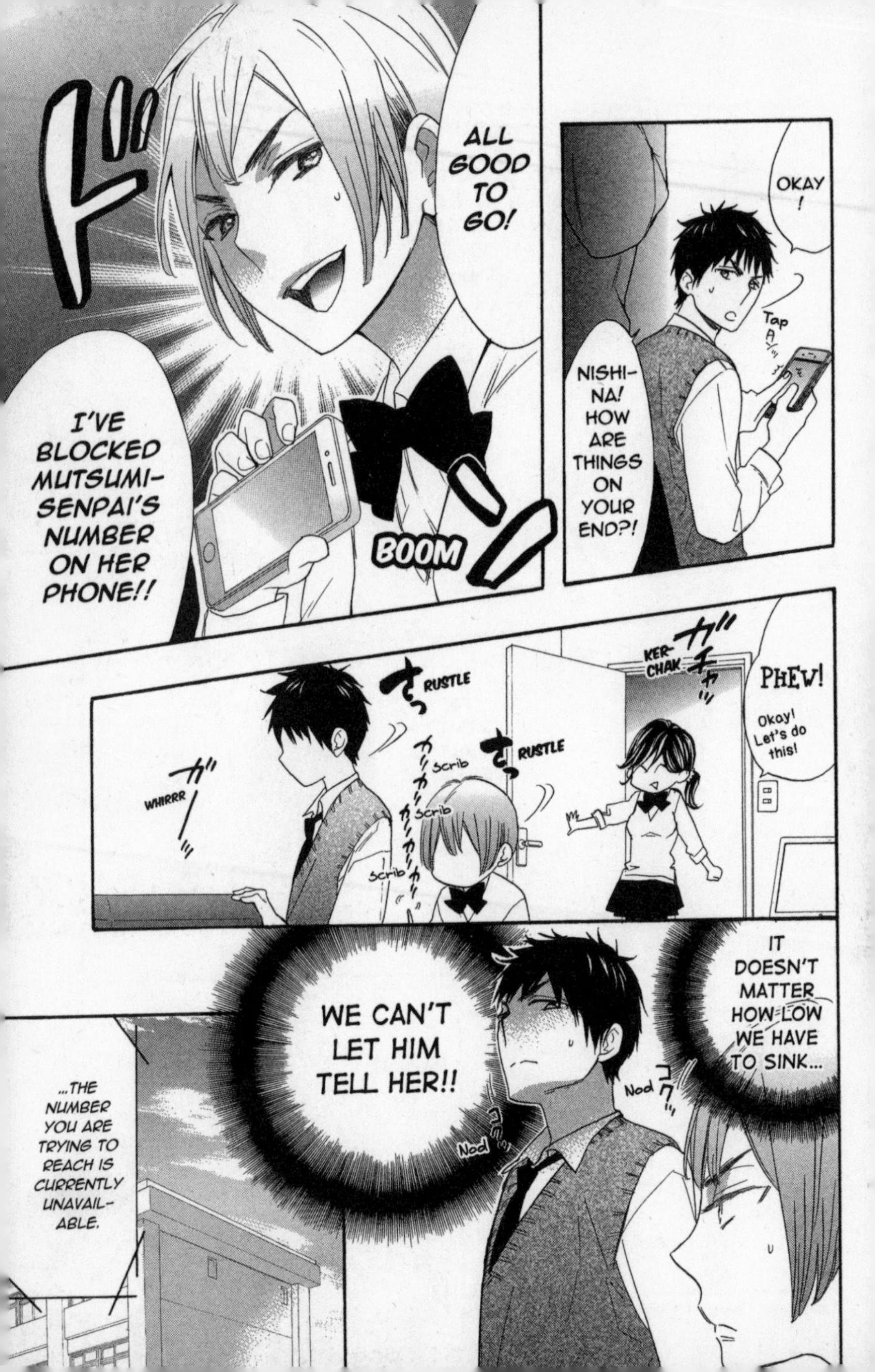
OKAY!
Tap
NISHINA! HOW ARE THINGS ON YOUR END?!
ALL GOOD TO GO!
I'VE BLOCKED MUTSUMI-SENPAI'S NUMBER ON HER PHONE!!
BOOM
PHEW!
Okay! Let's do this!
KER-CHAK
RUSTLE
RUSTLE
Scrib
Scrib
Scrib
WHIRRR
IT DOESN'T MATTER HOW LOW WE HAVE TO SINK...
Nod
WE CAN'T LET HIM TELL HER!!
Nod
...THE NUMBER YOU ARE TRYING TO REACH IS CURRENTLY UNAVAILABLE.

*Ono no Imoko: A Japanese diplomat in the late 6th and early 7th century.

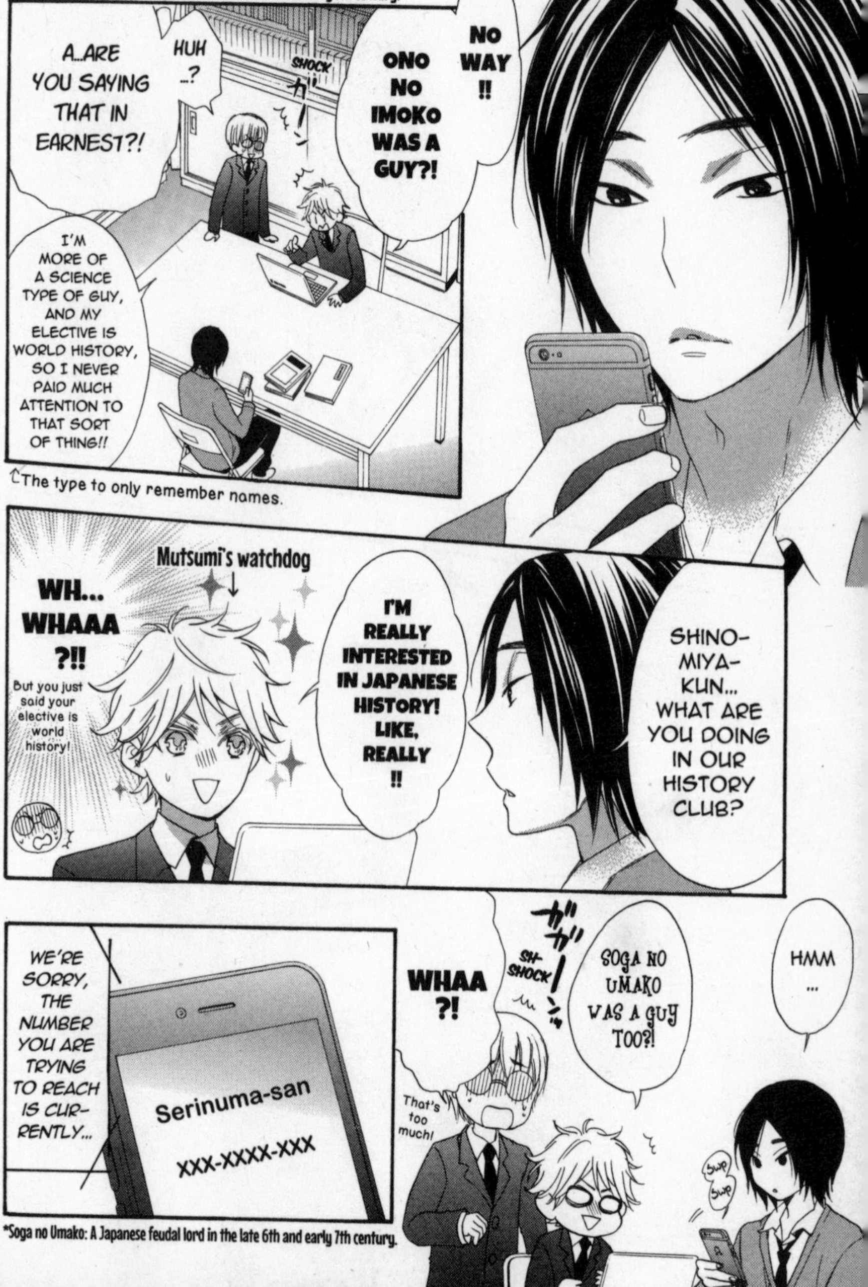
NO WAY!!
ONO NO IMOKO WAS A GUY?!
HUH...?
A...ARE YOU SAYING THAT IN EARNEST?!
SHOCK
I'M MORE OF A SCIENCE TYPE OF GUY, AND MY ELECTIVE IS WORLD HISTORY, SO I NEVER PAID MUCH ATTENTION TO THAT SORT OF THING!!
The type to only remember names.
SHINO-MIYA-KUN... WHAT ARE YOU DOING IN OUR HISTORY CLUB?
I'M REALLY INTERESTED IN JAPANESE HISTORY! LIKE, REALLY!!
Mutsumi's watchdog
WH... WHAAA?!!
But you just said your elective is world history!
HMM...
SOGA NO UMAKO WAS A GUY TOO?!
SH-SHOCK
WHAA?!
That's too much!
Swp
Swp
WE'RE SORRY, THE NUMBER YOU ARE TRYING TO REACH IS CUR-RENTLY...
Serinuma-san
XXX-XXXX-XXX

*Soga no Umako: A Japanese feudal lord in the late 6th and early 7th century.

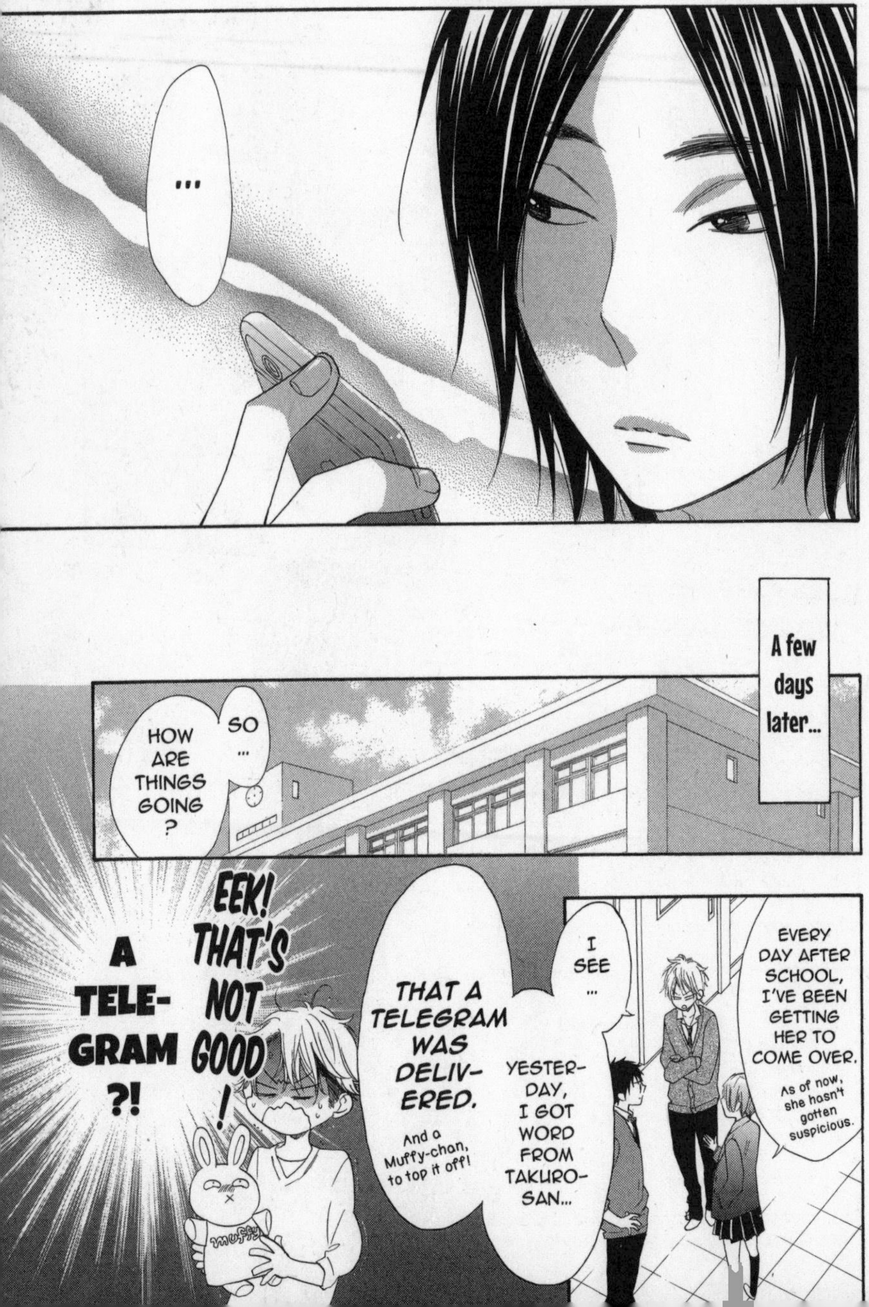
...
A few days later...
SO ...
HOW ARE THINGS GOING ?
EVERY DAY AFTER SCHOOL, I'VE BEEN GETTING HER TO COME OVER.
As of now, she hasn't gotten suspicious.
I SEE ...
YESTERDAY, I GOT WORD FROM TAKURO-SAN...
THAT A TELEGRAM WAS DELIVERED.
And a Muffy-chan, to top it off!
EEK! THAT'S NOT GOOD!
A TELEGRAM ?!
muffy

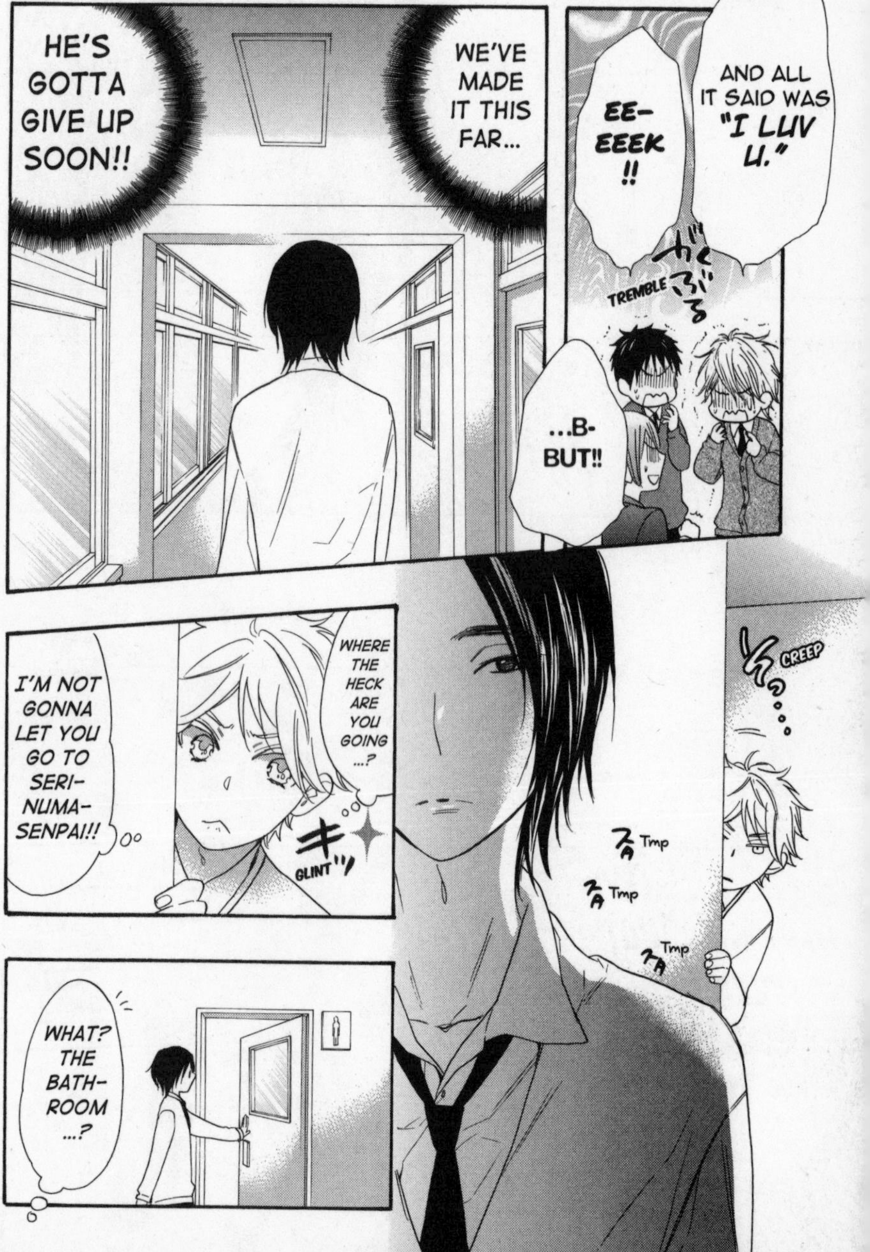
AND ALL IT SAID WAS "I LUV U."
EE-EEEK!!
TREMBLE
...B-BUT!!
WE'VE MADE IT THIS FAR...
HE'S GOTTA GIVE UP SOON!!
CREEP
Tmp
Tmp
Tmp
WHERE THE HECK ARE YOU GOING ...?
I'M NOT GONNA LET YOU GO TO SERI-NUMA-SENPAI!!
GLINT
WHAT? THE BATH-ROOM ...?

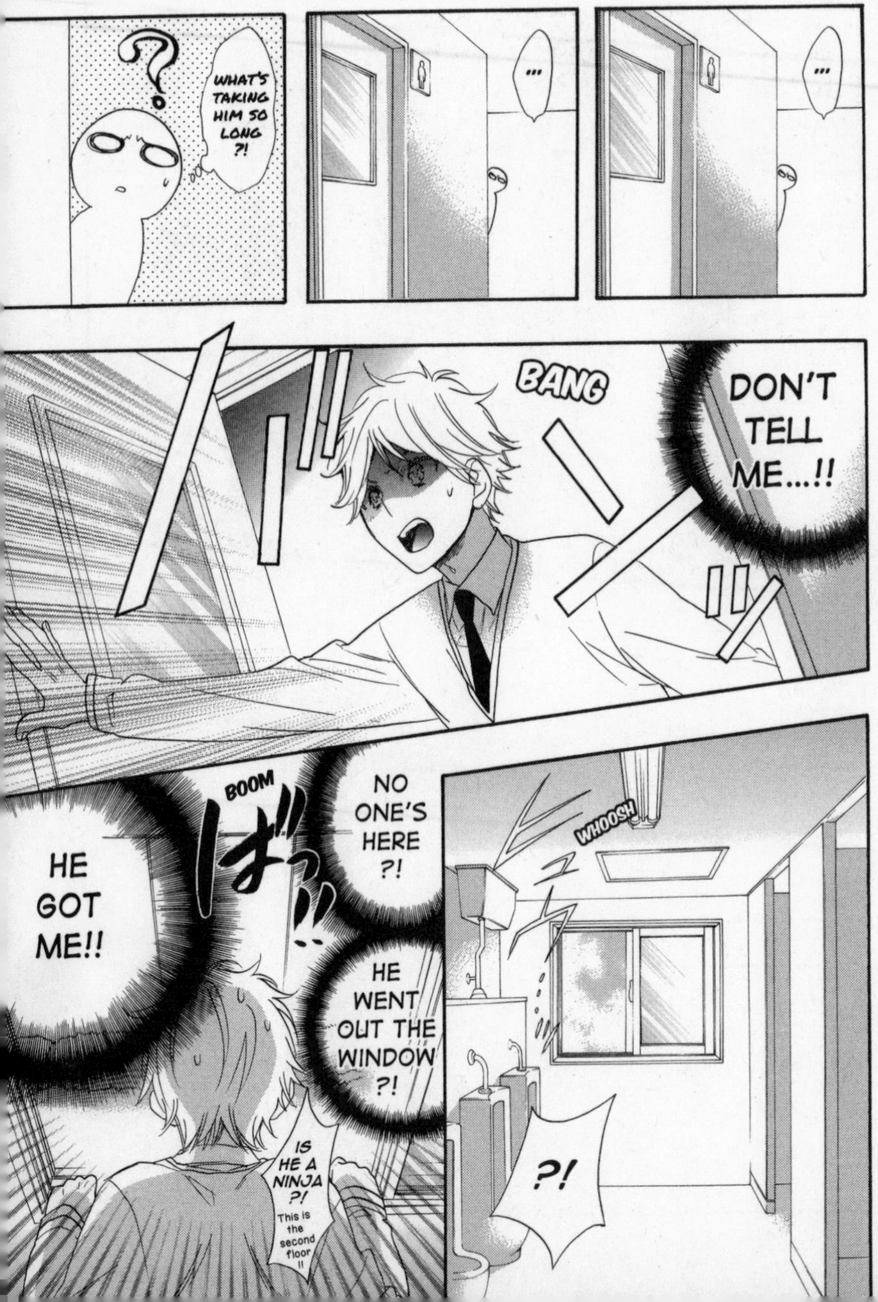
...
...
?
WHAT'S TAKING HIM SO LONG ?!
BANG
DON'T TELL ME...!!
WHOOSH
?!
BOOM
ばっ!!
NO ONE'S HERE ?!
HE WENT OUT THE WINDOW ?!
HE GOT ME!!
IS HE A NINJA ?!
This is the second floor !!

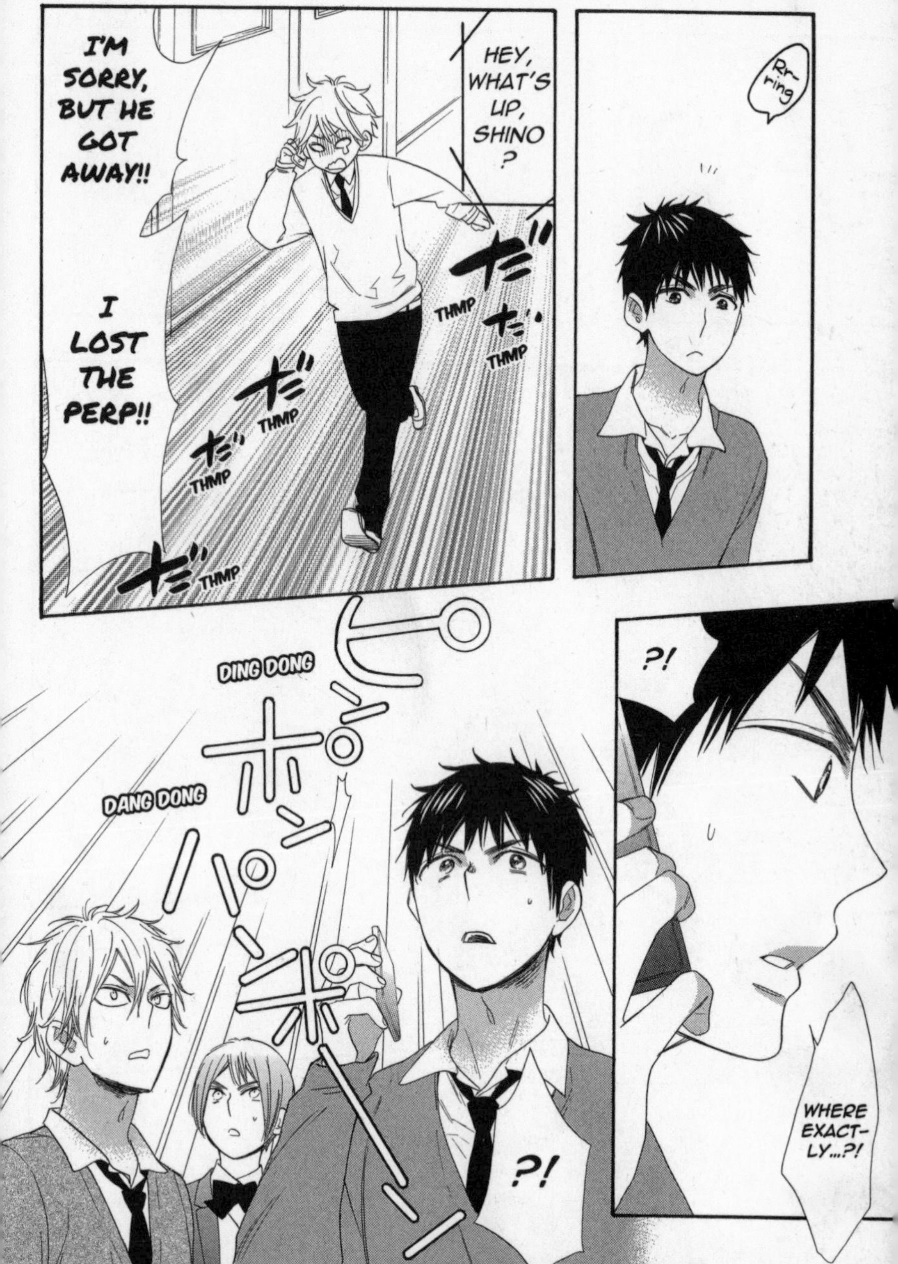
Rr-ring
HEY, WHAT'S UP, SHINO?
I'M SORRY, BUT HE GOT AWAY!!
I LOST THE PERP!!
THMP
THMP
THMP
THMP
THMP
?!
WHERE EXACTLY...?!
DING DONG
DANG DONG
?!

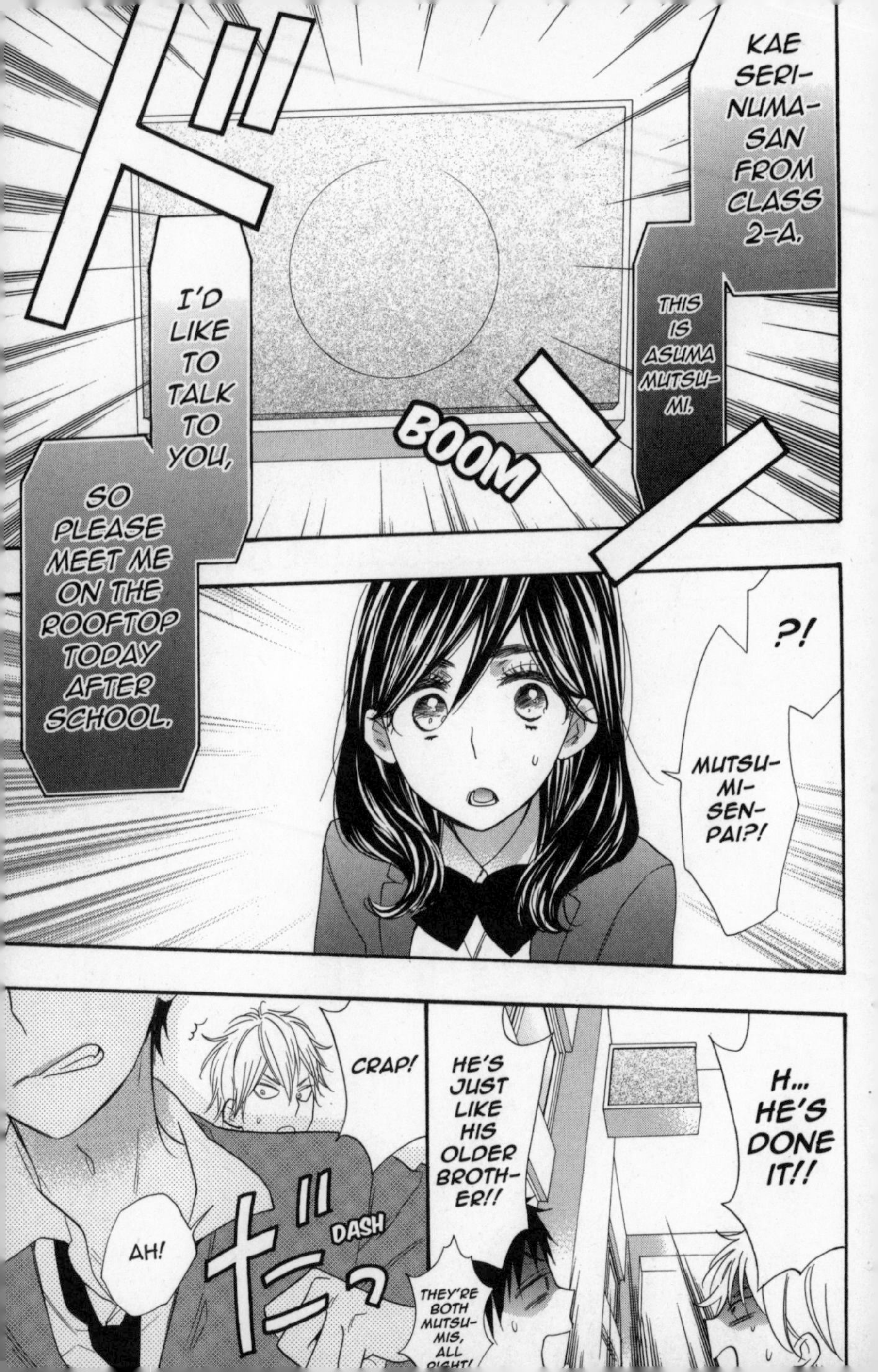
KAE SERI-NUMA-SAN FROM CLASS 2-A.
THIS IS ASUMA MUTSU-MI.
BOOM
I'D LIKE TO TALK TO YOU,
SO PLEASE MEET ME ON THE ROOFTOP TODAY AFTER SCHOOL.
?!
MUTSU-MI-SEN-PAI?!
H... HE'S DONE IT!!
HE'S JUST LIKE HIS OLDER BROTH-ER!!
THEY'RE BOTH MUTSU-MIS, ALL RIGHT!
CRAP!
DASH
AH!

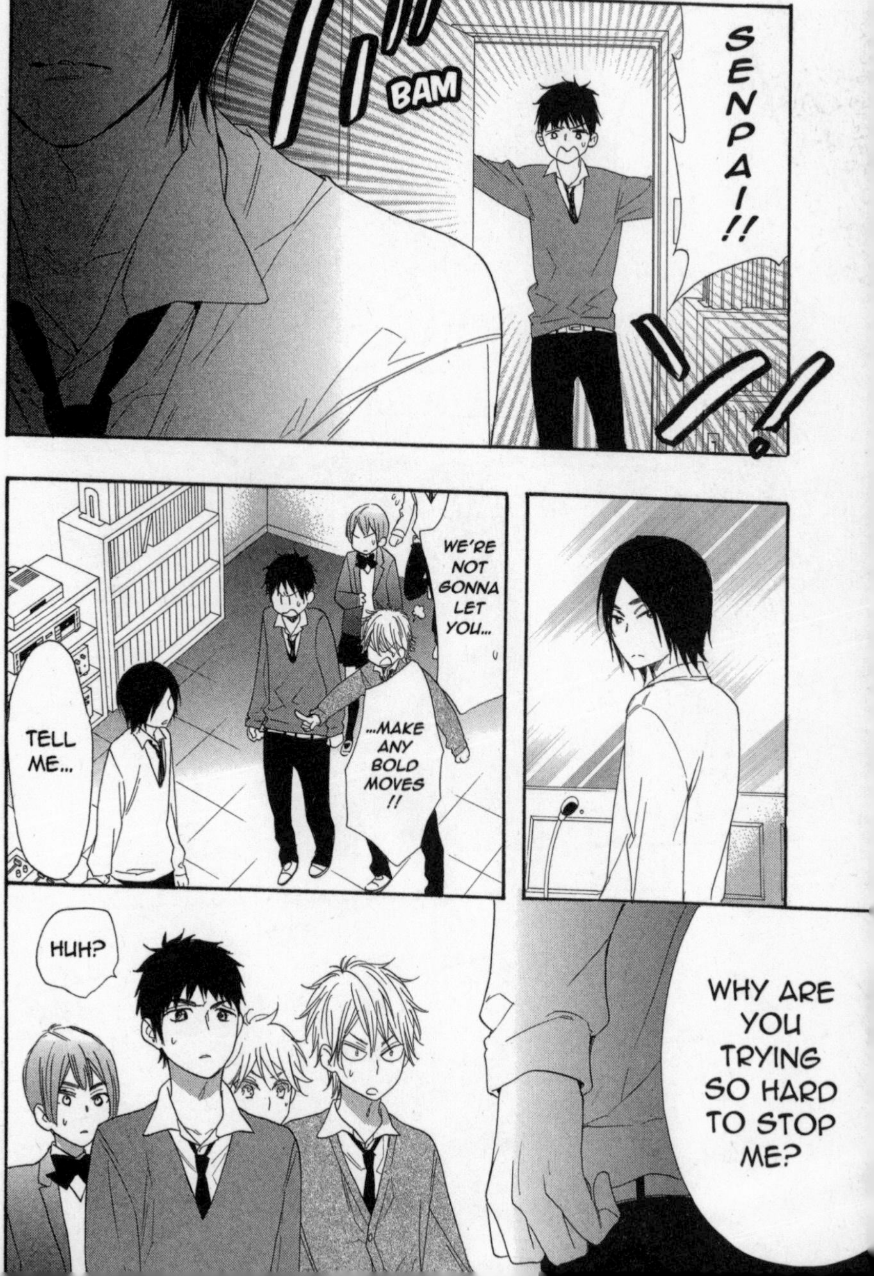
SENPAI!!
BAM
WE'RE NOT GONNA LET YOU...
...MAKE ANY BOLD MOVES!!
TELL ME...
WHY ARE YOU TRYING SO HARD TO STOP ME?
HUH?

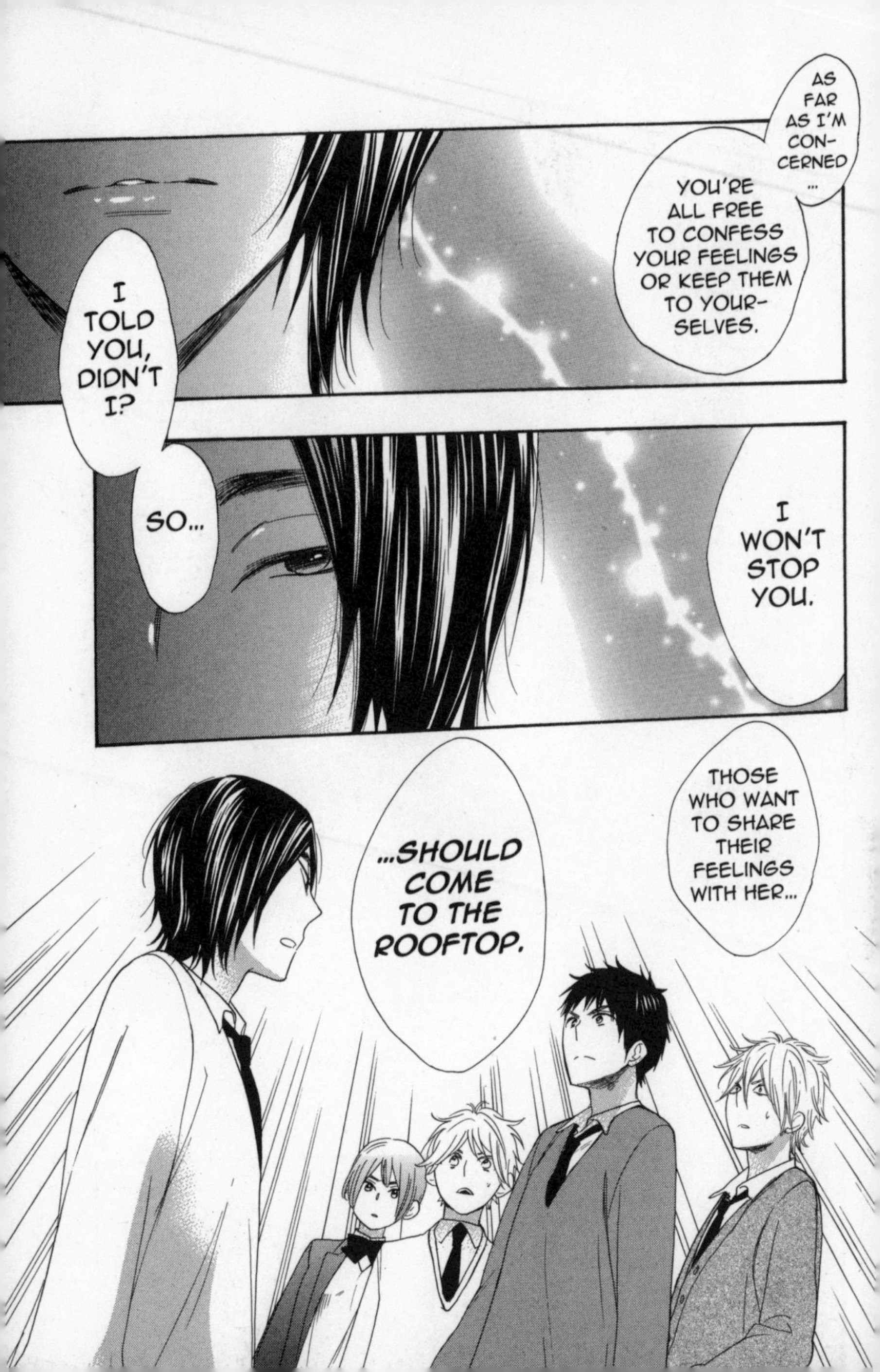
AS FAR AS I'M CON-CERNED...
YOU'RE ALL FREE TO CONFESS YOUR FEELINGS OR KEEP THEM TO YOUR-SELVES.
I TOLD YOU, DIDN'T I?
I WON'T STOP YOU.
SO...
THOSE WHO WANT TO SHARE THEIR FEELINGS WITH HER...
...SHOULD COME TO THE ROOFTOP.

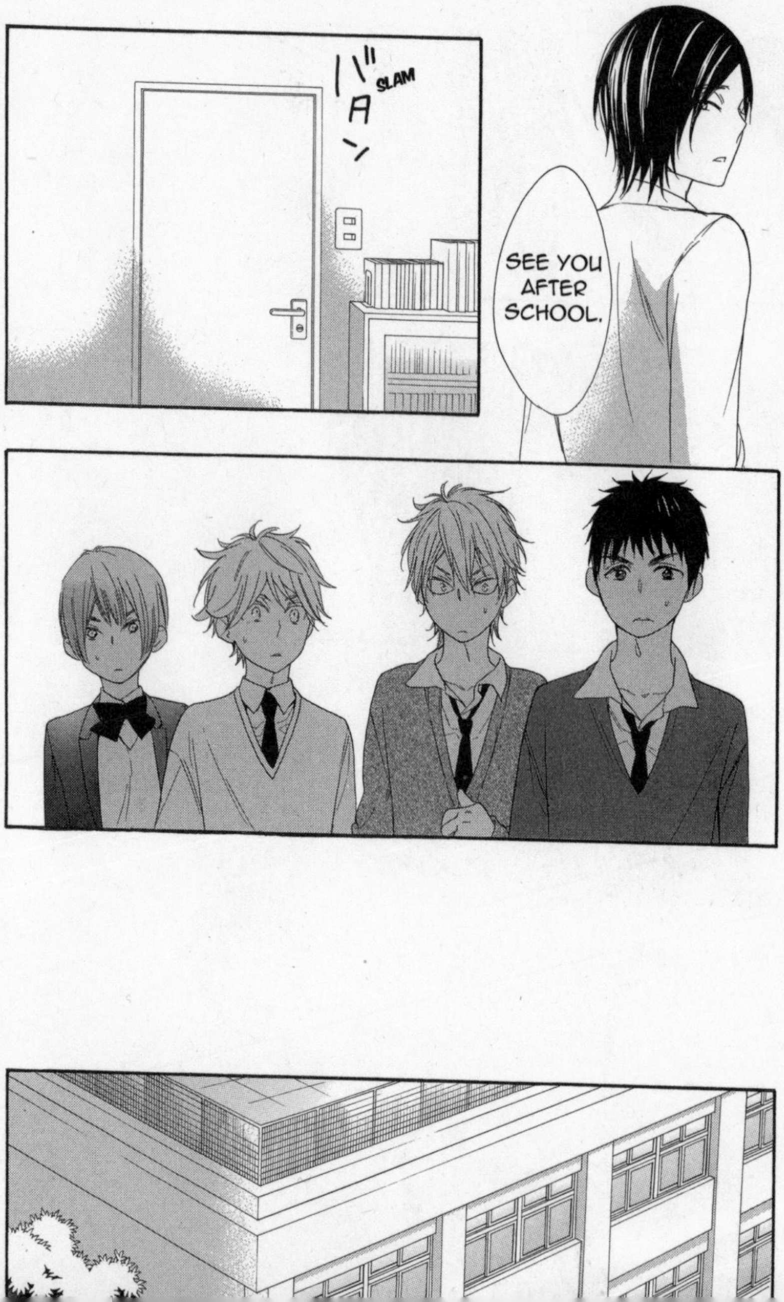
SEE YOU AFTER SCHOOL.
バタン
SLAM

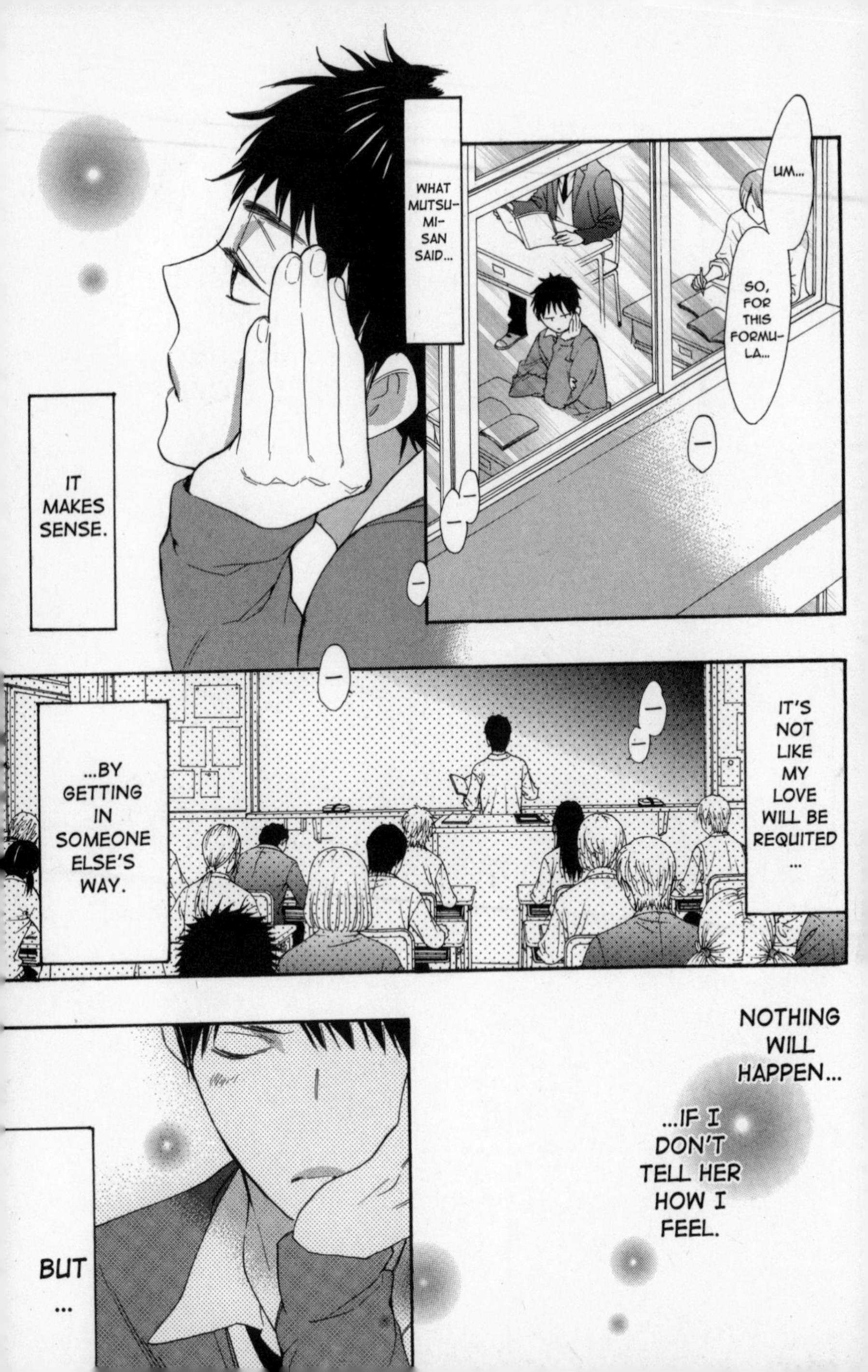
UM...
SO, FOR THIS FORMULA...
WHAT MUTSUMI-SAN SAID...
IT MAKES SENSE.
IT'S NOT LIKE MY LOVE WILL BE REQUITED...
...BY GETTING IN SOMEONE ELSE'S WAY.
NOTHING WILL HAPPEN...
...IF I DON'T TELL HER HOW I FEEL.
BUT ...

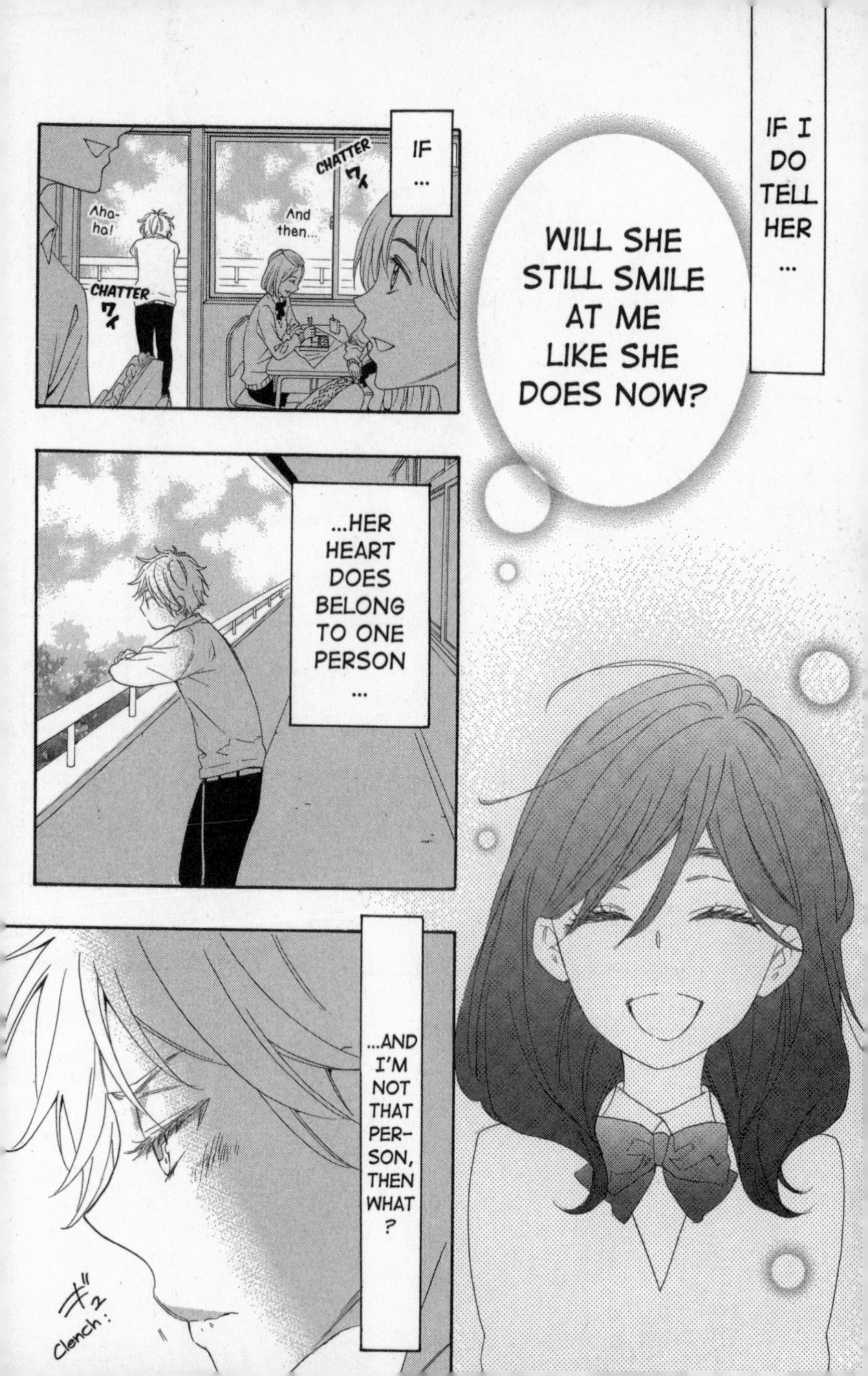
IF I DO TELL HER ...
WILL SHE STILL SMILE AT ME LIKE SHE DOES NOW?
IF ...
CHATTER
And then...
Aha-ha!
CHATTER
...HER HEART DOES BELONG TO ONE PERSON ...
...AND I'M NOT THAT PERSON, THEN WHAT ?
Clench:

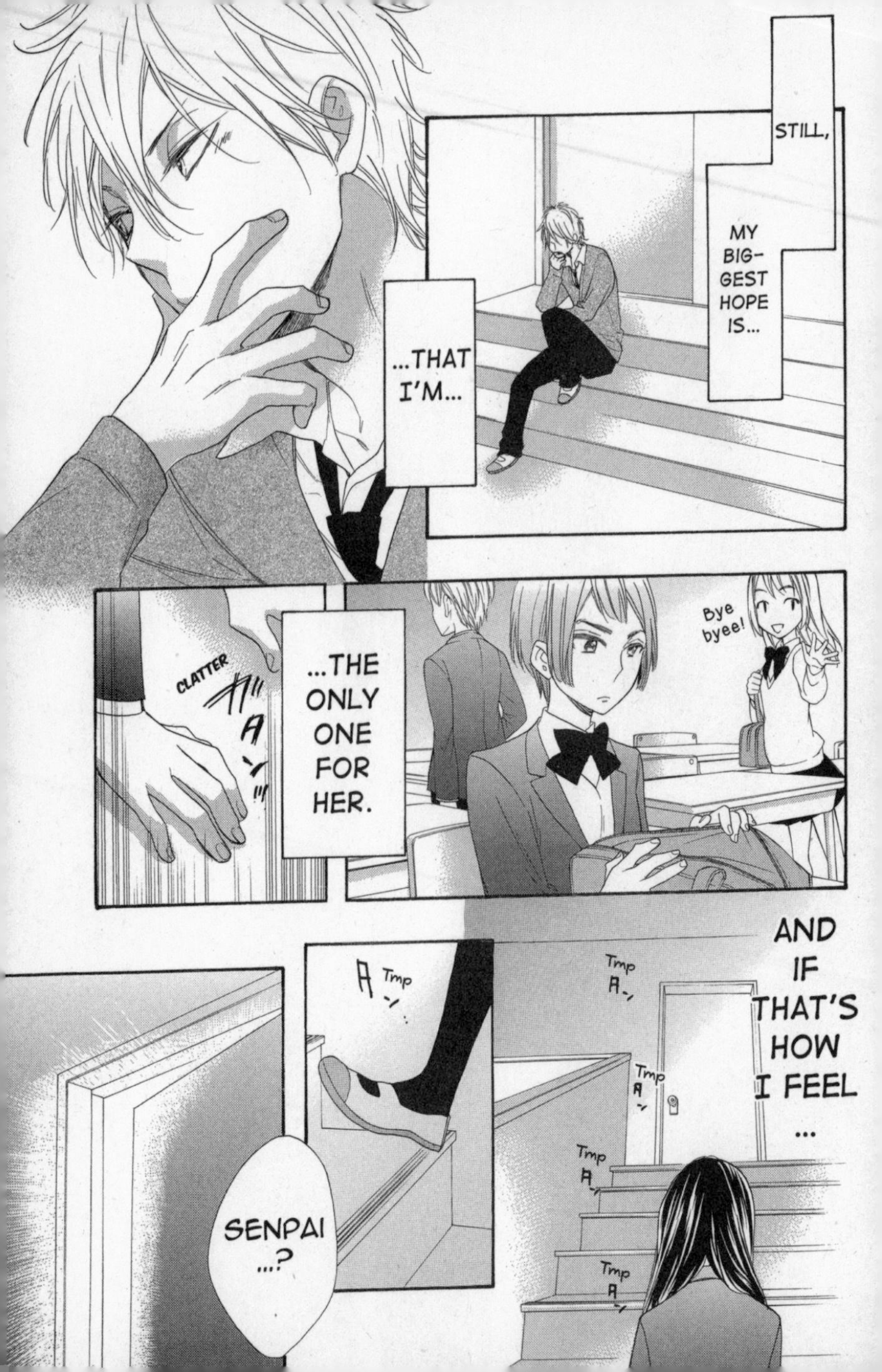
STILL,
MY BIG-GEST HOPE IS...
...THAT I'M...
Bye byee!
...THE ONLY ONE FOR HER.
CLATTER
AND IF THAT'S HOW I FEEL ...
Tmp
Tmp
Tmp
Tmp
Tmp
SENPAI ...?

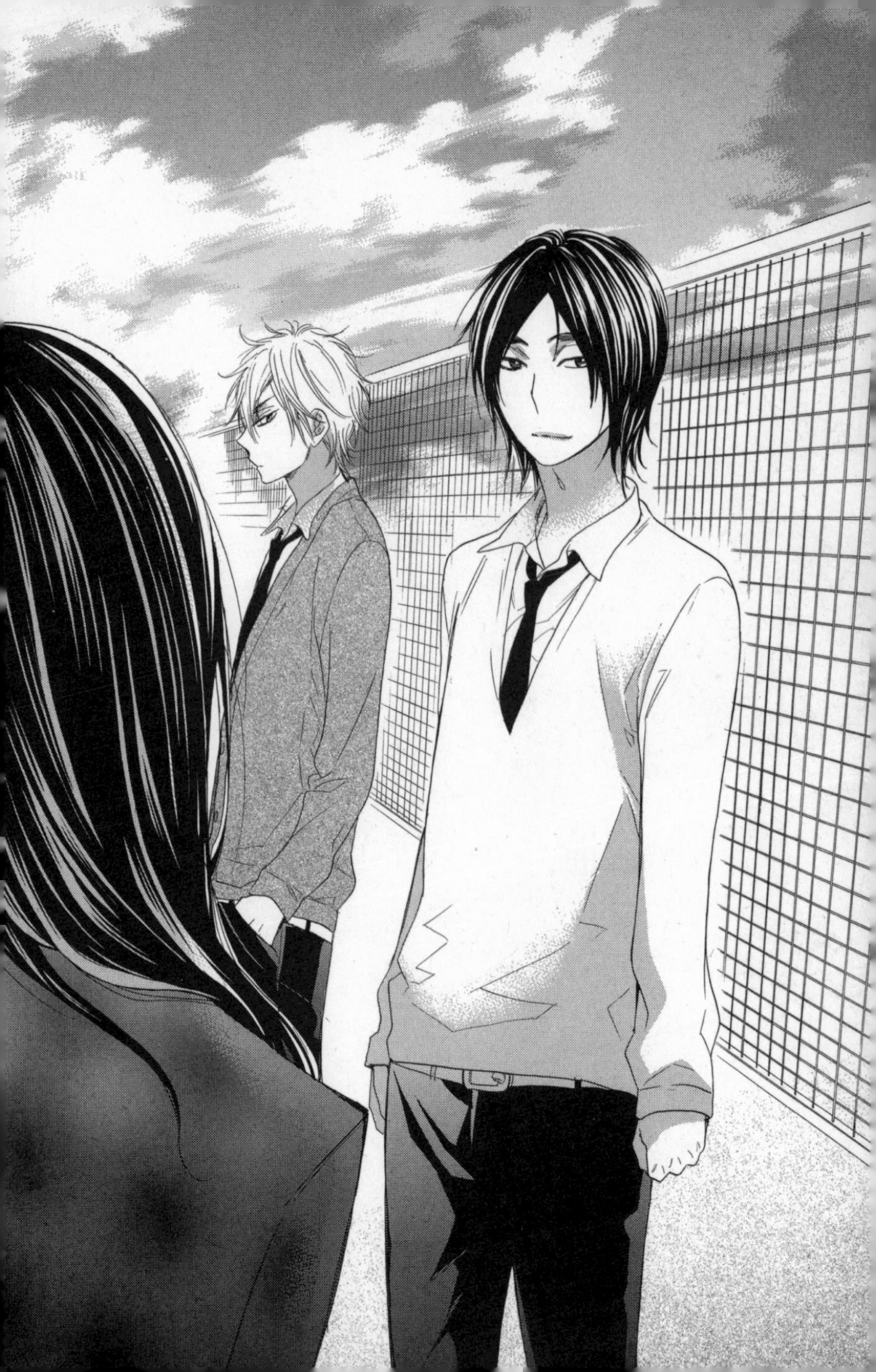

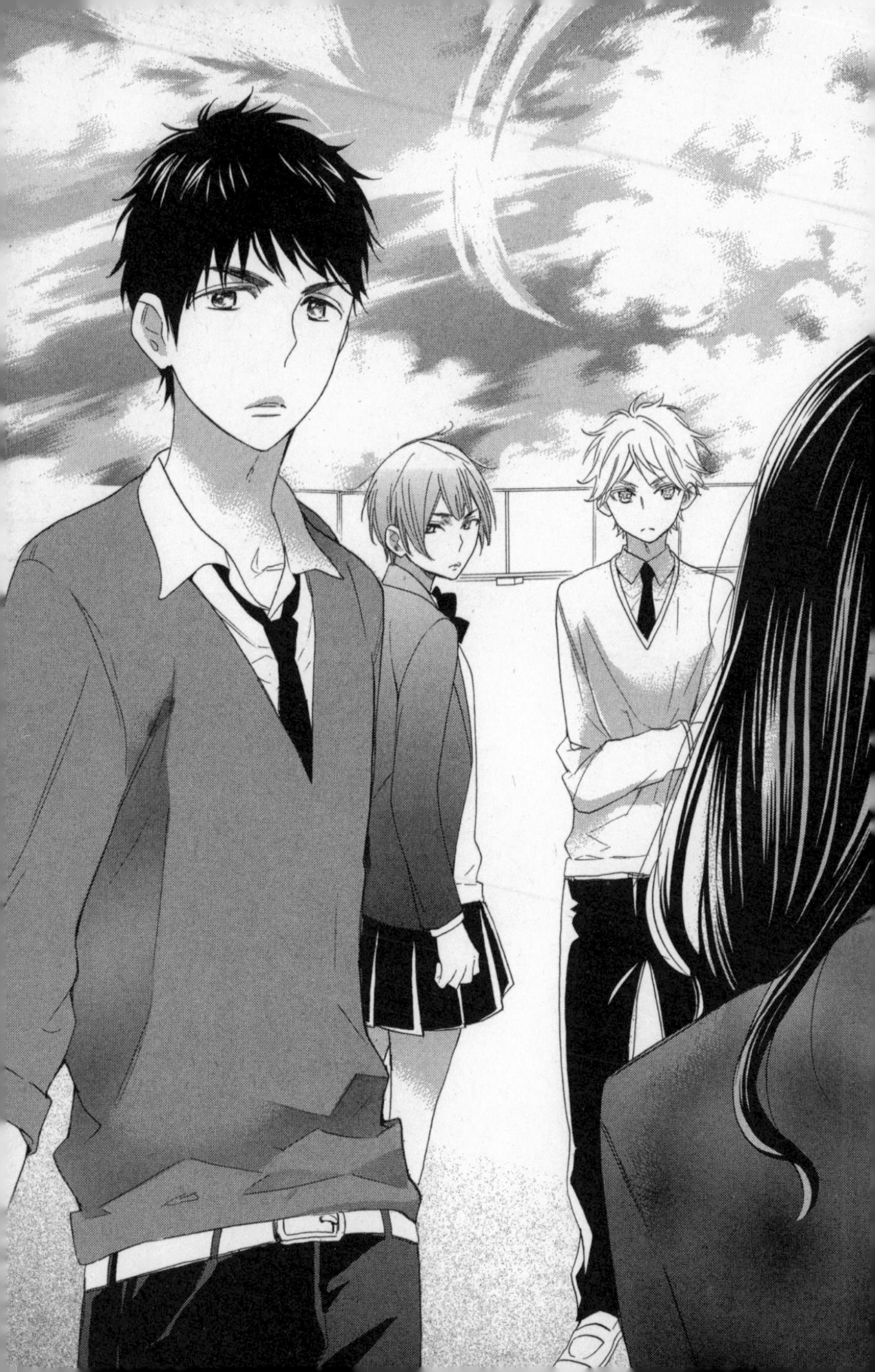

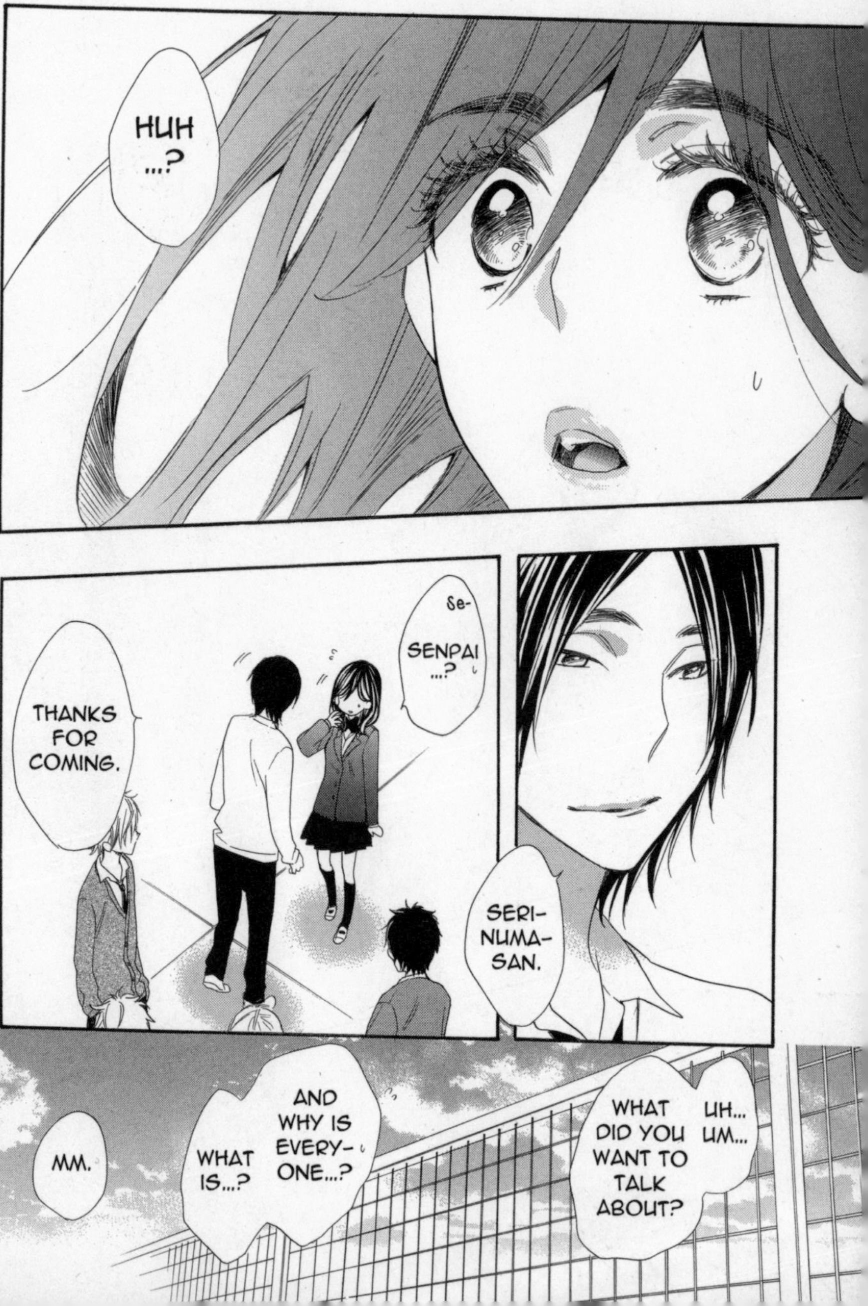
HUH ...?
SERI-NUMA-SAN.
Se-SENPAI ...?
THANKS FOR COMING.
UH... UM...
WHAT DID YOU WANT TO TALK ABOUT?
AND WHY IS EVERY-ONE...?
WHAT IS...?
MM.

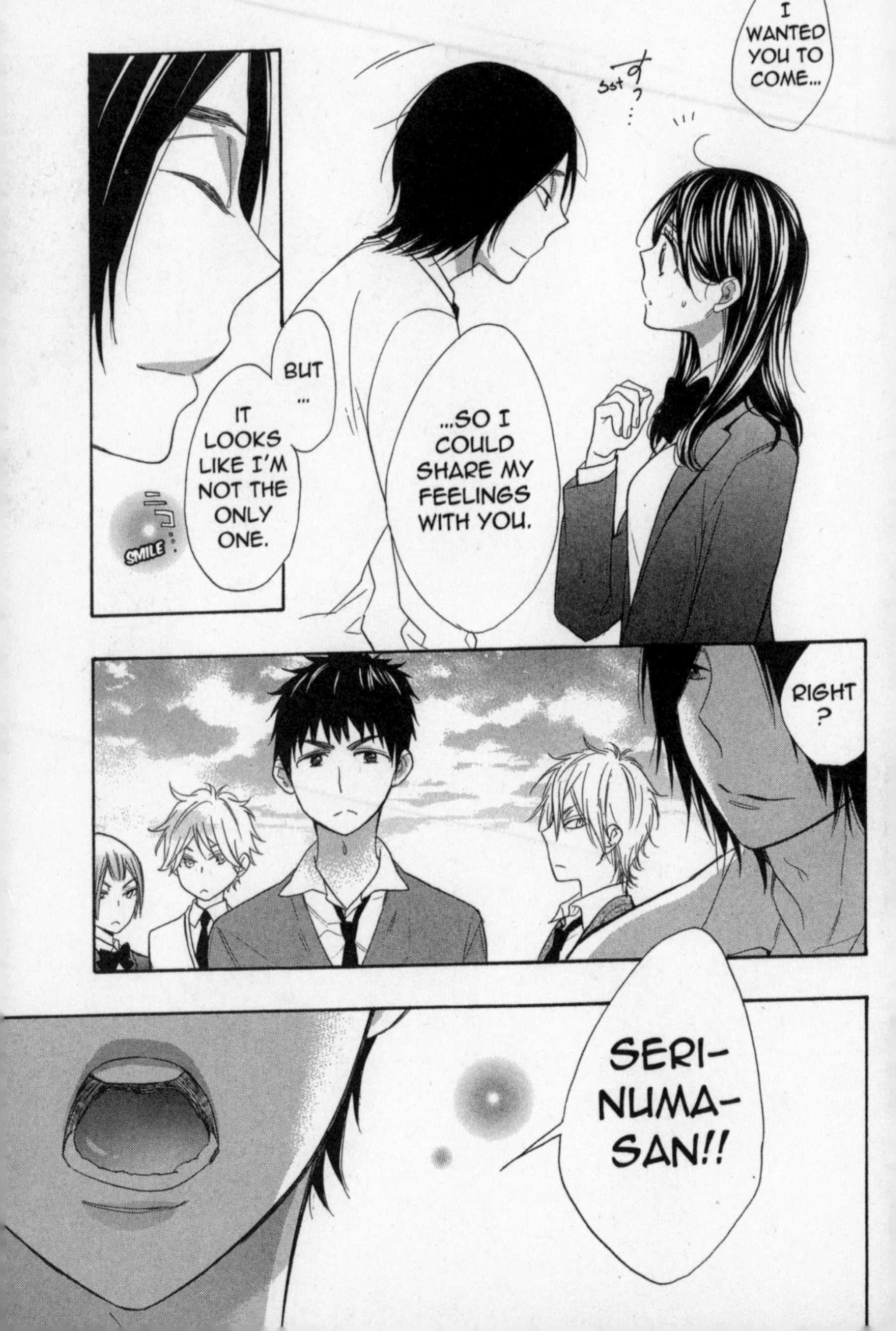
I WANTED YOU TO COME...
Sst す
...SO I COULD SHARE MY FEELINGS WITH YOU.
BUT ...
IT LOOKS LIKE I'M NOT THE ONLY ONE.
ニコ SMILE
RIGHT?
SERI-NUMA-SAN!!

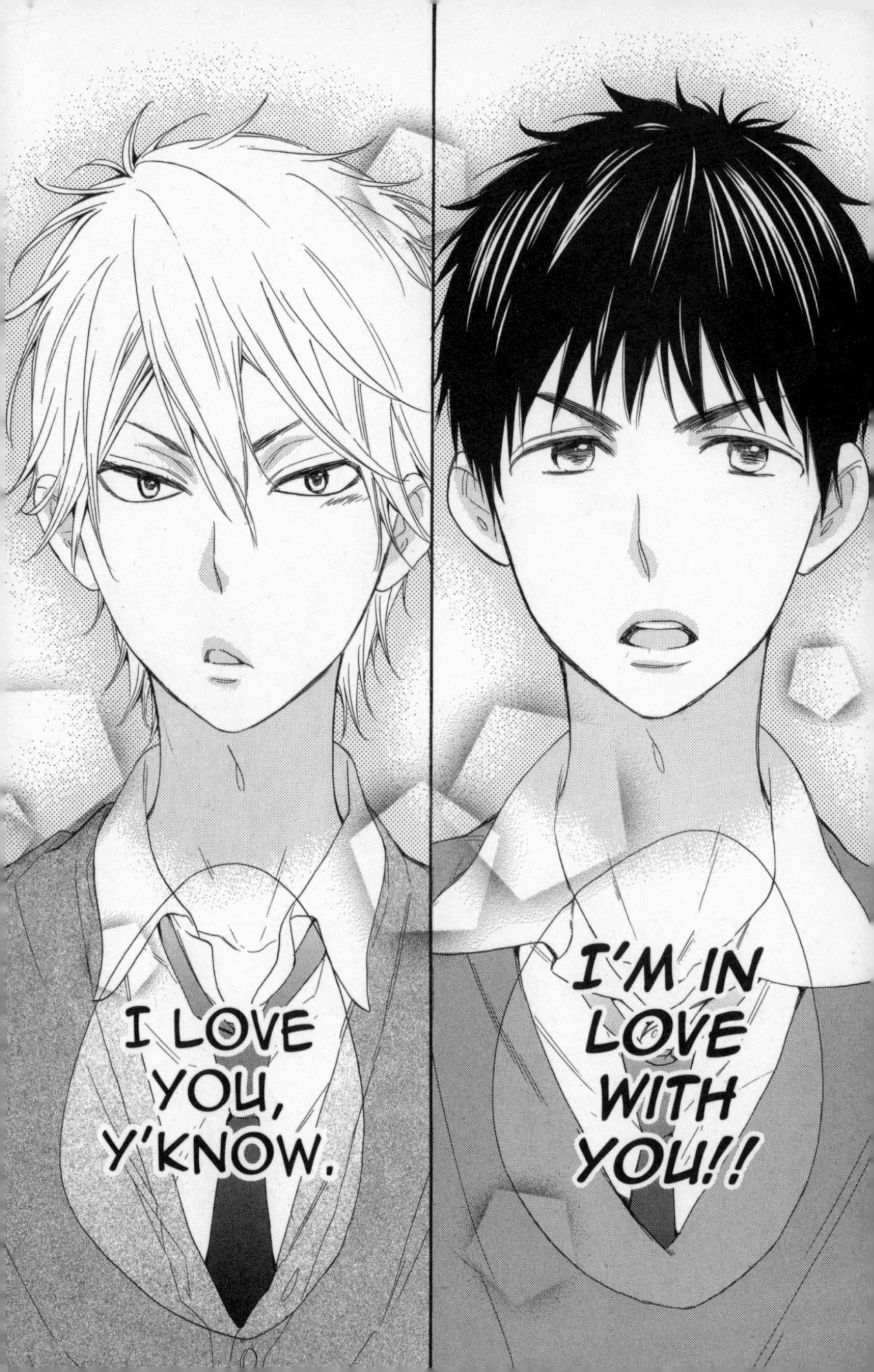
I'M IN LOVE WITH YOU!!
I LOVE YOU, Y'KNOW.

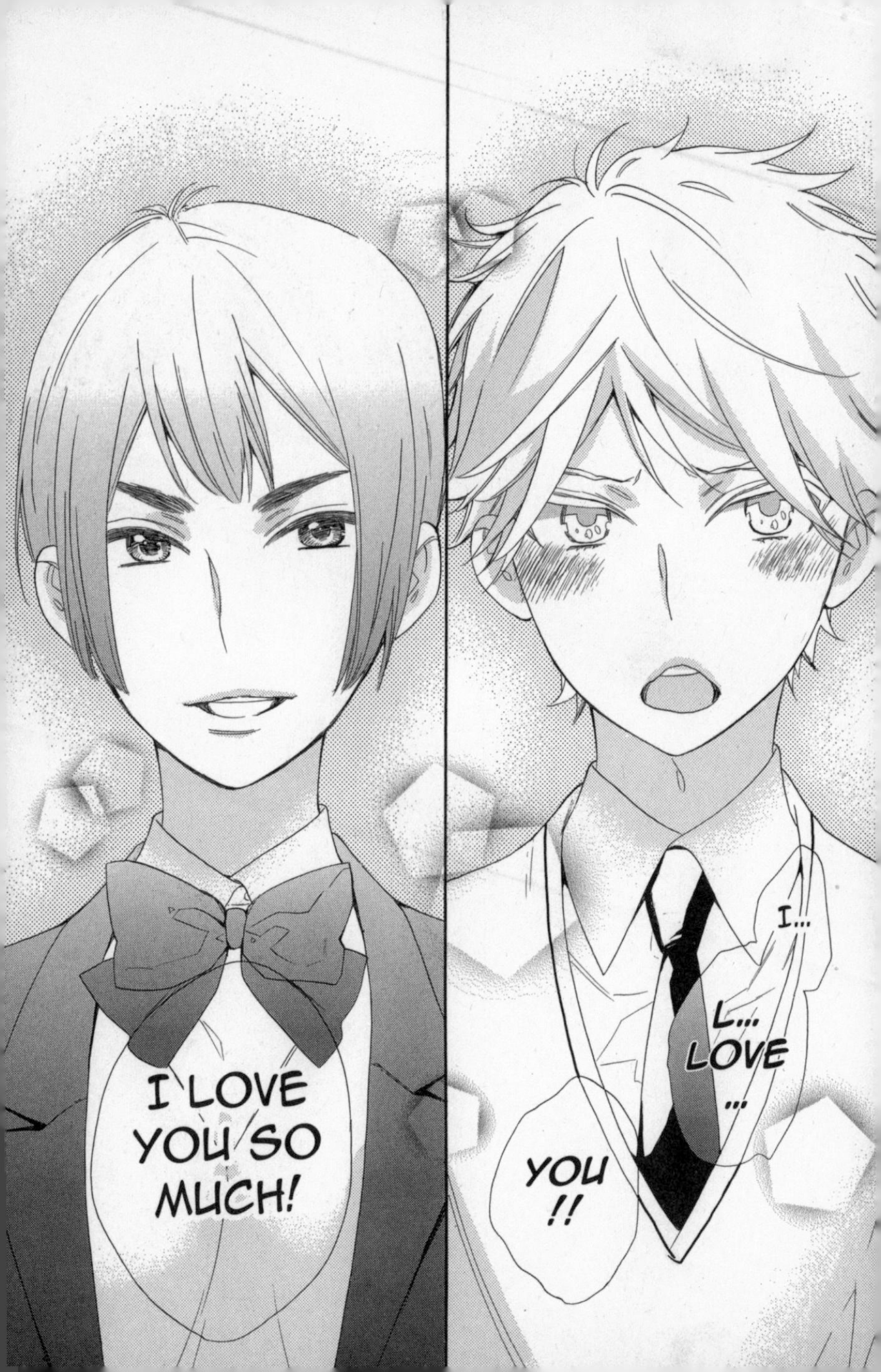
I...
L... LOVE ...
YOU !!
I LOVE YOU SO MUCH!

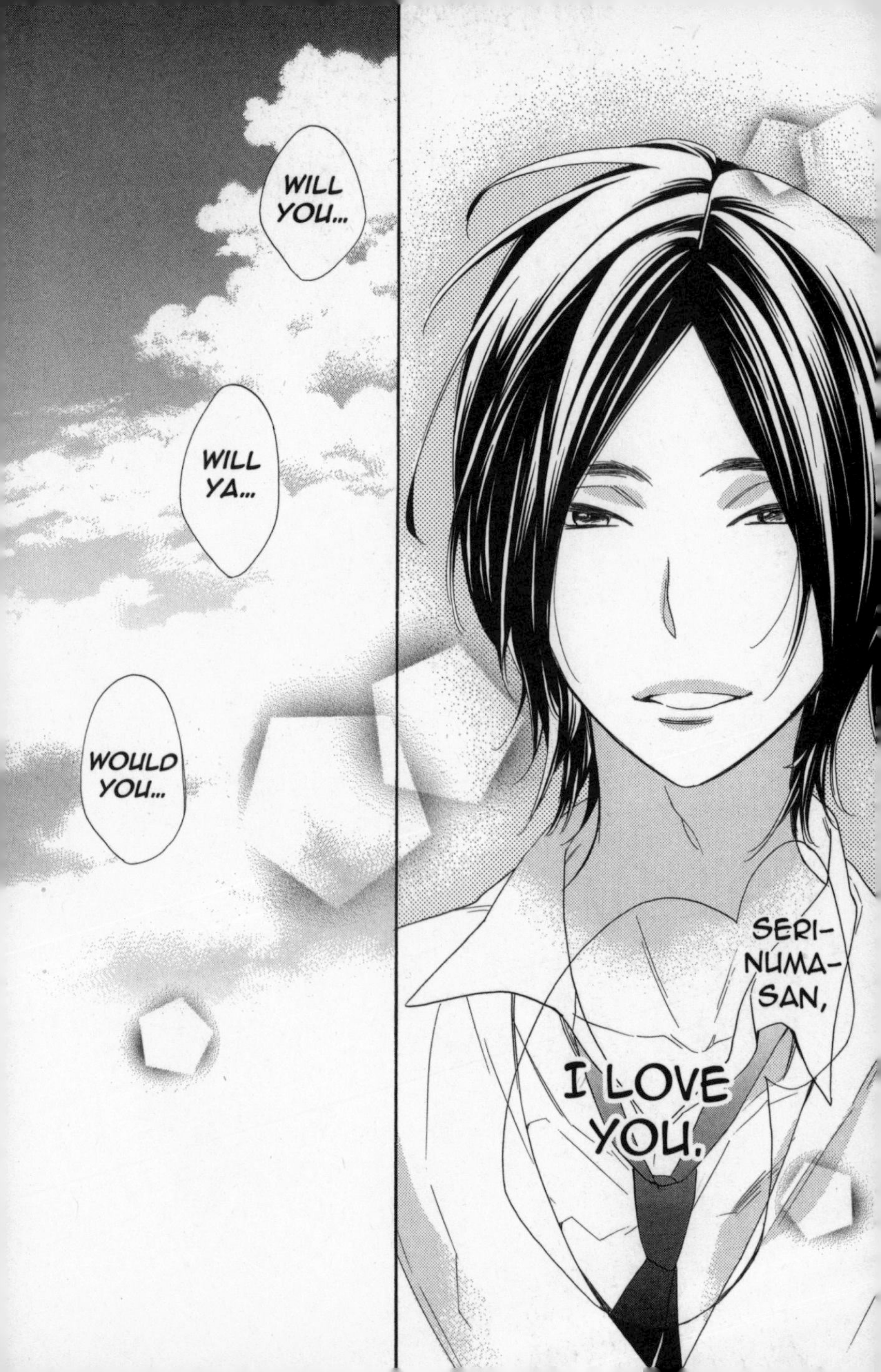
SERI-NUMA-SAN,
I LOVE YOU.
WILL YOU...
WILL YA...
WOULD YOU...

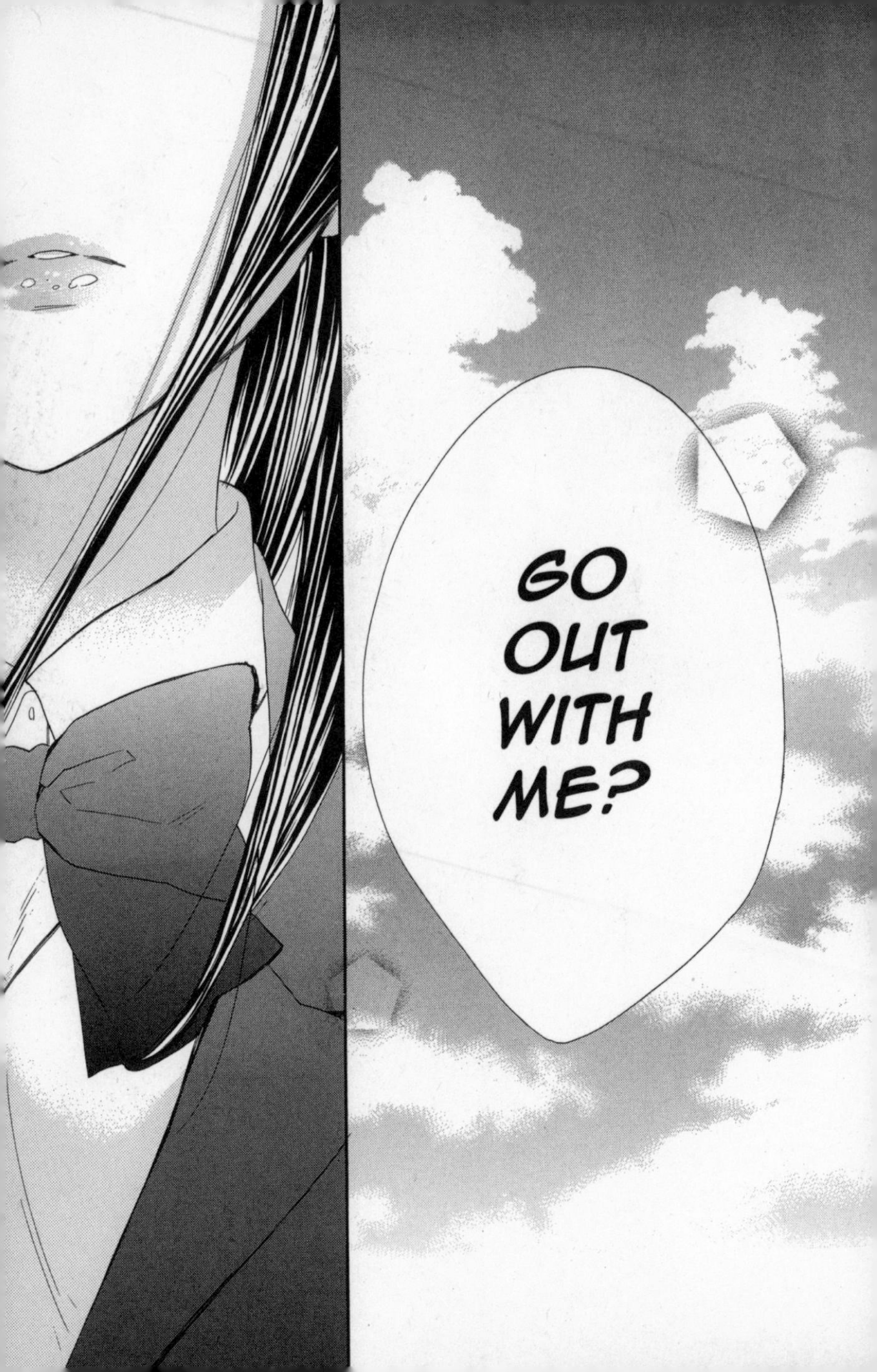
GO OUT WITH ME?

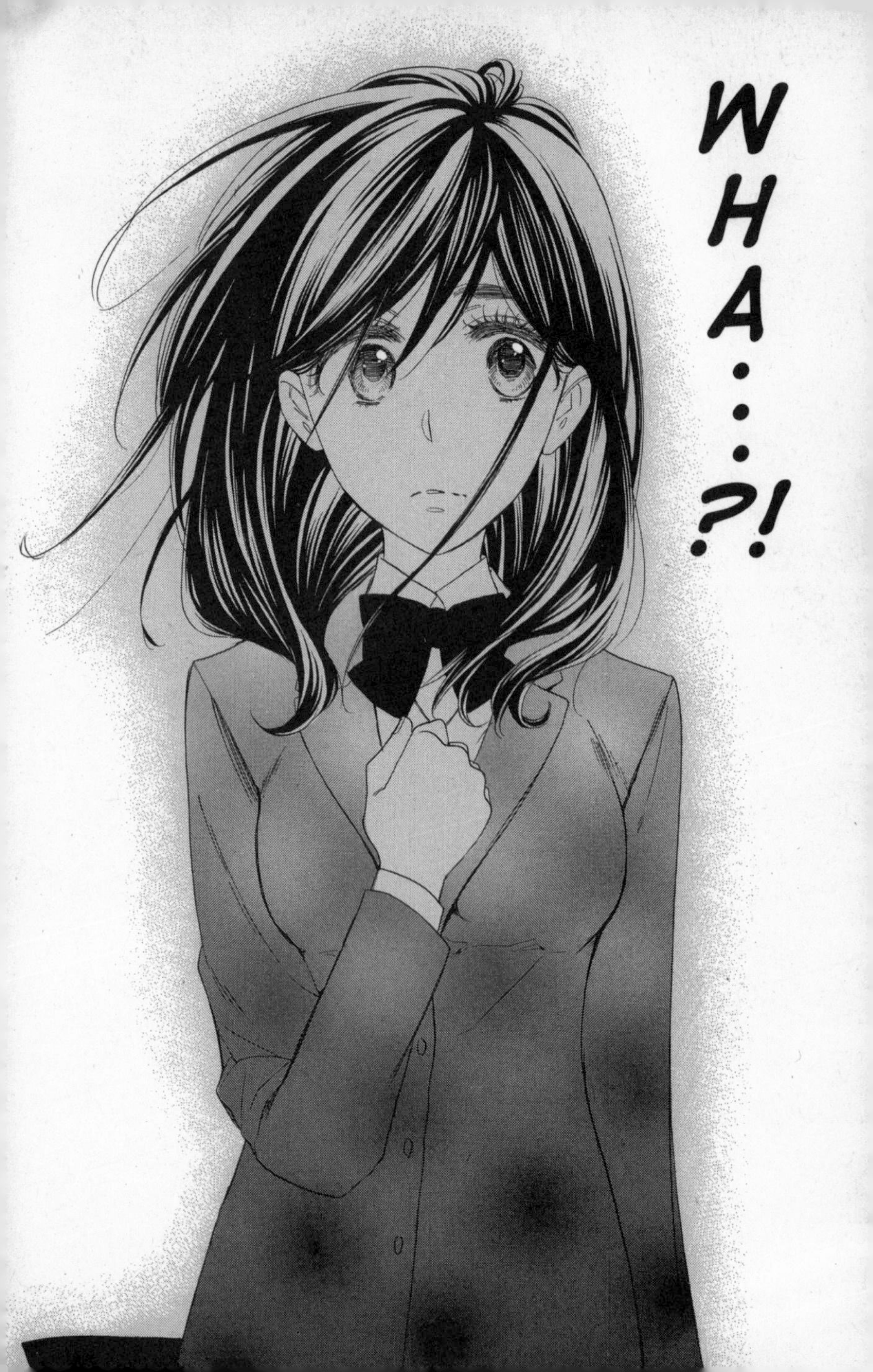
WHA...?!

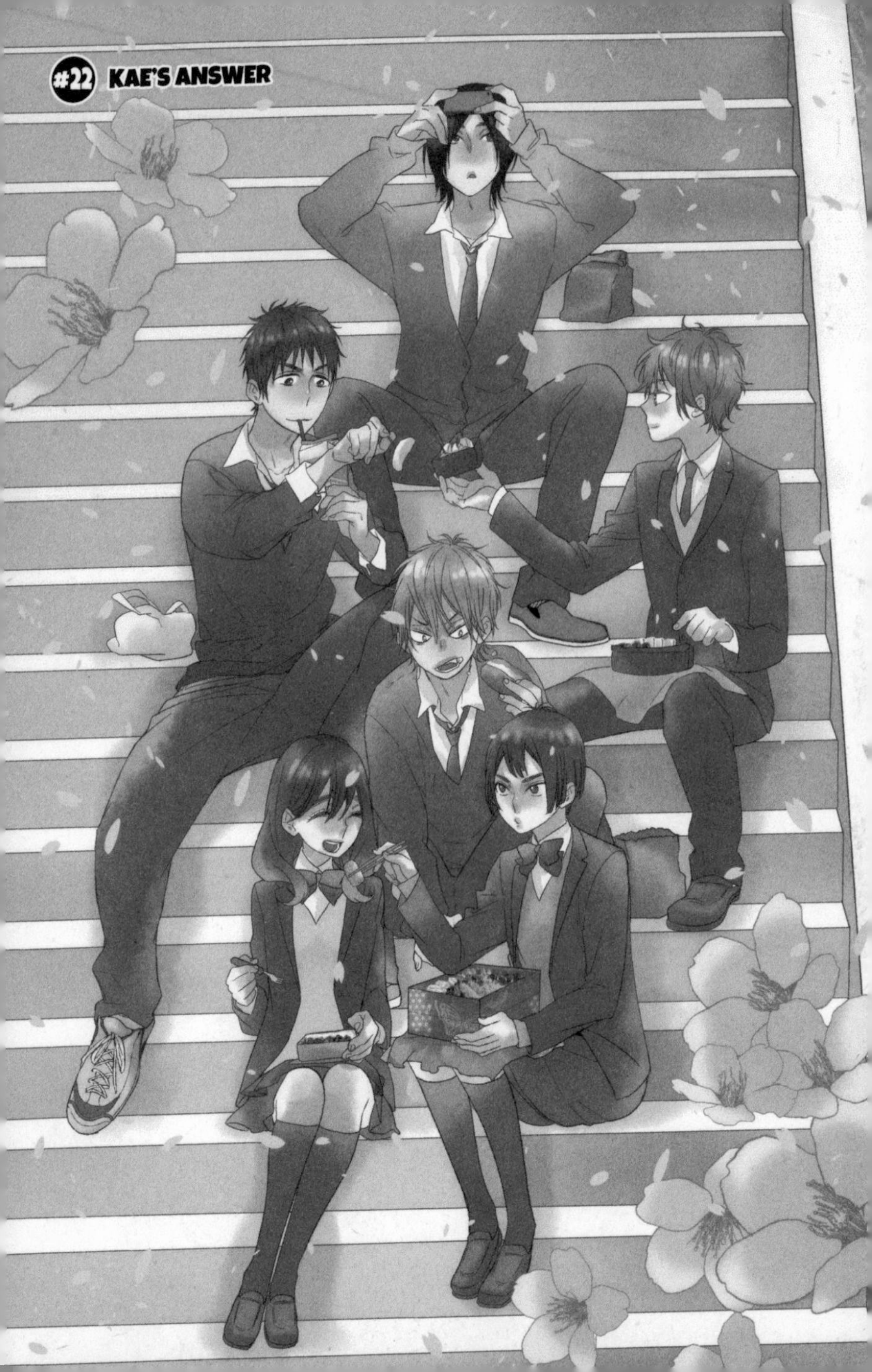
#22 KAE'S ANSWER

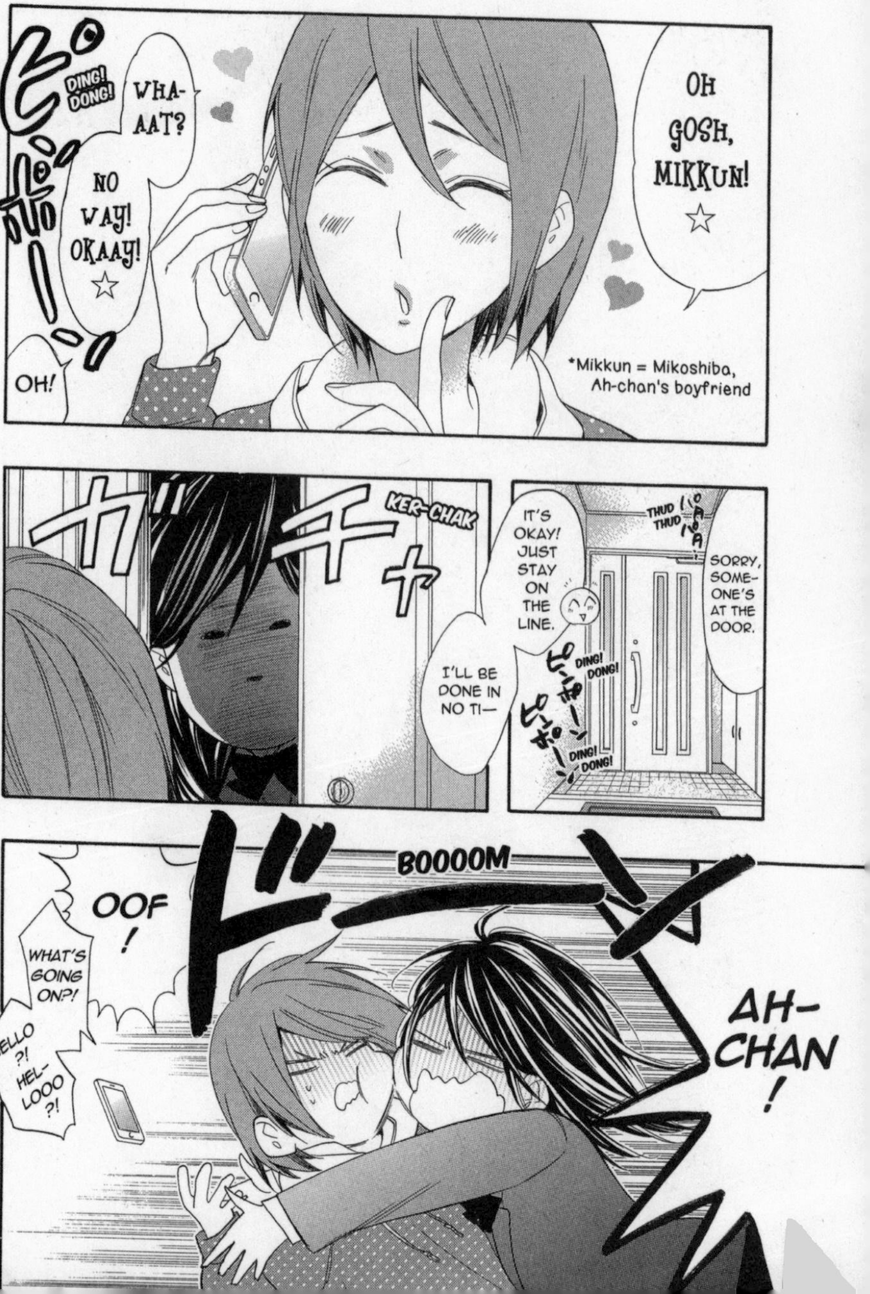
OH GOSH, MIKKUN! ☆
*Mikkun = Mikoshiba, Ah-chan's boyfriend
DING! DONG!
WHA-AAT?
NO WAY! OKAAY! ☆
OH!
SORRY, SOME-ONE'S AT THE DOOR.
THUD THUD
IT'S OKAY! JUST STAY ON THE LINE.
DING! DONG!
I'LL BE DONE IN NO TI—
DING! DONG!
KER-CHAK
BOOOOM
AH-CHAN!
OOF!
WHAT'S GOING ON?!
HELLO?! HEL-LOOO?!

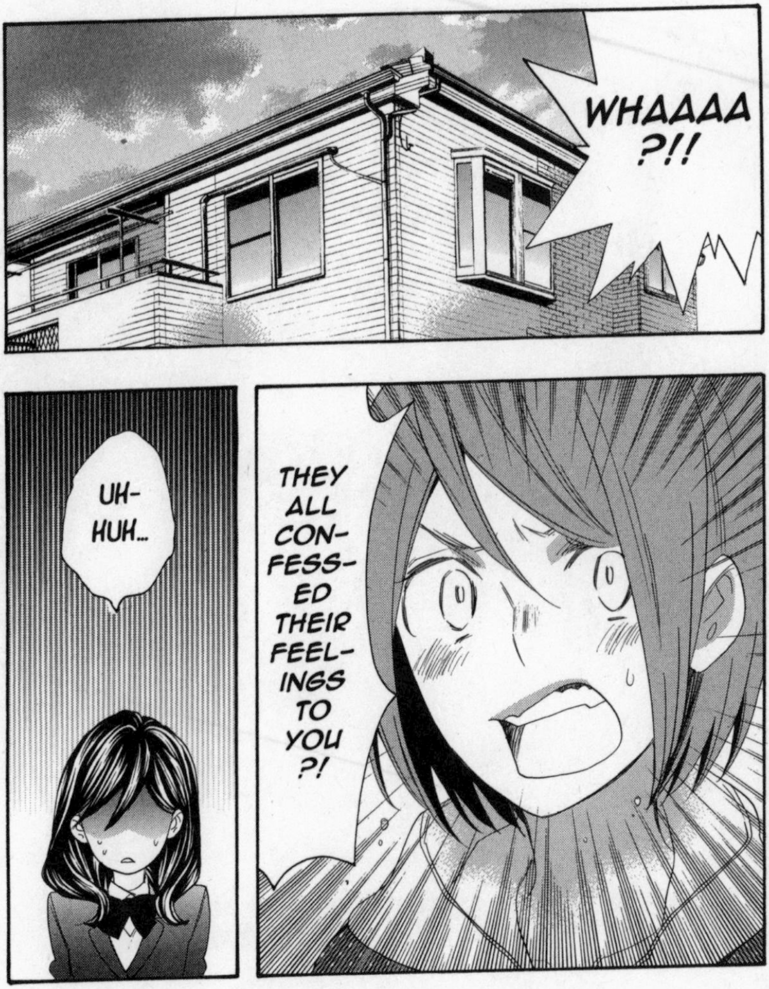
WHAAAA ?!!
THEY ALL CON-FESS-ED THEIR FEEL-INGS TO YOU ?!
UH-HUH...

KiSS HiM, NOT ME!

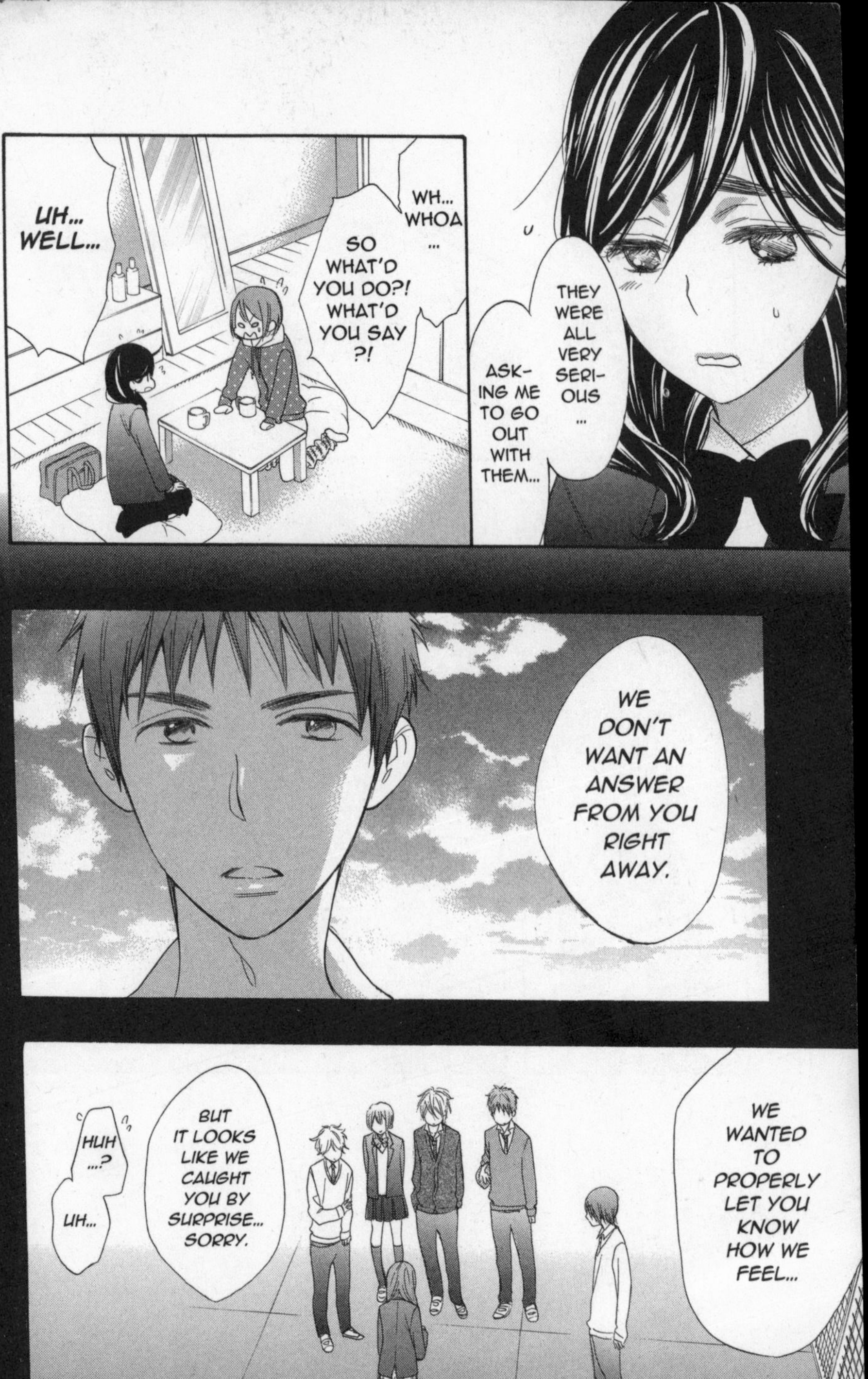

THEY WERE ALL VERY SERIOUS...
ASKING ME TO GO OUT WITH THEM...
WH... WHOA...
SO WHAT'D YOU DO?! WHAT'D YOU SAY?!
UH... WELL...
WE DON'T WANT AN ANSWER FROM YOU RIGHT AWAY.
WE WANTED TO PROPERLY LET YOU KNOW HOW WE FEEL...
BUT IT LOOKS LIKE WE CAUGHT YOU BY SURPRISE... SORRY.
HUH...?
UH...

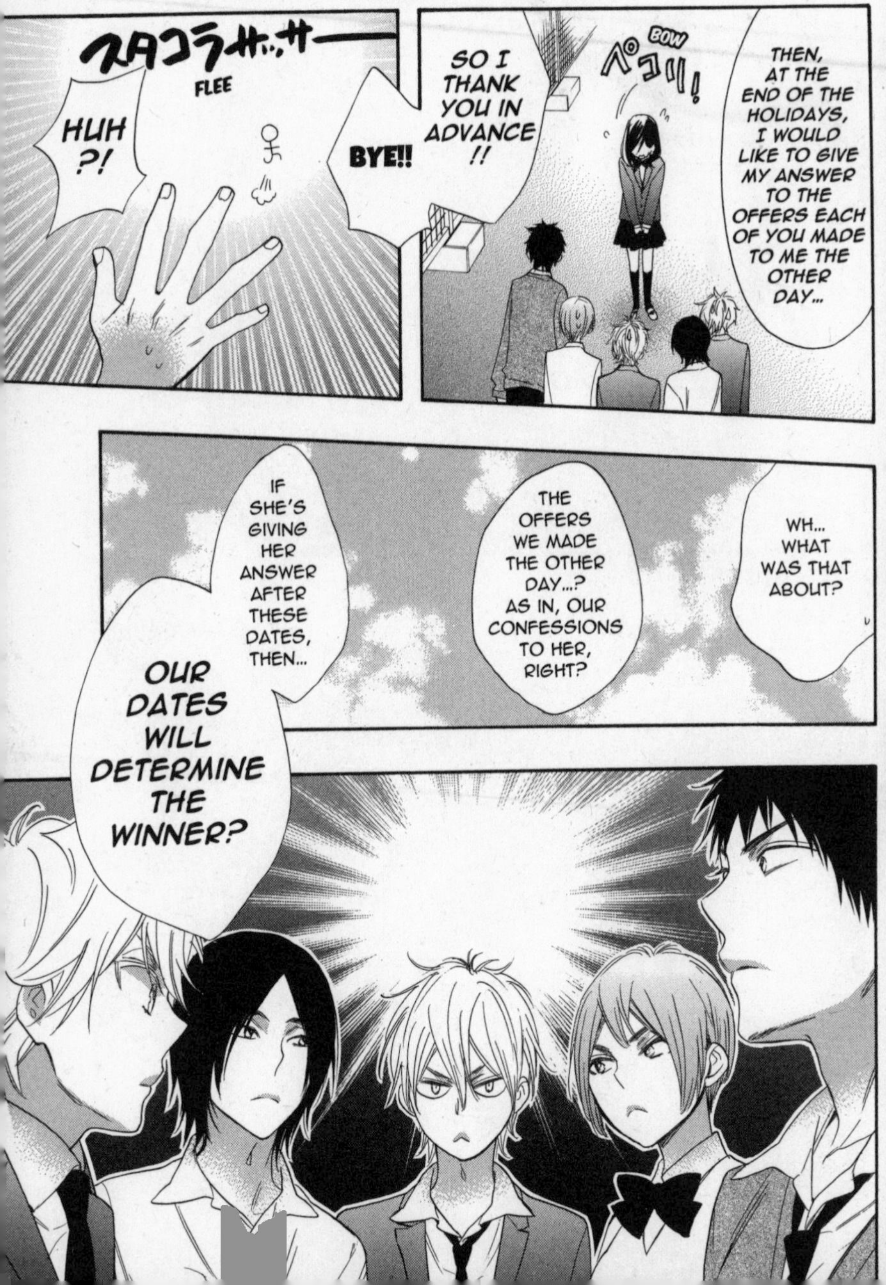
THEN, AT THE END OF THE HOLIDAYS, I WOULD LIKE TO GIVE MY ANSWER TO THE OFFERS EACH OF YOU MADE TO ME THE OTHER DAY...
ペコリ!
BOW
SO I THANK YOU IN ADVANCE !!
BYE!!
スタコラサッサー
FLEE
HUH ?!
WH... WHAT WAS THAT ABOUT?
THE OFFERS WE MADE THE OTHER DAY...? AS IN, OUR CONFESSIONS TO HER, RIGHT?
IF SHE'S GIVING HER ANSWER AFTER THESE DATES, THEN...
OUR DATES WILL DETERMINE THE WINNER?

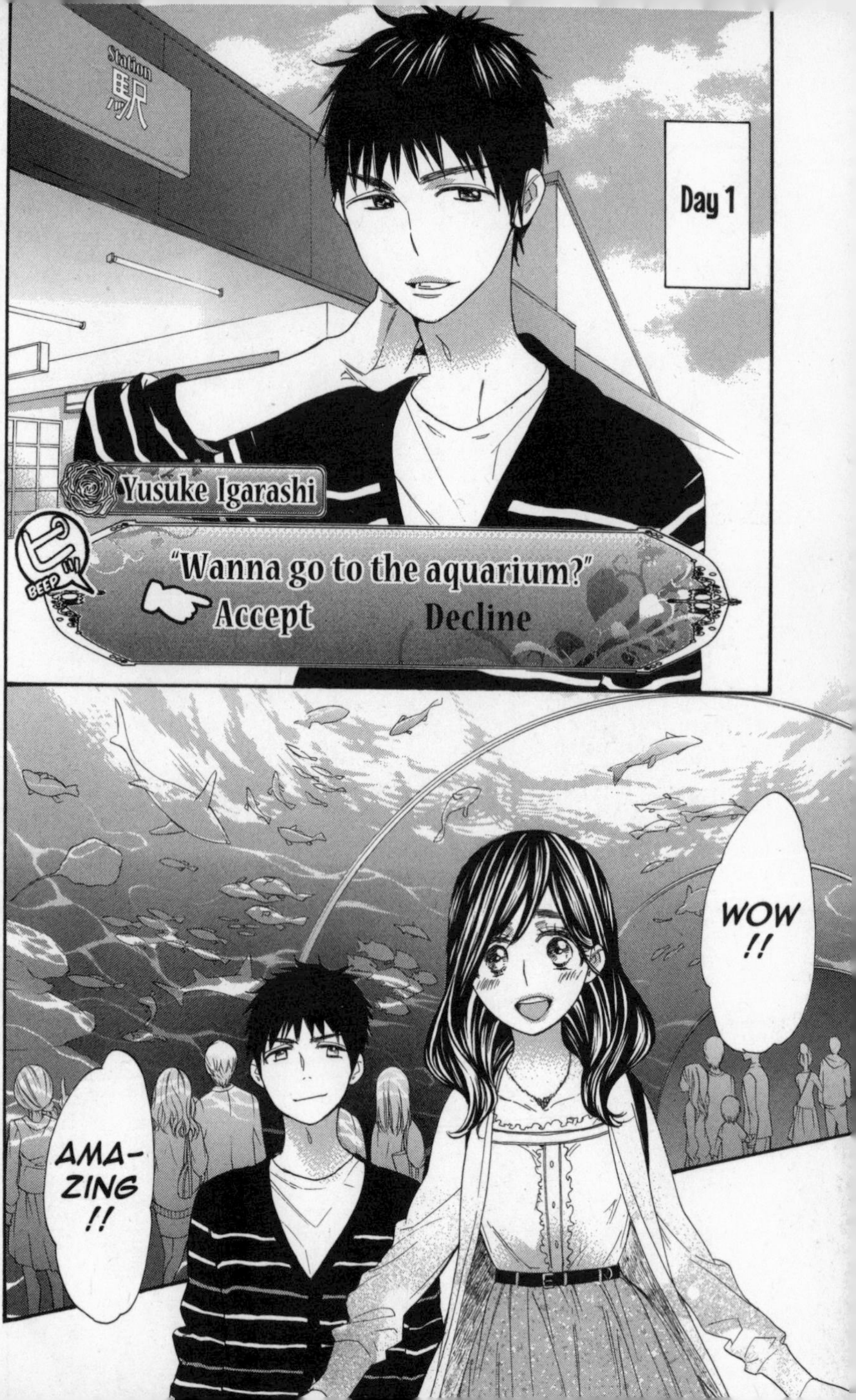
Day 1
Station 駅
Yusuke Igarashi
BEEP
"Wanna go to the aquarium?"
Accept
Decline
WOW !!
AMA-ZING !!

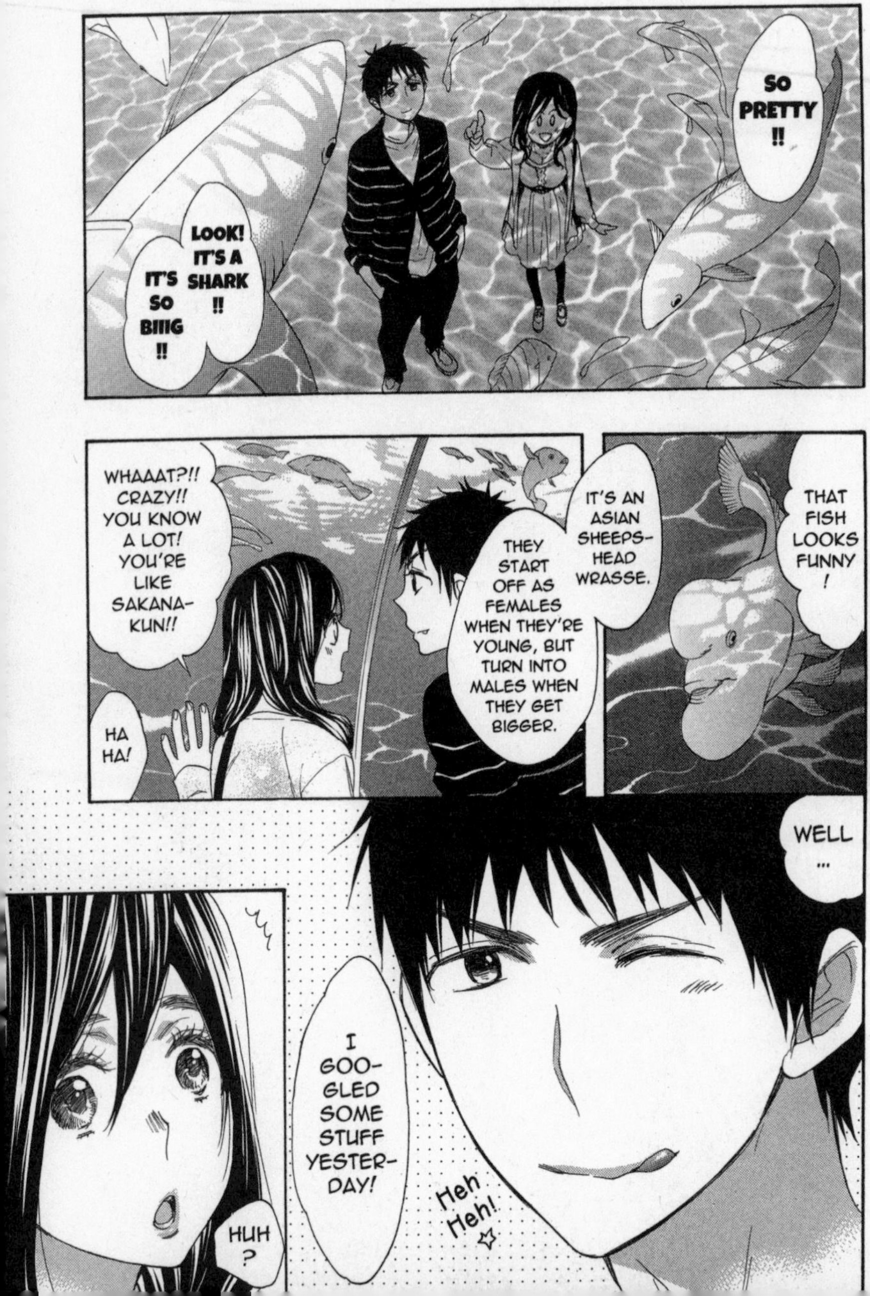
SO PRETTY!!
LOOK! IT'S A SHARK!!
IT'S SO BIIIG!!
THAT FISH LOOKS FUNNY!
IT'S AN ASIAN SHEEPS-HEAD WRASSE.
THEY START OFF AS FEMALES WHEN THEY'RE YOUNG, BUT TURN INTO MALES WHEN THEY GET BIGGER.
WHAAAT?!! CRAZY!! YOU KNOW A LOT! YOU'RE LIKE SAKANA-KUN!!
HA HA!
WELL...
I GOO-GLED SOME STUFF YESTER-DAY!
Heh Heh!
HUH?

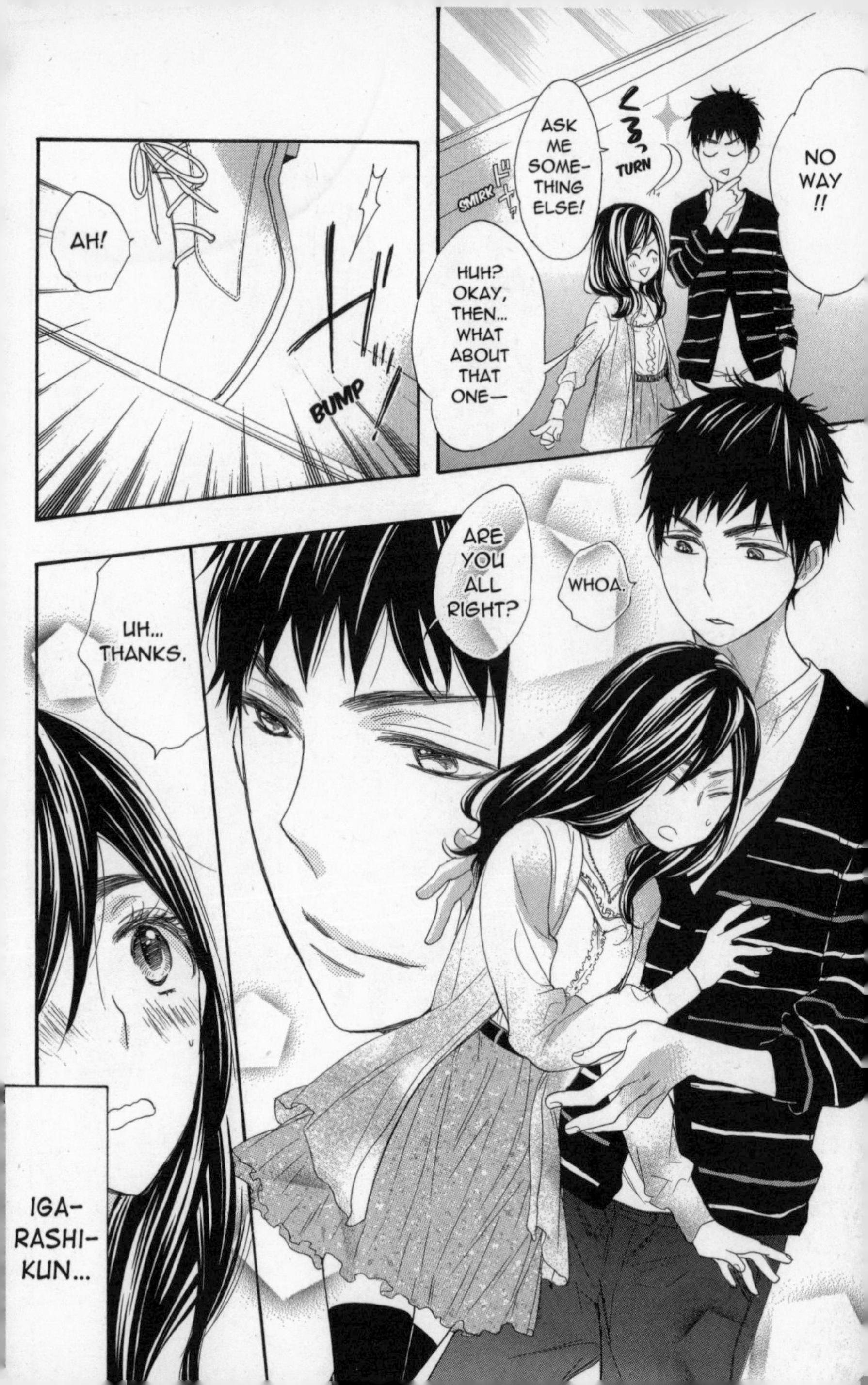
NO WAY!!
ASK ME SOME-THING ELSE!
TURN
SMIRK
HUH? OKAY, THEN... WHAT ABOUT THAT ONE—
AH!
BUMP
ARE YOU ALL RIGHT?
WHOA.
UH... THANKS.
IGA-RASHI-KUN...

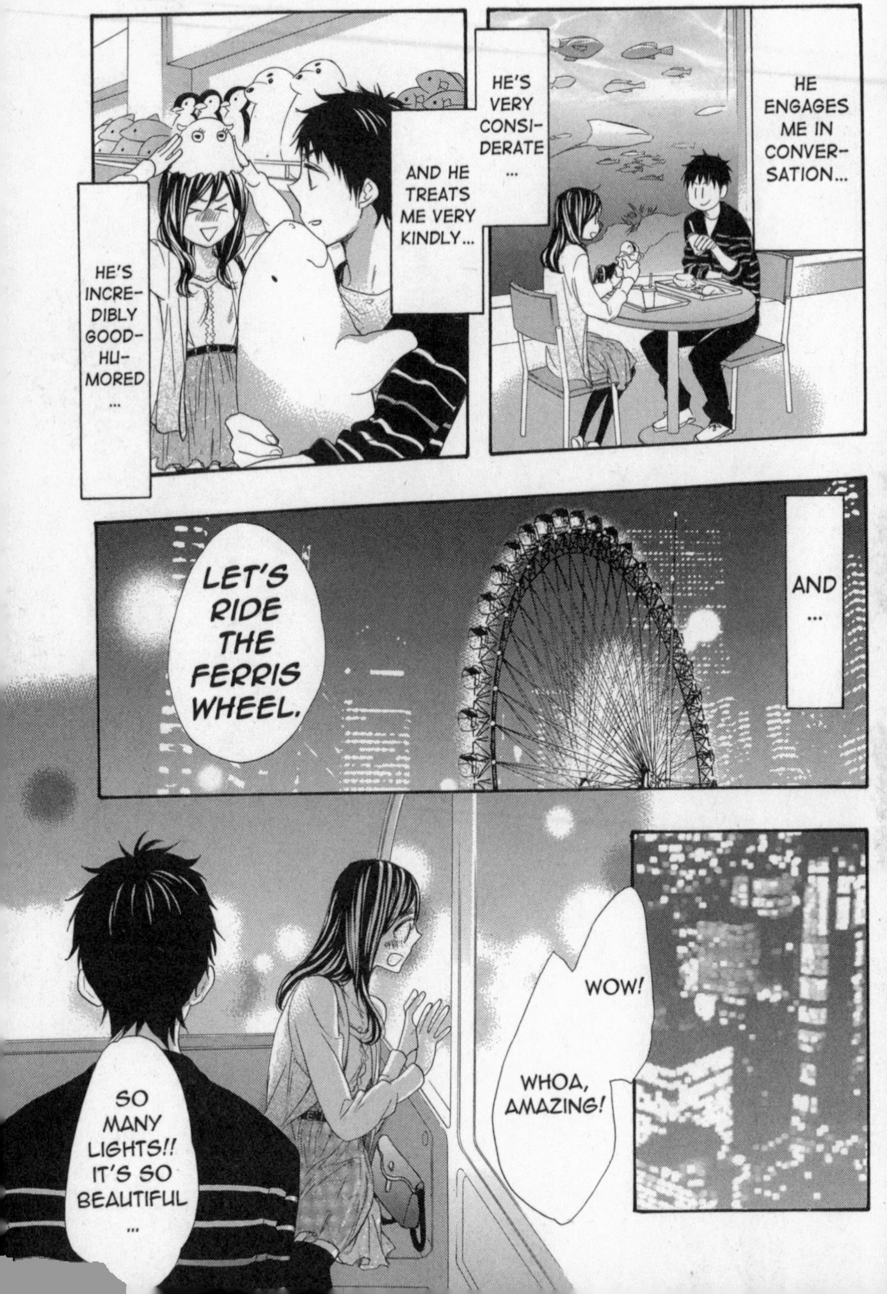
HE ENGAGES ME IN CONVERSATION...
HE'S VERY CONSIDERATE ...
AND HE TREATS ME VERY KINDLY...
HE'S INCREDIBLY GOOD-HUMORED ...
AND ...
LET'S RIDE THE FERRIS WHEEL.
WOW!
WHOA, AMAZING!
SO MANY LIGHTS!! IT'S SO BEAUTIFUL ...

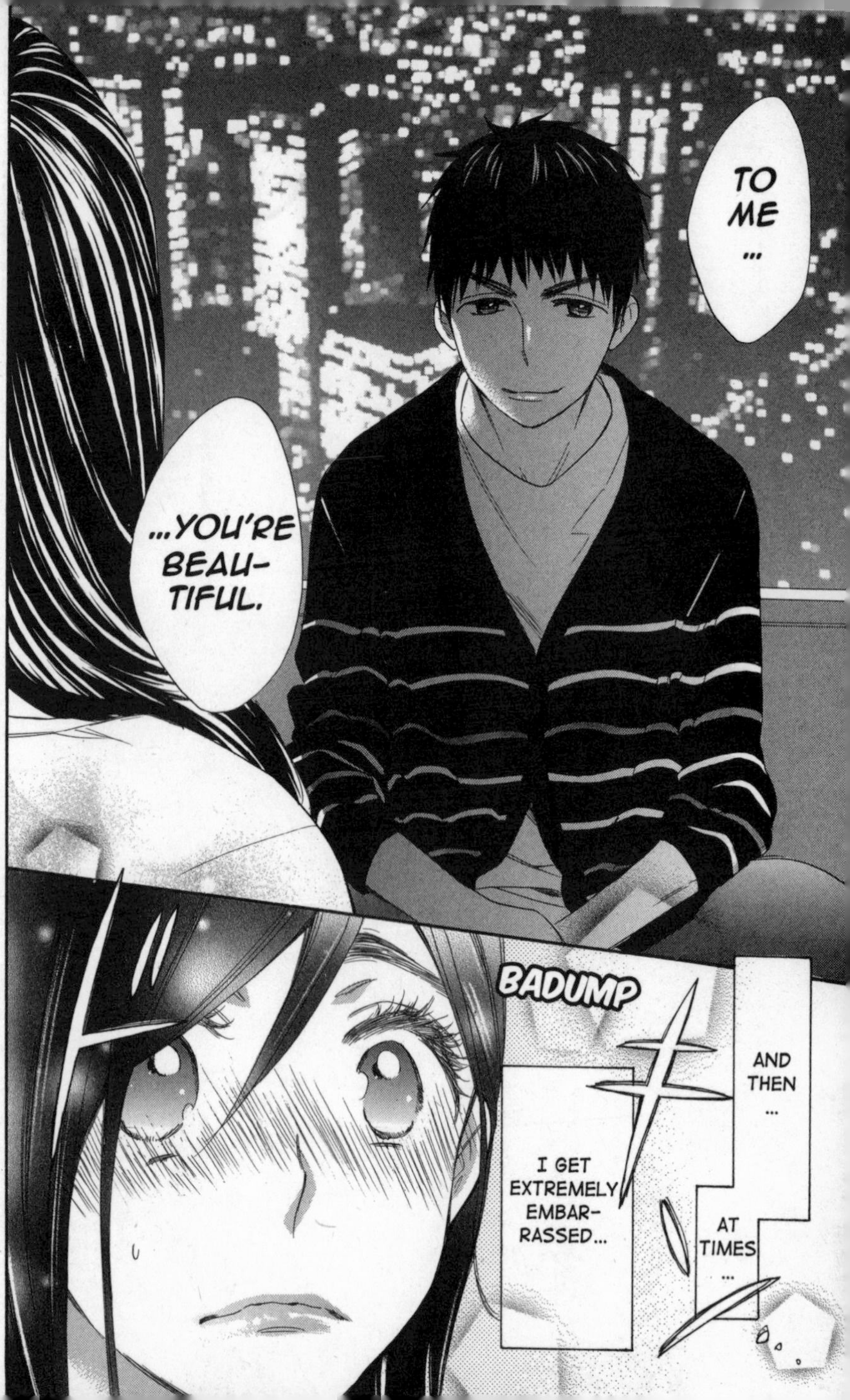
TO ME ...
...YOU'RE BEAU-TIFUL.
BADUMP
AND THEN ...
AT TIMES ...
I GET EXTREMELY EMBAR-RASSED...

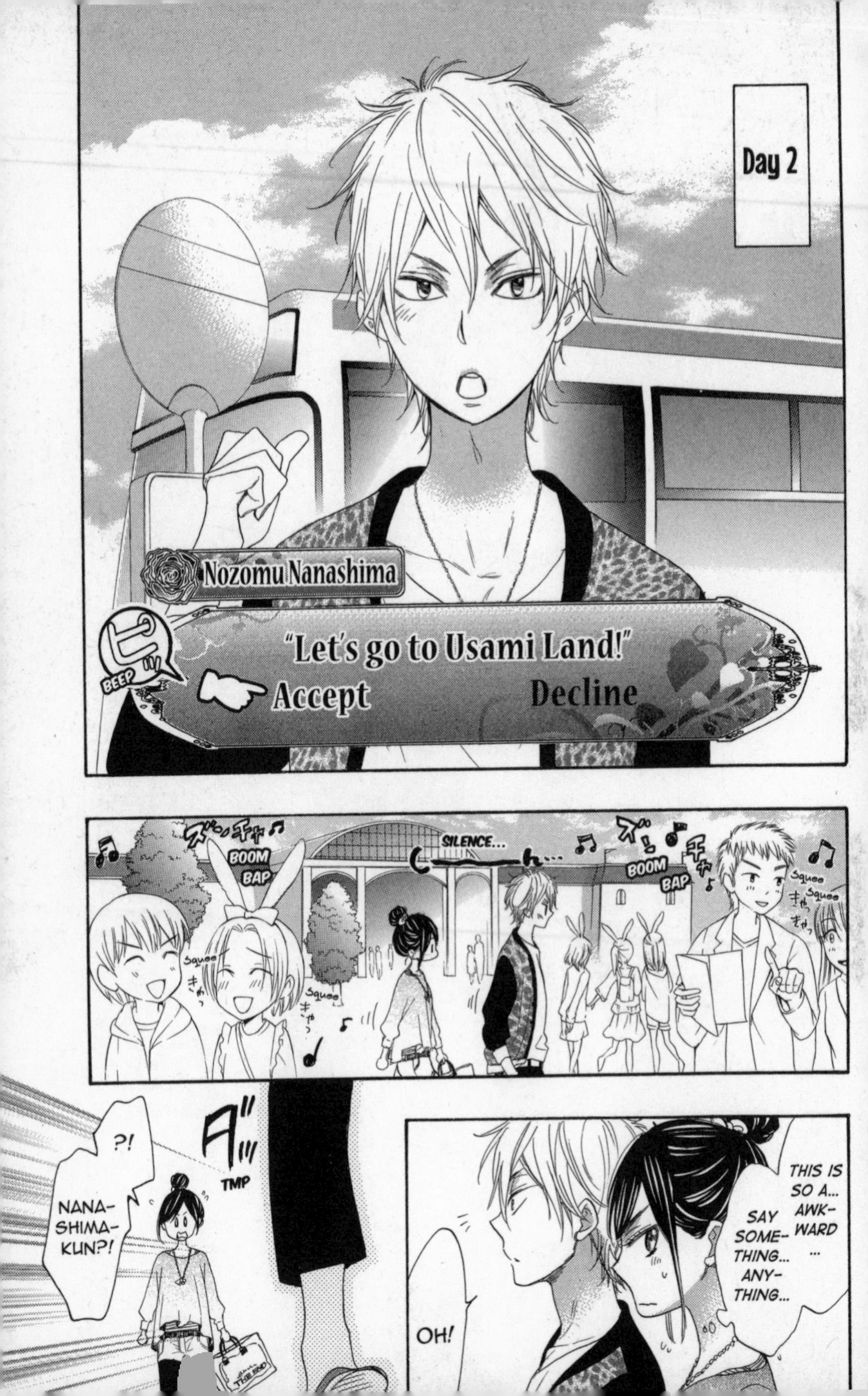
Day 2
Nozomu Nanashima
BEEP
"Let's go to Usami Land!"
Accept
Decline
Squee
Squee
BOOM BAP
SILENCE...
BOOM BAP
Squee
Squee
THIS IS SO A... AWK-WARD ...
SAY SOME-THING... ANY-THING...
OH!
TMP
?!
NANA-SHIMA-KUN?!

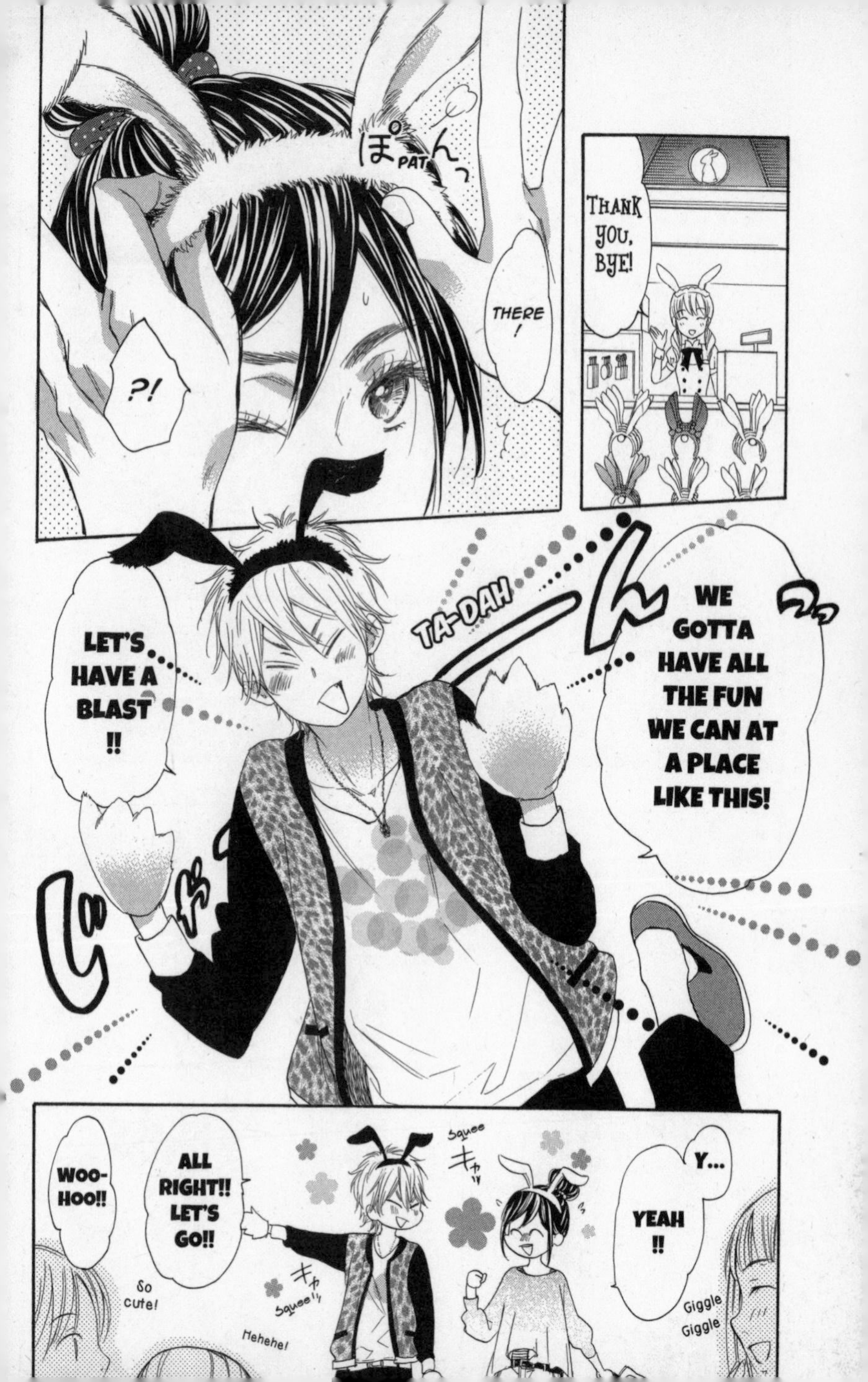
THANK YOU, BYE!
ぽんっ
PAT
THERE!
?!
WE GOTTA HAVE ALL THE FUN WE CAN AT A PLACE LIKE THIS!
TA-DAH
LET'S HAVE A BLAST!!
Y... YEAH!!
Giggle Giggle
キャ
Squee
ALL RIGHT!! LET'S GO!!
WOO-HOO!!
キャ
Squee
So cute!
Hehehe!

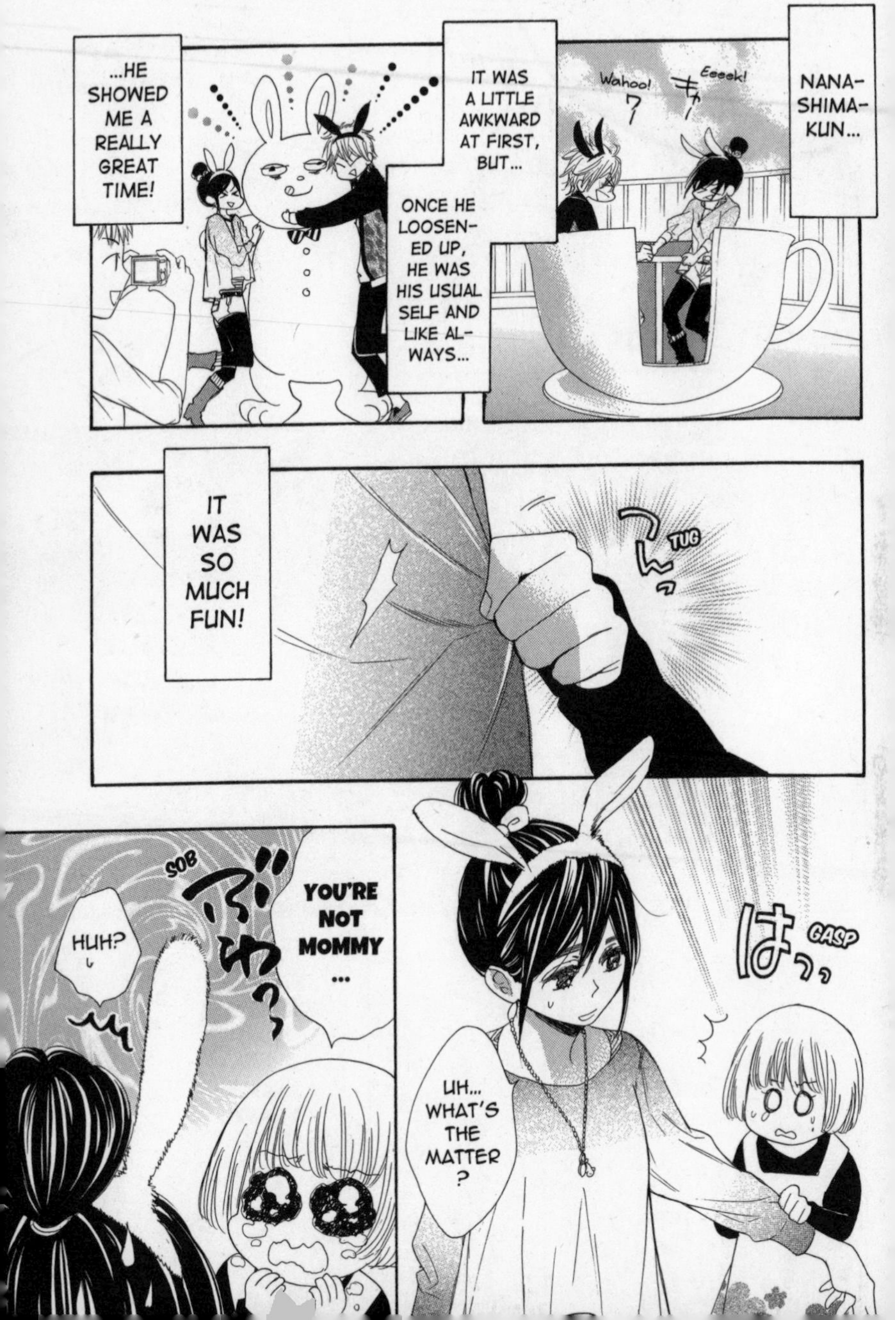
NANA-SHIMA-KUN...
Eeeek!
Wahoo!
IT WAS A LITTLE AWKWARD AT FIRST, BUT...
ONCE HE LOOSEN-ED UP, HE WAS HIS USUAL SELF AND LIKE AL-WAYS...
...HE SHOWED ME A REALLY GREAT TIME!
IT WAS SO MUCH FUN!
TUG
GASP
UH... WHAT'S THE MATTER?
YOU'RE NOT MOMMY...
SOB
HUH?

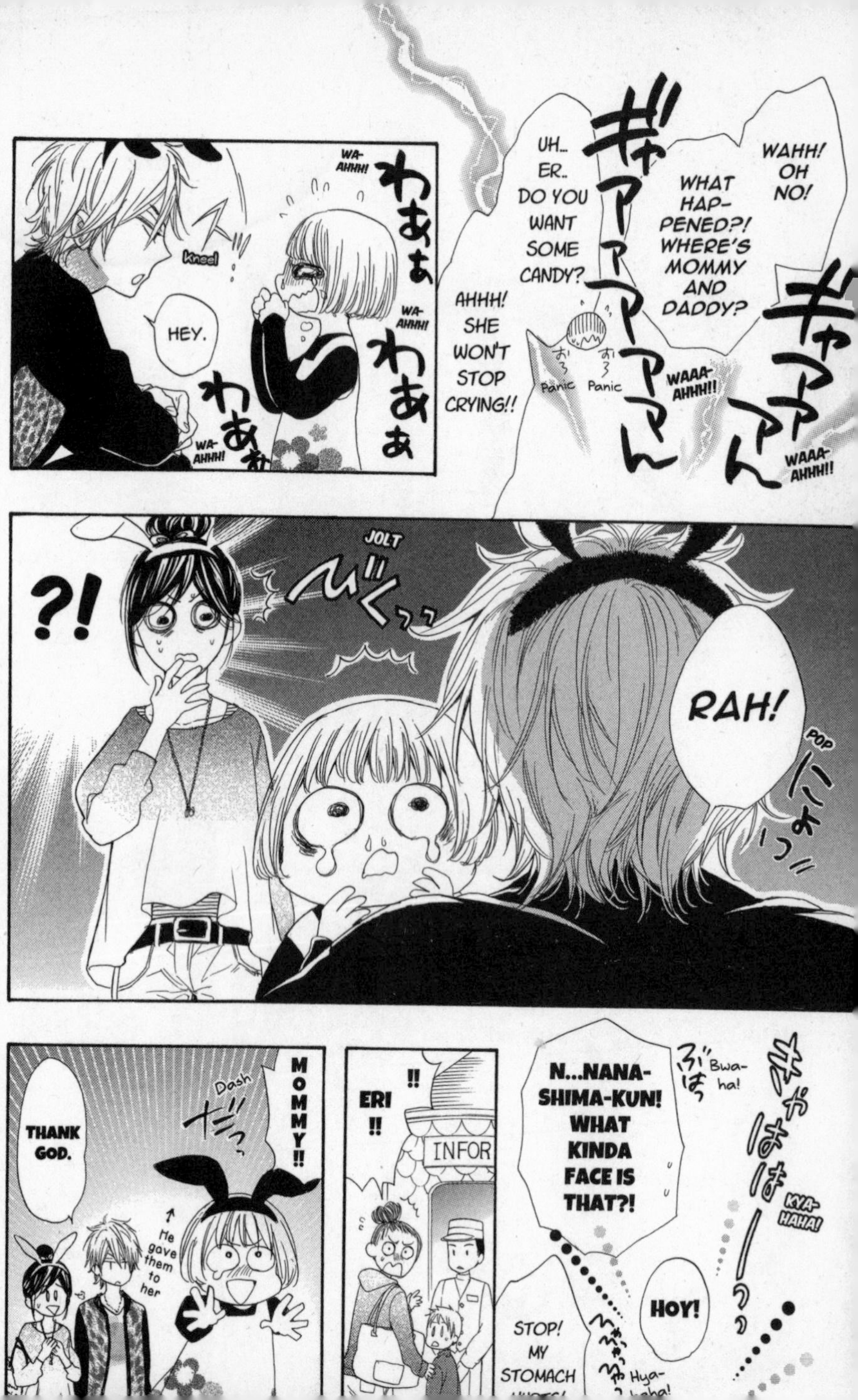

WAHH! OH NO!
WHAT HAP-PENED?! WHERE'S MOMMY AND DADDY?
ギャアアアん
WAAA-AHHH!!
UH... ER.. DO YOU WANT SOME CANDY?
ギャアアアアん
WAAA-AHHH!!
おろ Panic
おろ Panic
AHHH! SHE WON'T STOP CRYING!!
わぁぁ
WA-AHHH!
わぁぁ
WA-AHHH!
わぁぁ
WA-AHHH!
Kneel
HEY.
RAH!
にょっ
POP
びくっ
JOLT
?!
きゃははーっっ
KYA-HAHA!
ぶはっ
Bwa-ha!
N...NANA-SHIMA-KUN! WHAT KINDA FACE IS THAT?!
HOY!
Hya-haha!
STOP! MY STOMACH
!!
ERI!!
INFOR
MOMMY!!
Dash
THANK GOD.
He gave them to her

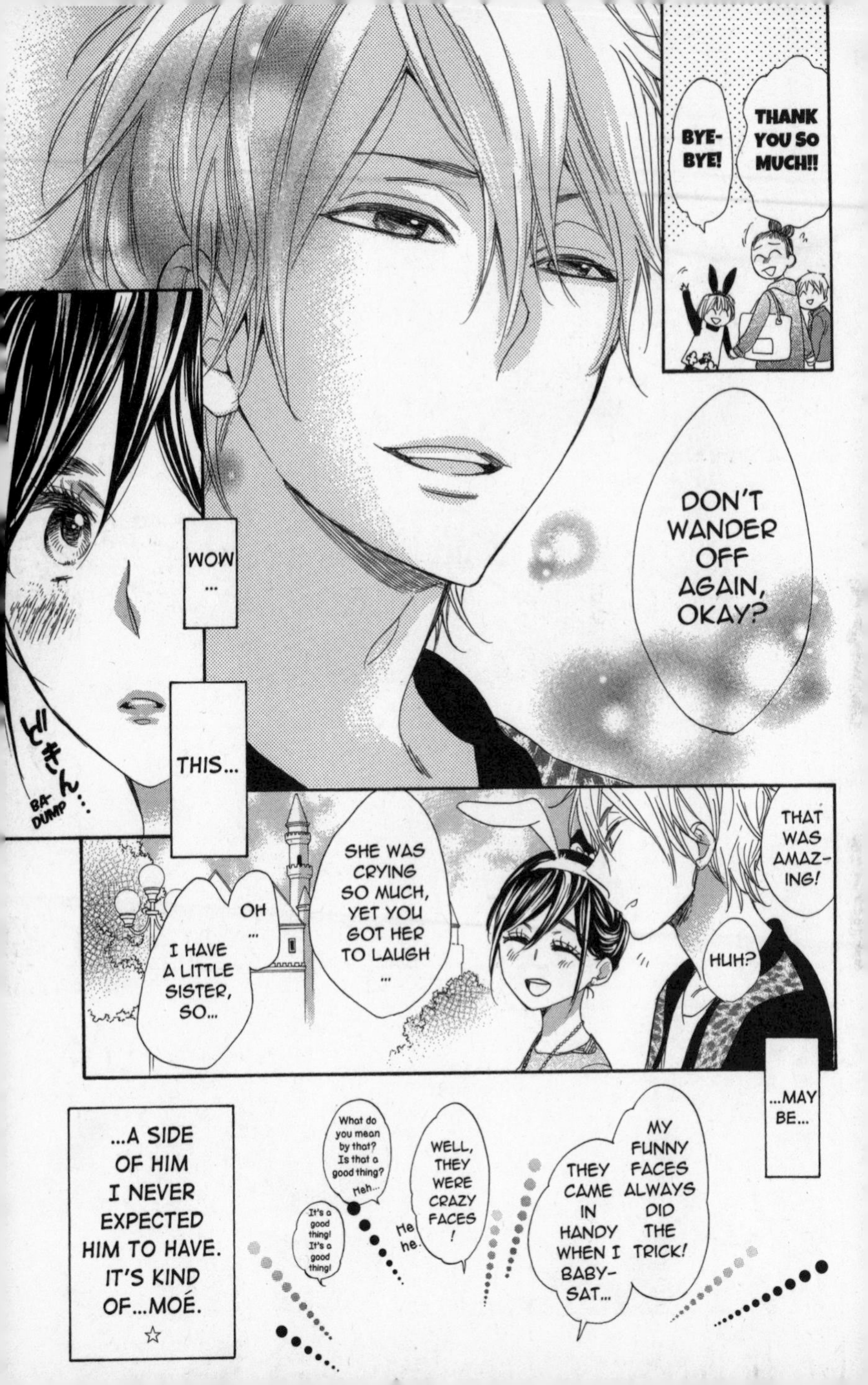
THANK YOU SO MUCH!!
BYE-BYE!
DON'T WANDER OFF AGAIN, OKAY?
WOW...
THIS...
どきん… BA-DUMP
THAT WAS AMAZING!
HUH?
SHE WAS CRYING SO MUCH, YET YOU GOT HER TO LAUGH...
OH... I HAVE A LITTLE SISTER, SO...
...MAY BE...
MY FUNNY FACES ALWAYS DID THE TRICK!
THEY CAME IN HANDY WHEN I BABY-SAT...
WELL, THEY WERE CRAZY FACES!
He he.
What do you mean by that? Is that a good thing?
Heh...
It's a good thing! It's a good thing!
...A SIDE OF HIM I NEVER EXPECTED HIM TO HAVE. IT'S KIND OF...MOÉ. ☆

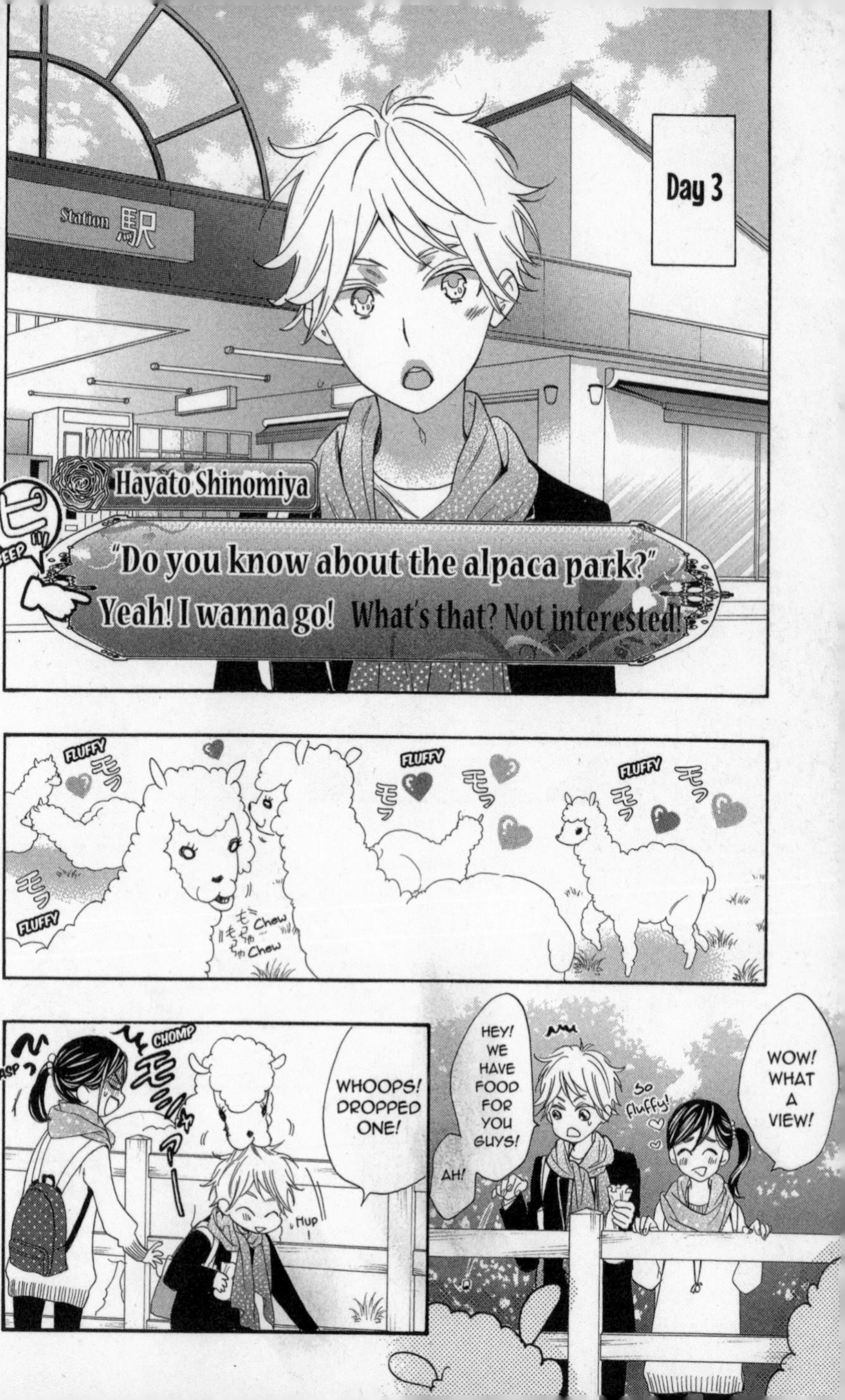
Day 3
Station 駅
Hayato Shinomiya
BEEP
"Do you know about the alpaca park?"
Yeah! I wanna go!
What's that? Not interested!
FLUFFY
FLUFFY
FLUFFY
FLUFFY
Chew Chew
WOW! WHAT A VIEW!
So fluffy!
HEY! WE HAVE FOOD FOR YOU GUYS!
AH!
WHOOPS! DROPPED ONE!
Hup!
CHOMP
GASP

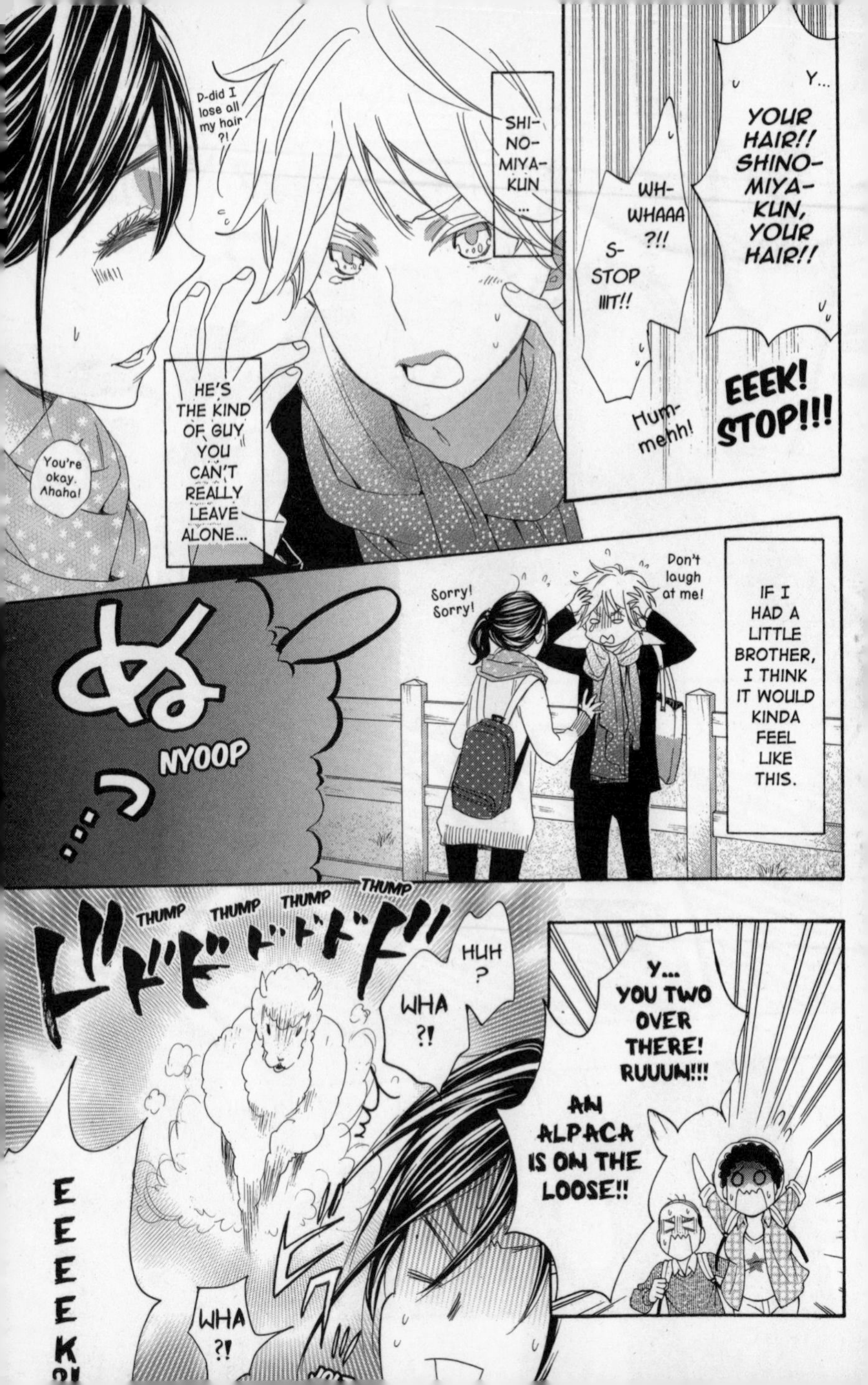
Y...
YOUR HAIR!! SHINO-MIYA-KUN, YOUR HAIR!!
EEEK! STOP!!!
WH-WHAAA?!!
S-STOP IIIT!!
Hum-mehh!
SHI-NO-MIYA-KUN...
D-did I lose all my hair?!
HE'S THE KIND OF GUY YOU CAN'T REALLY LEAVE ALONE...
You're okay. Ahaha!
IF I HAD A LITTLE BROTHER, I THINK IT WOULD KINDA FEEL LIKE THIS.
Don't laugh at me!
Sorry! Sorry!
ぬっ...
NYOOP
Y... YOU TWO OVER THERE! RUUUN!!!
AN ALPACA IS ON THE LOOSE!!
ドドドドドドド
THUMP THUMP THUMP THUMP
HUH?
WHA?!
WHA?!
EEEEEK

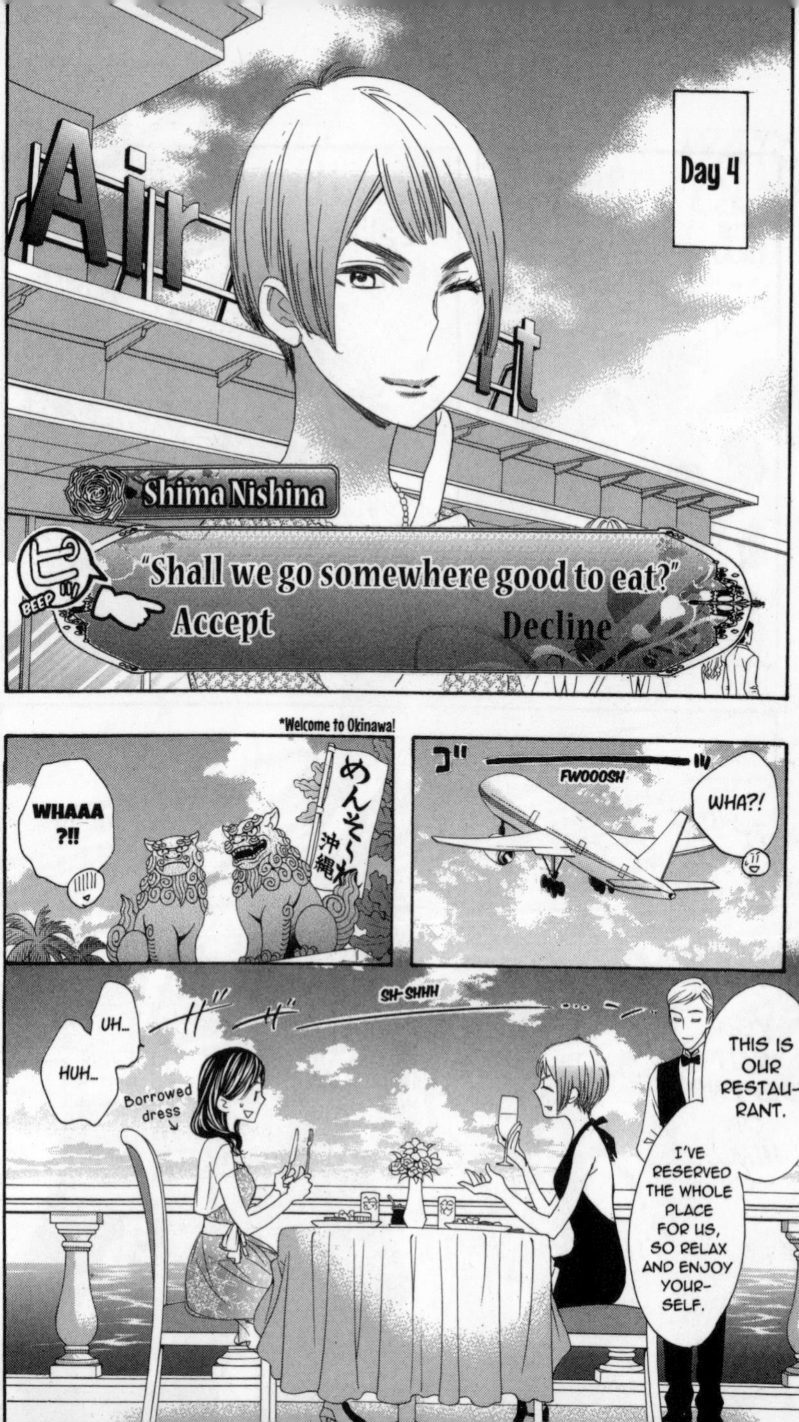
Day 4
Shima Nishina
ピッ BEEP
"Shall we go somewhere good to eat?"
Accept
Decline
ゴ"
FWOOOSH
WHA?!
*Welcome to Okinawa!
めんそ〜れ沖縄
WHAAA?!!
THIS IS OUR RESTAURANT.
I'VE RESERVED THE WHOLE PLACE FOR US, SO RELAX AND ENJOY YOURSELF.
SH-SHHH
UH...
HUH...
Borrowed dress

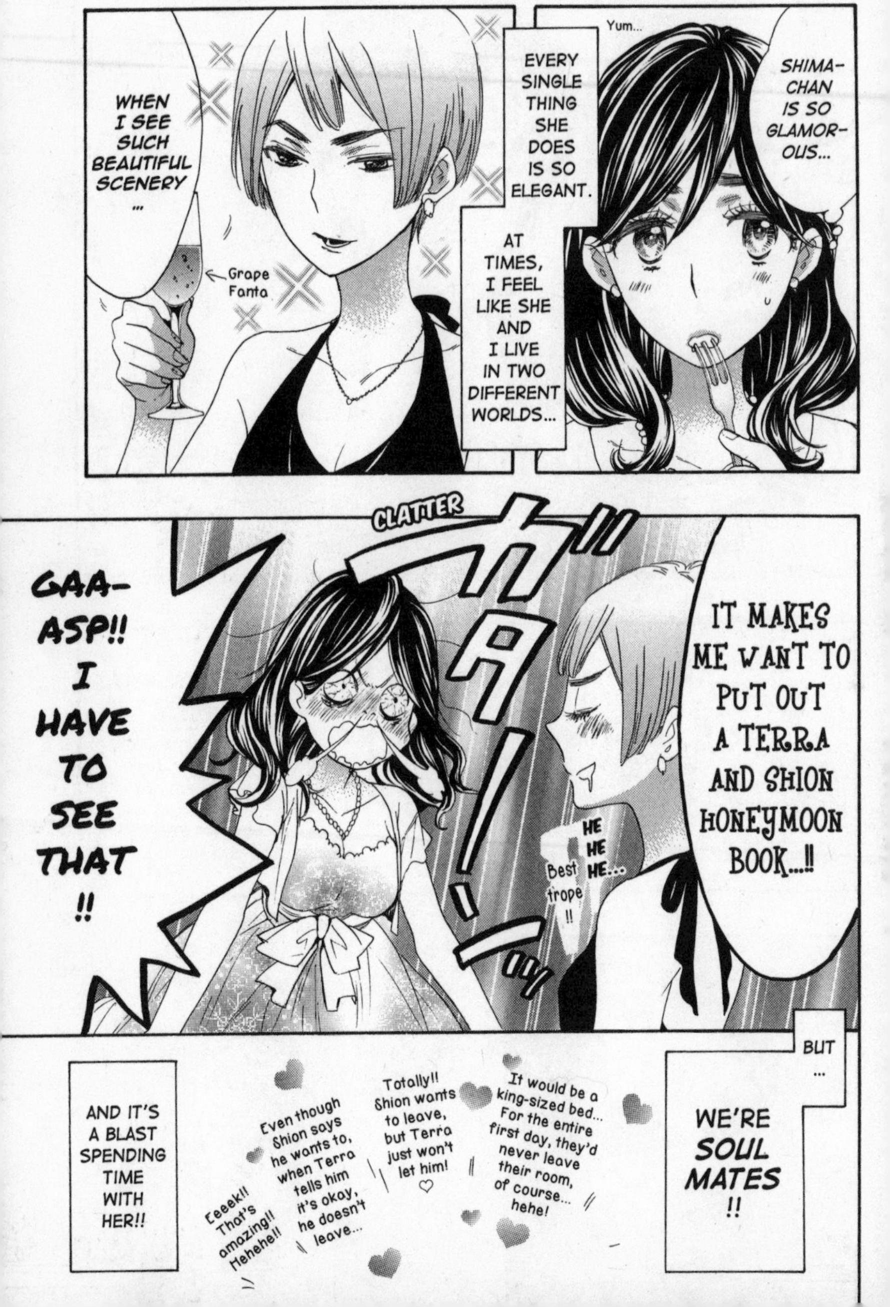
Yum...
SHIMA-CHAN IS SO GLAMOROUS...
EVERY SINGLE THING SHE DOES IS SO ELEGANT.
AT TIMES, I FEEL LIKE SHE AND I LIVE IN TWO DIFFERENT WORLDS...
WHEN I SEE SUCH BEAUTIFUL SCENERY ...
Grape Fanta
CLATTER
IT MAKES ME WANT TO PUT OUT A TERRA AND SHION HONEYMOON BOOK...!!
HE HE HE...
Best trope !!
GAA-ASP!! I HAVE TO SEE THAT !!
BUT ...
WE'RE SOUL MATES !!
It would be a king-sized bed... For the entire first day, they'd never leave their room, of course... hehe!
Totally!! Shion wants to leave, but Terra just won't let him! ♡
Even though Shion says he wants to, when Terra tells him it's okay, he doesn't leave...
Eeeek!! That's amazing!! Hehehe!!
AND IT'S A BLAST SPENDING TIME WITH HER!!

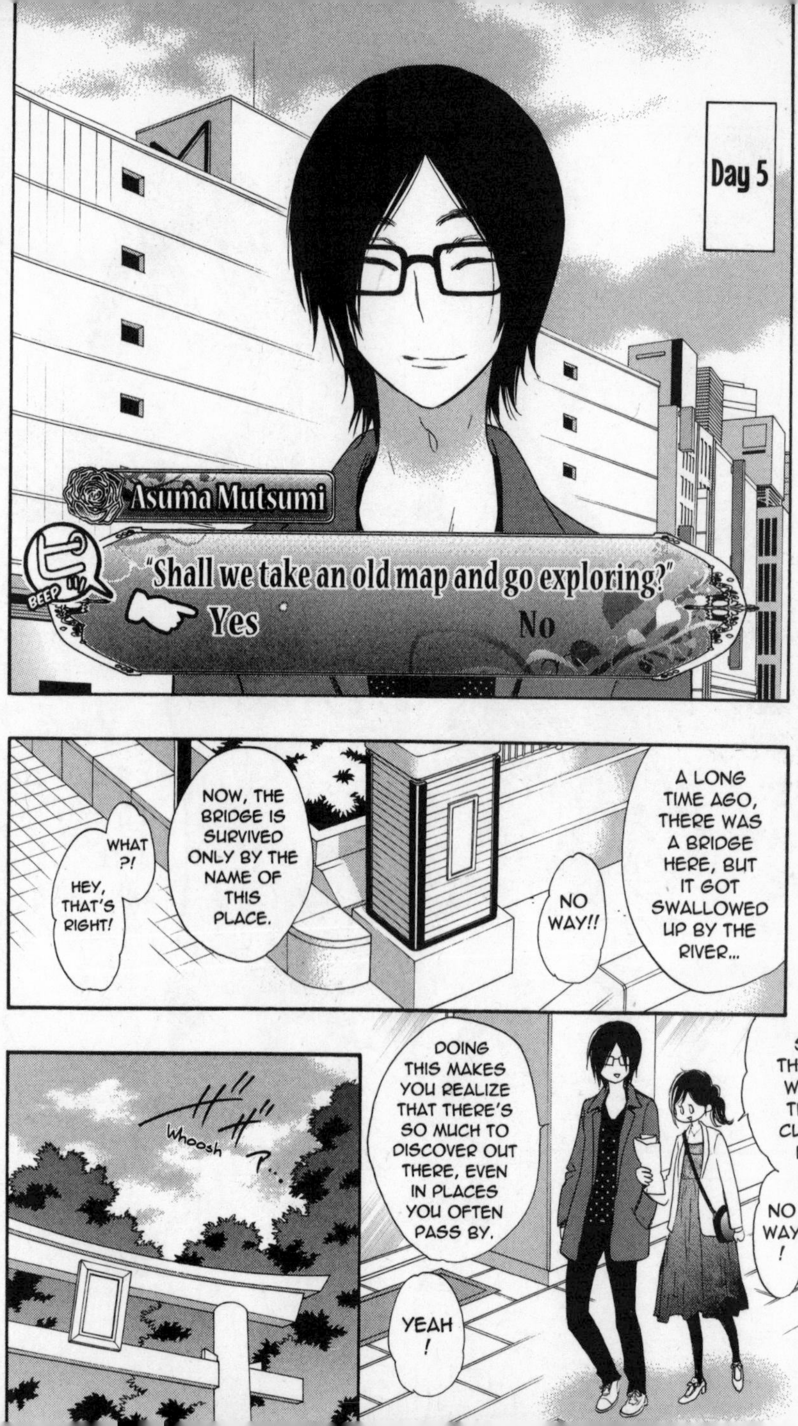
Day 5
Asuma Mutsumi
BEEP
"Shall we take an old map and go exploring?"
Yes
No
A LONG TIME AGO, THERE WAS A BRIDGE HERE, BUT IT GOT SWALLOWED UP BY THE RIVER...
NO WAY!!
NOW, THE BRIDGE IS SURVIVED ONLY BY THE NAME OF THIS PLACE.
WHAT?!
HEY, THAT'S RIGHT!
SO THAT'S WHAT THAT CURVE IS!
NO WAY!
DOING THIS MAKES YOU REALIZE THAT THERE'S SO MUCH TO DISCOVER OUT THERE, EVEN IN PLACES YOU OFTEN PASS BY.
YEAH!
Whoosh

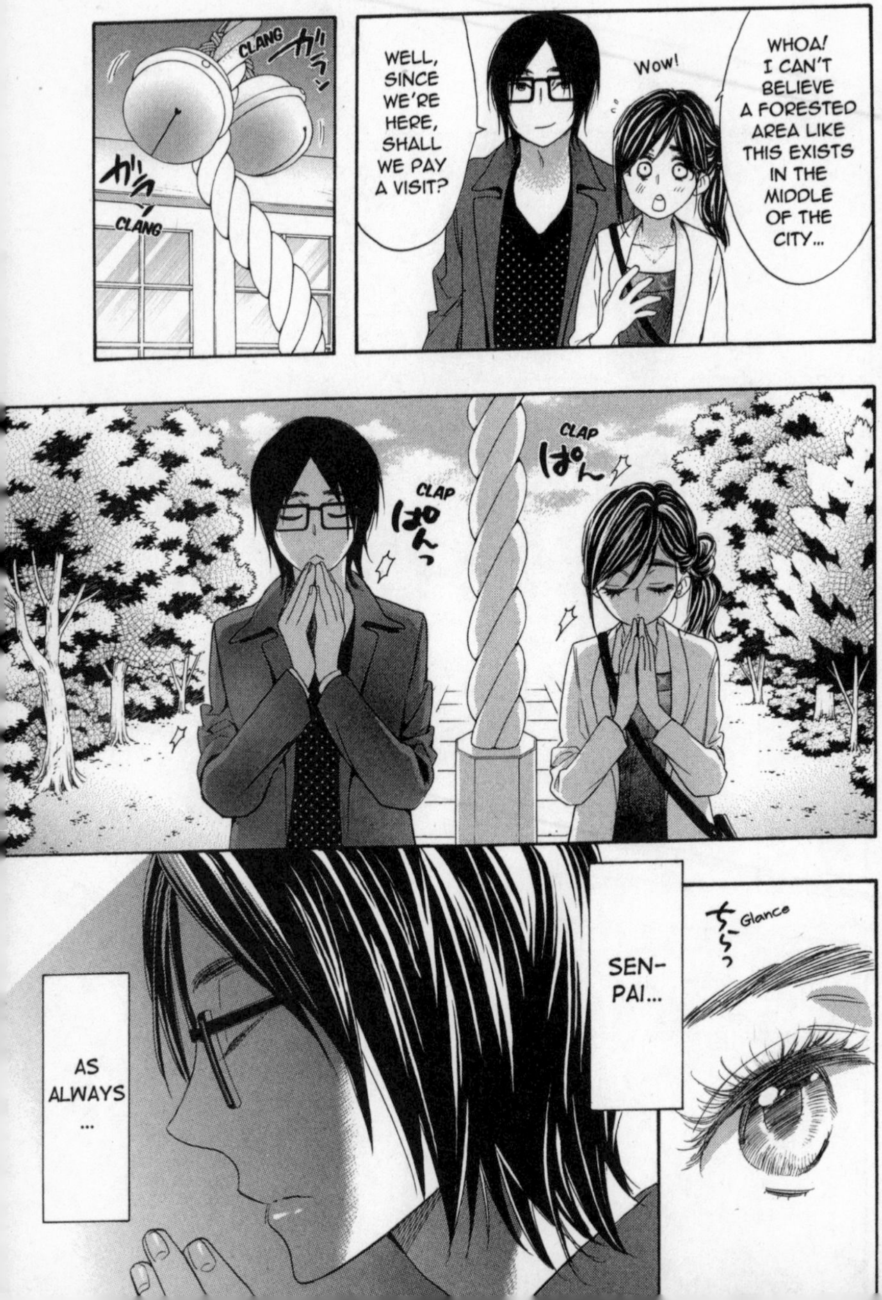
WHOA! I CAN'T BELIEVE A FORESTED AREA LIKE THIS EXISTS IN THE MIDDLE OF THE CITY...
Wow!
WELL, SINCE WE'RE HERE, SHALL WE PAY A VISIT?
CLANG
CLANG
CLAP
CLAP
Glance
SEN-PAI...
AS ALWAYS ...

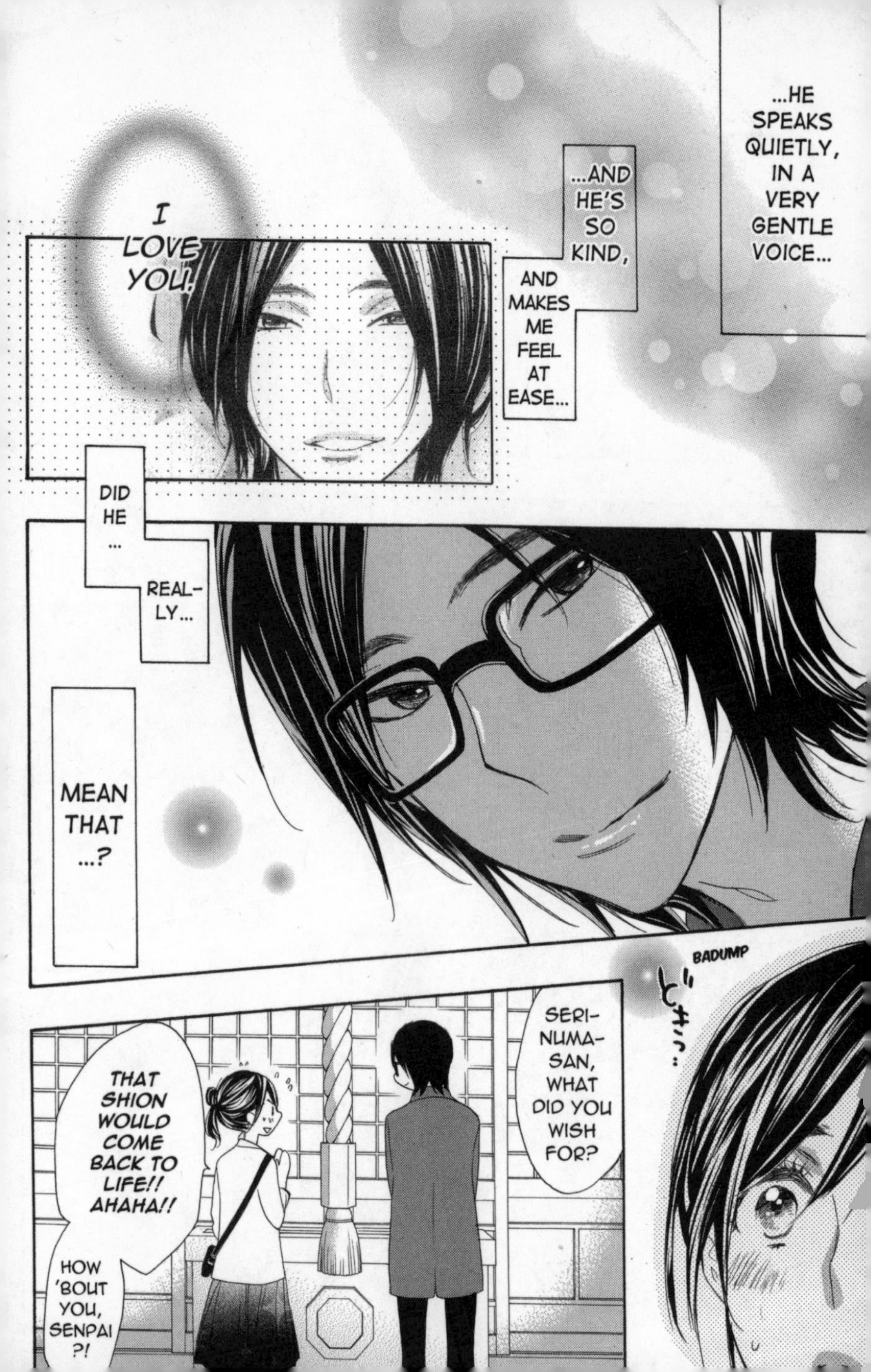
...HE SPEAKS QUIETLY, IN A VERY GENTLE VOICE...
...AND HE'S SO KIND,
AND MAKES ME FEEL AT EASE...
I LOVE YOU.
DID HE ...
REALLY...
MEAN THAT ...?
BADUMP
どきっ..
SERI-NUMA-SAN, WHAT DID YOU WISH FOR?
THAT SHION WOULD COME BACK TO LIFE!! AHAHA!!
HOW 'BOUT YOU, SENPAI?!

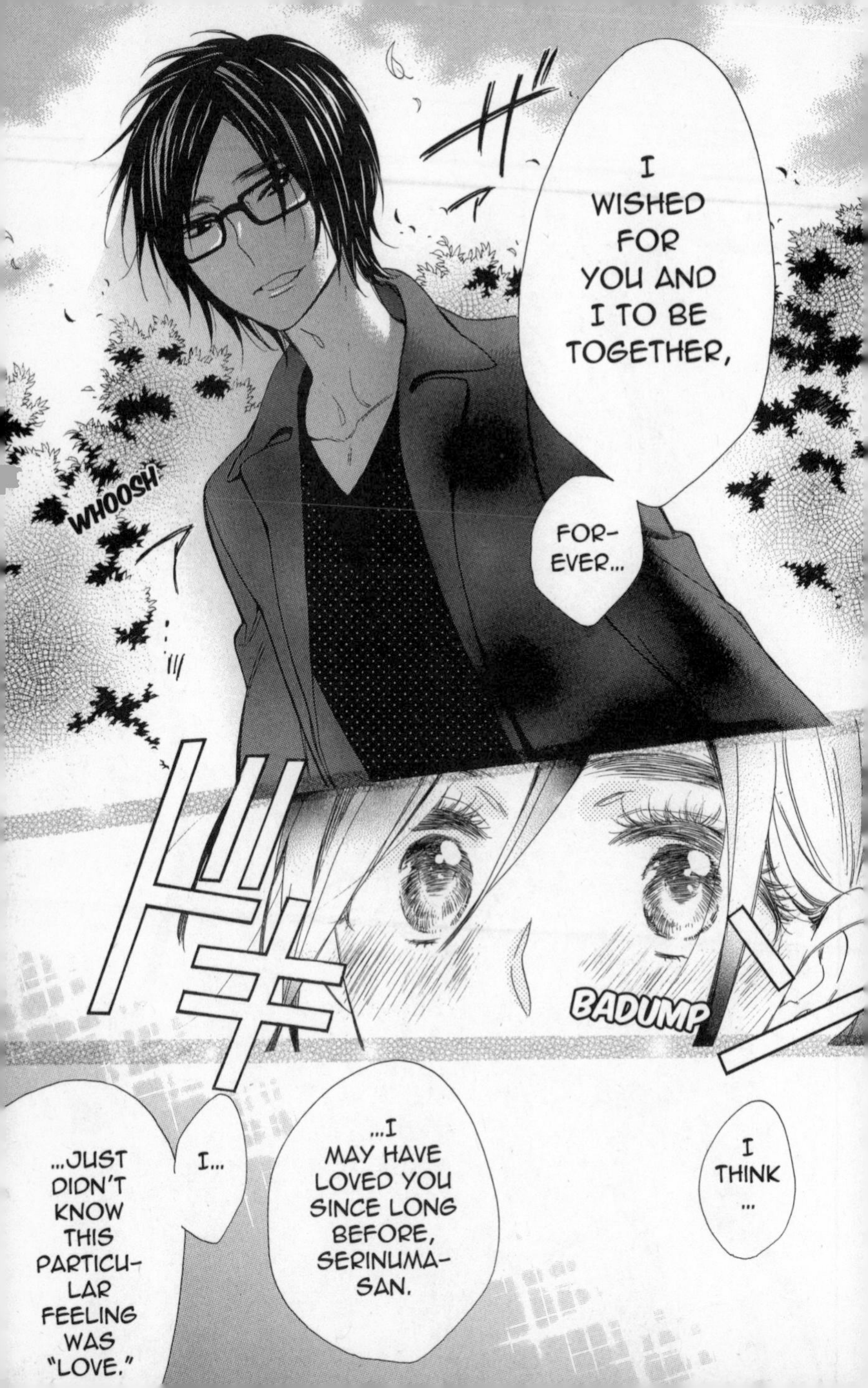
I WISHED FOR YOU AND I TO BE TOGETHER,
FOR-EVER...
WHOOSH
BADUMP
I THINK ...
...I MAY HAVE LOVED YOU SINCE LONG BEFORE, SERINUMA-SAN.
I...
...JUST DIDN'T KNOW THIS PARTICU-LAR FEELING WAS "LOVE."

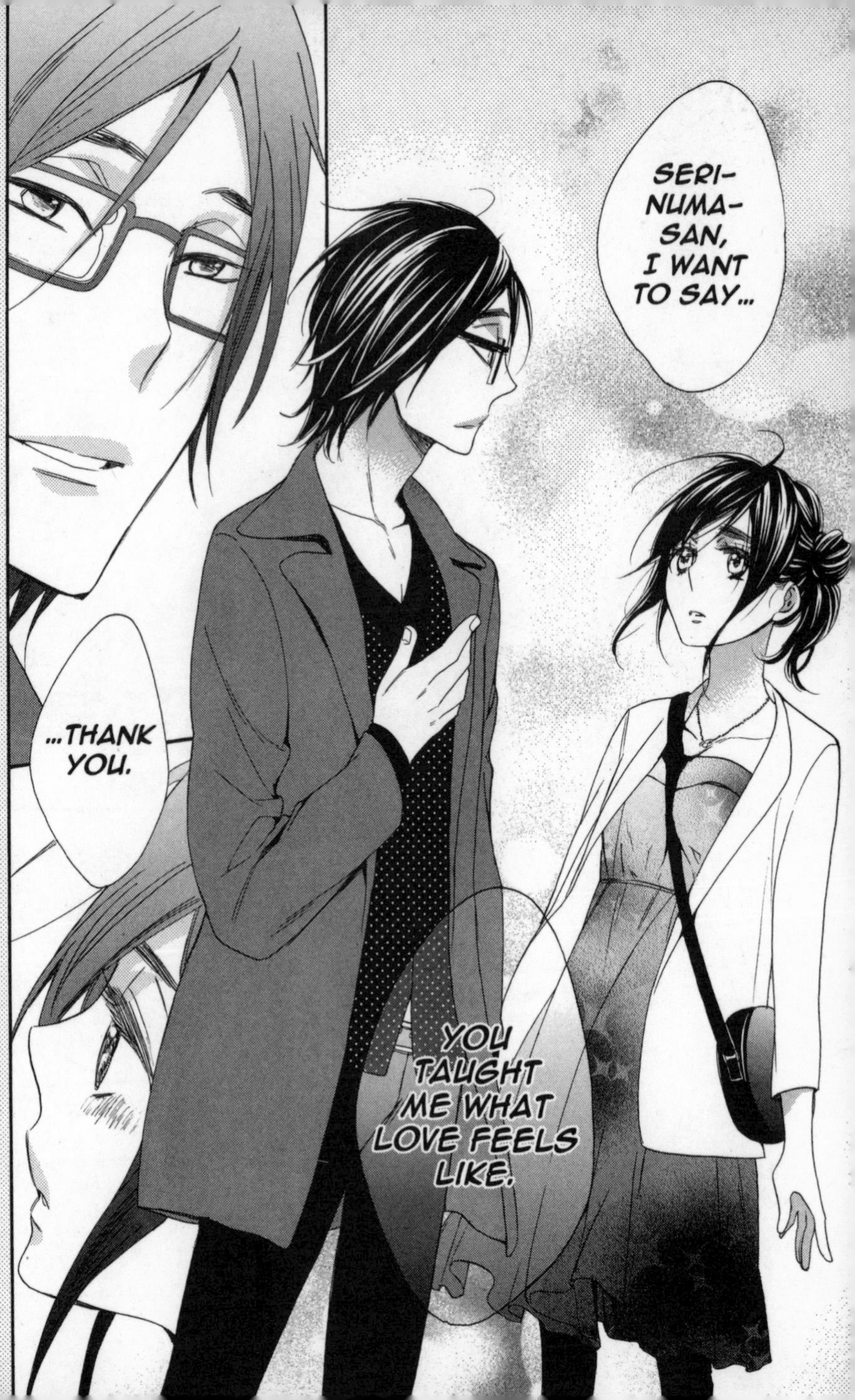
SERI-NUMA-SAN, I WANT TO SAY...
YOU TAUGHT ME WHAT LOVE FEELS LIKE.
...THANK YOU.

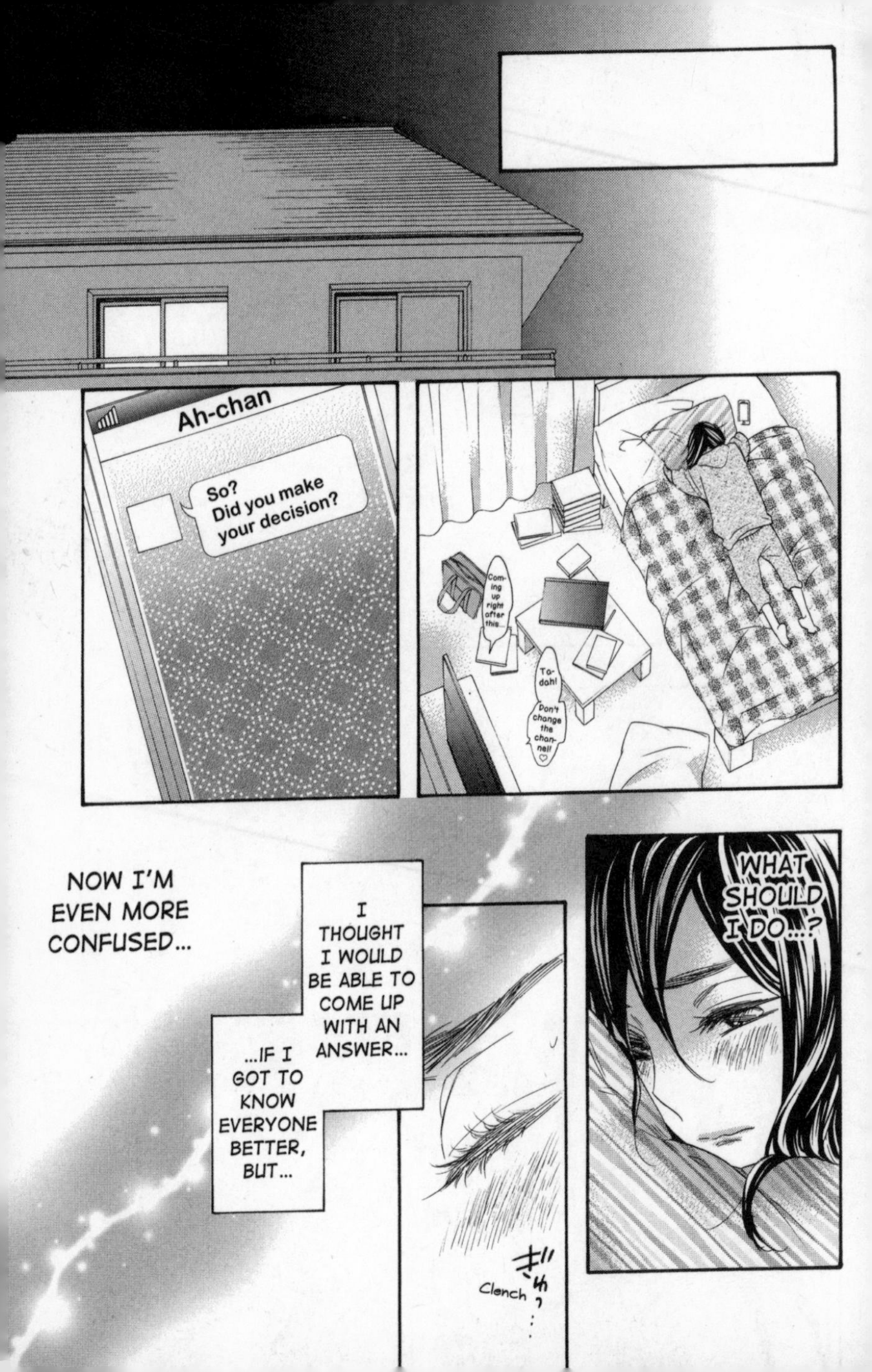

Coming up right after this...
Ta-dah!
Don't change the channel! ♡
Ah-chan
So? Did you make your decision?
WHAT SHOULD I DO...?
I THOUGHT I WOULD BE ABLE TO COME UP WITH AN ANSWER...
...IF I GOT TO KNOW EVERYONE BETTER, BUT...
Clench
NOW I'M EVEN MORE CONFUSED...

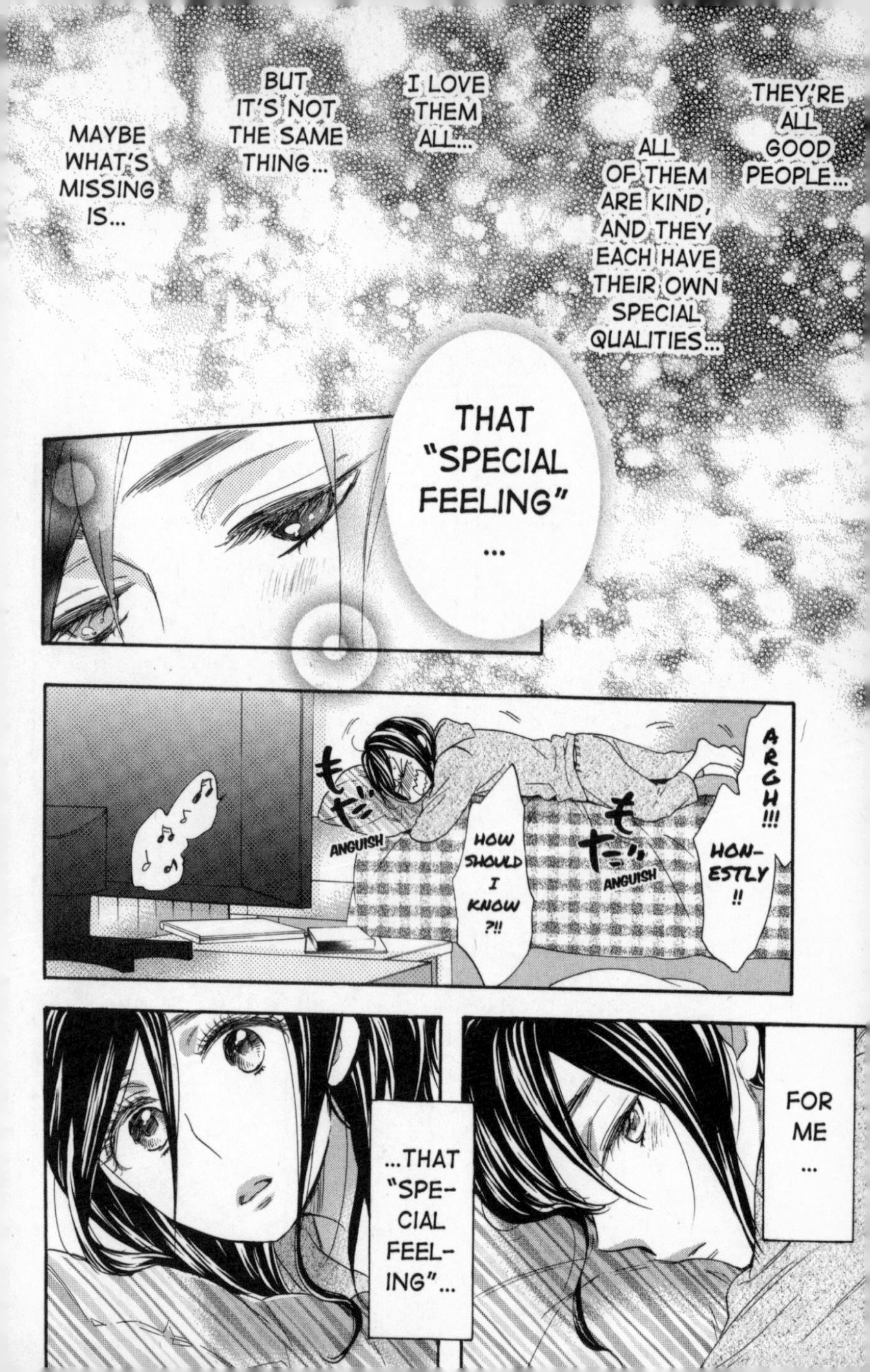
THEY'RE ALL GOOD PEOPLE...
ALL OF THEM ARE KIND, AND THEY EACH HAVE THEIR OWN SPECIAL QUALITIES...
I LOVE THEM ALL...
BUT IT'S NOT THE SAME THING...
MAYBE WHAT'S MISSING IS...
THAT "SPECIAL FEELING" ...
ARGH!!!
HON-ESTLY !!
ANGUISH
HOW SHOULD I KNOW ?!!
ANGUISH
FOR ME ...
...THAT "SPE-CIAL FEEL-ING"...

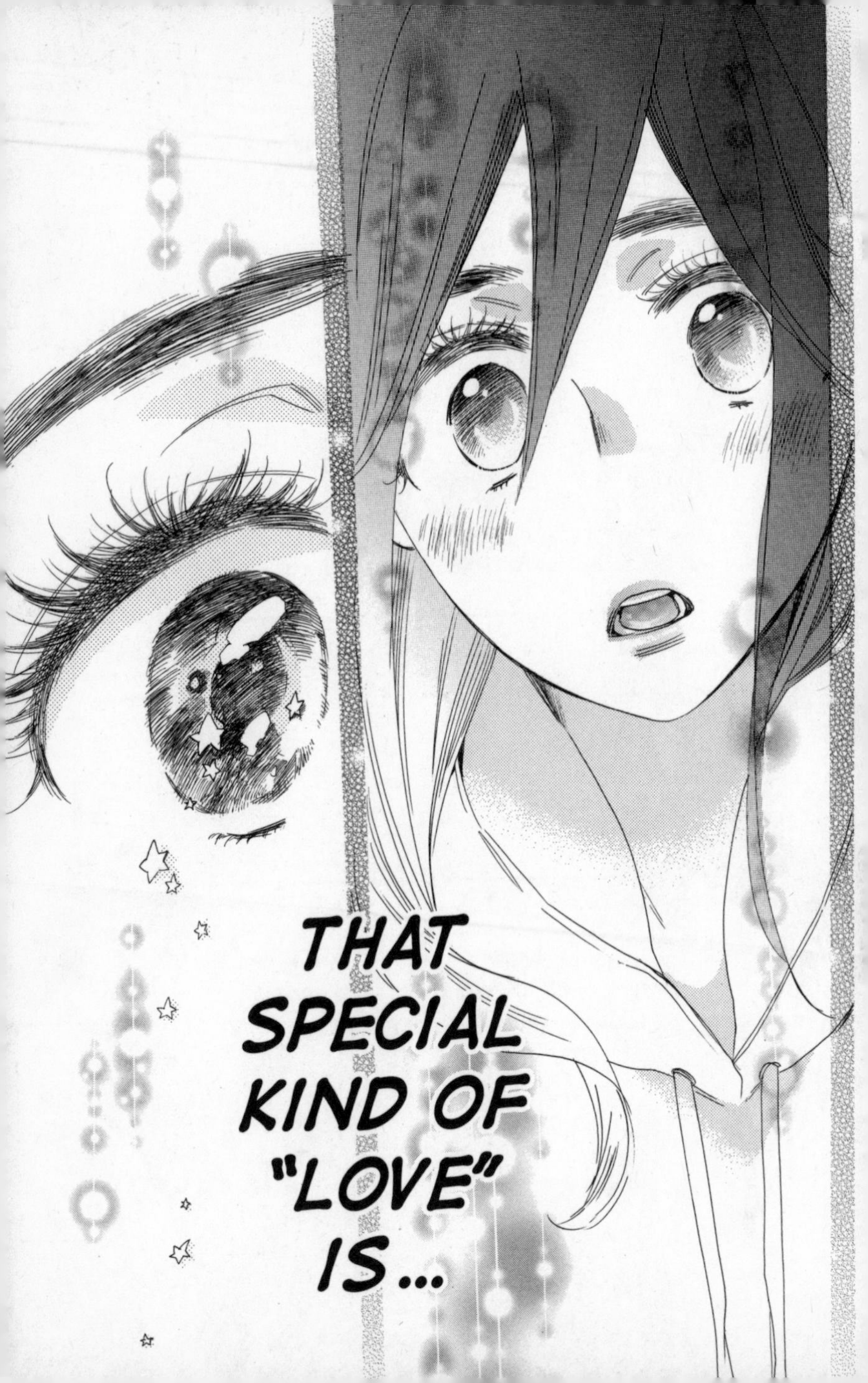
THAT SPECIAL KIND OF "LOVE" IS...

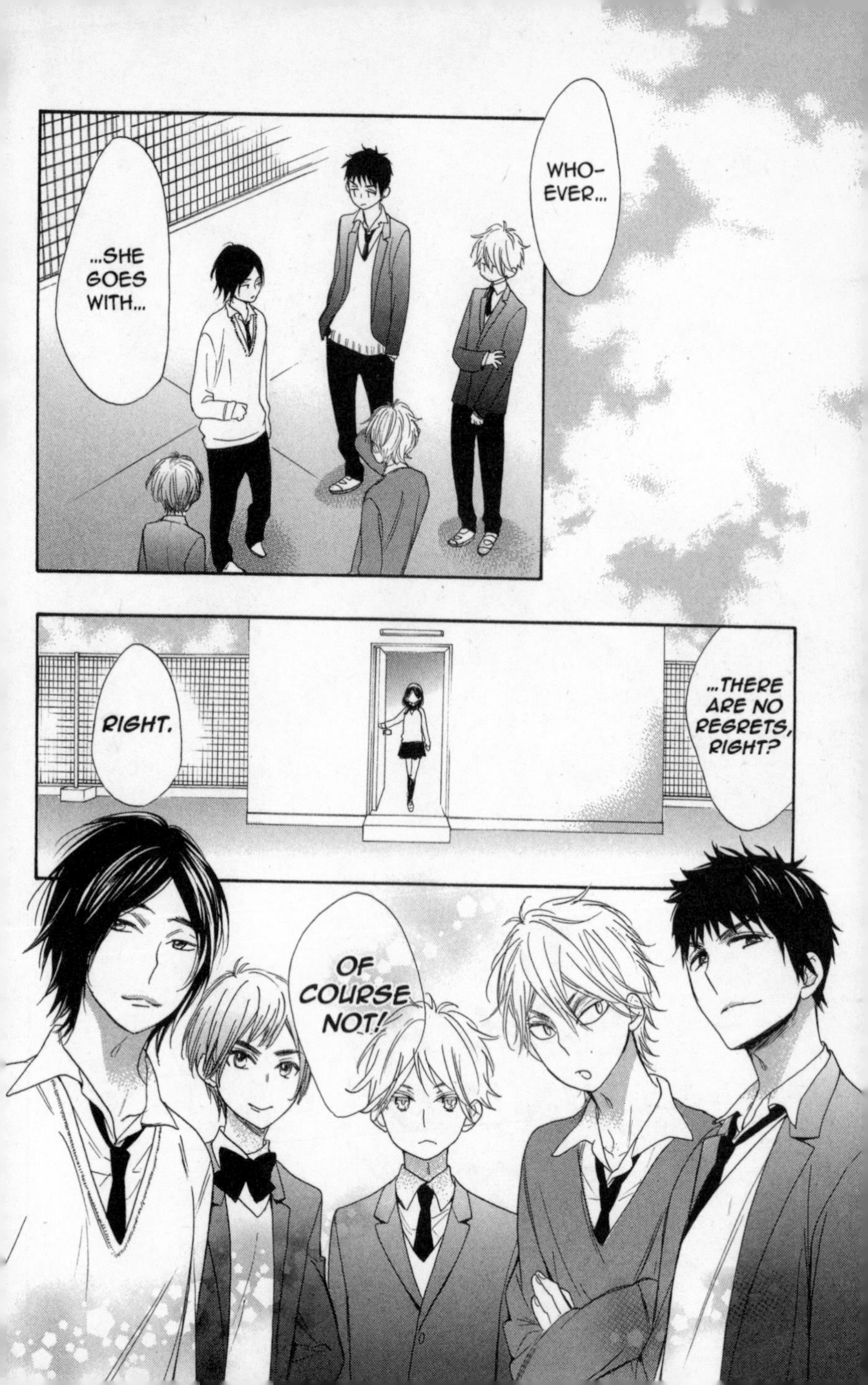
WHO-EVER...
...SHE GOES WITH...
...THERE ARE NO REGRETS, RIGHT?
RIGHT.
OF COURSE NOT!

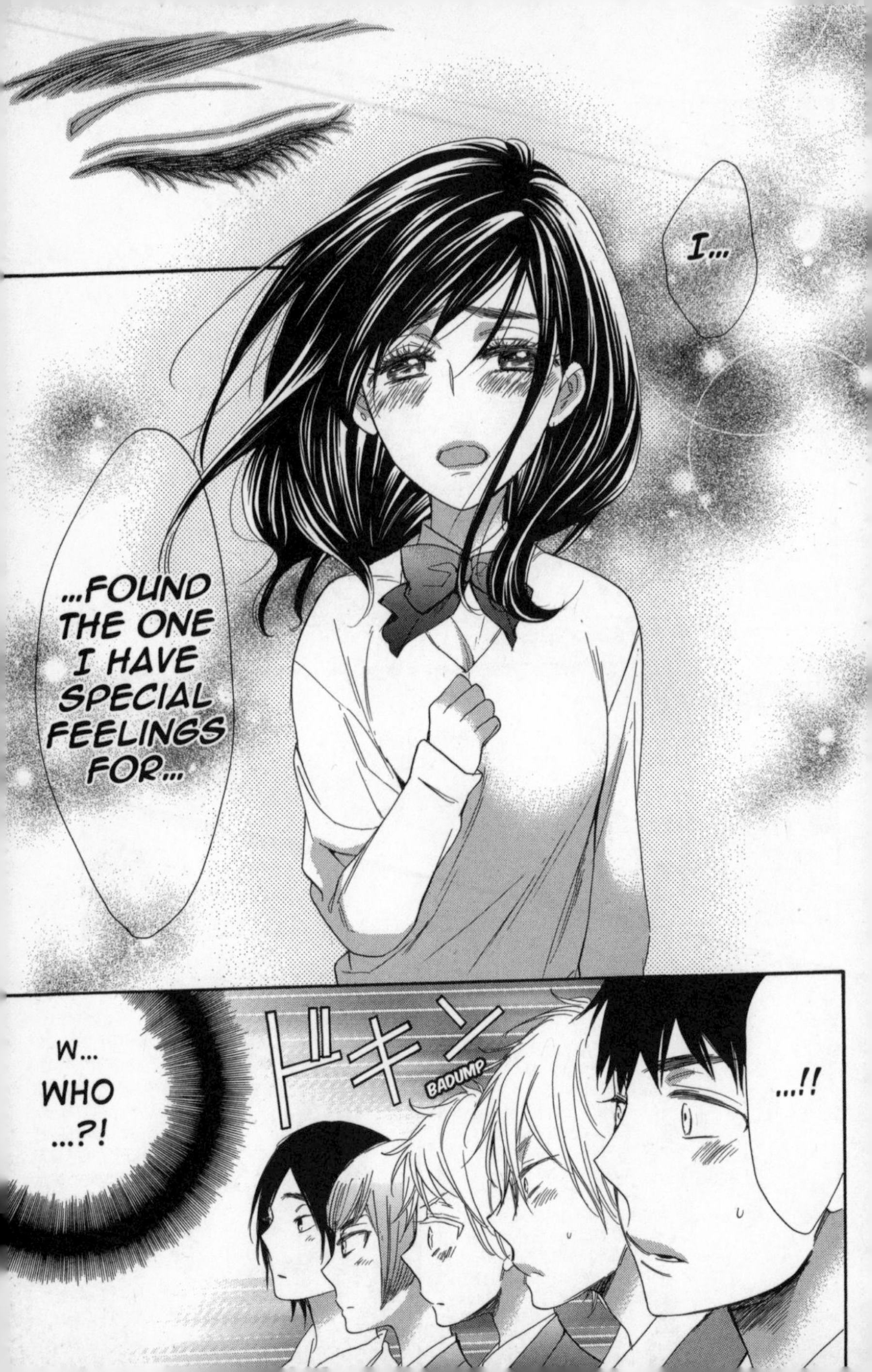
I...
...FOUND THE ONE I HAVE SPECIAL FEELINGS FOR...
...!!
ドキン
BADUMP
W... WHO ...?!

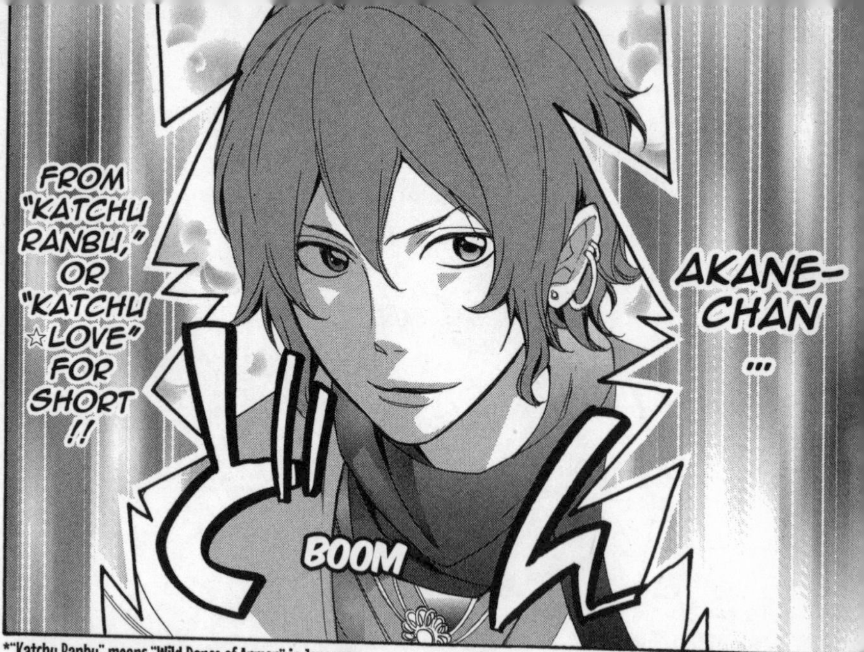
AKANE-CHAN ...
FROM "KATCHU RANBU," OR "KATCHU☆LOVE" FOR SHORT !!
BOOM

*"Katchu Ranbu" means "Wild Dance of Armor" in Japanese.

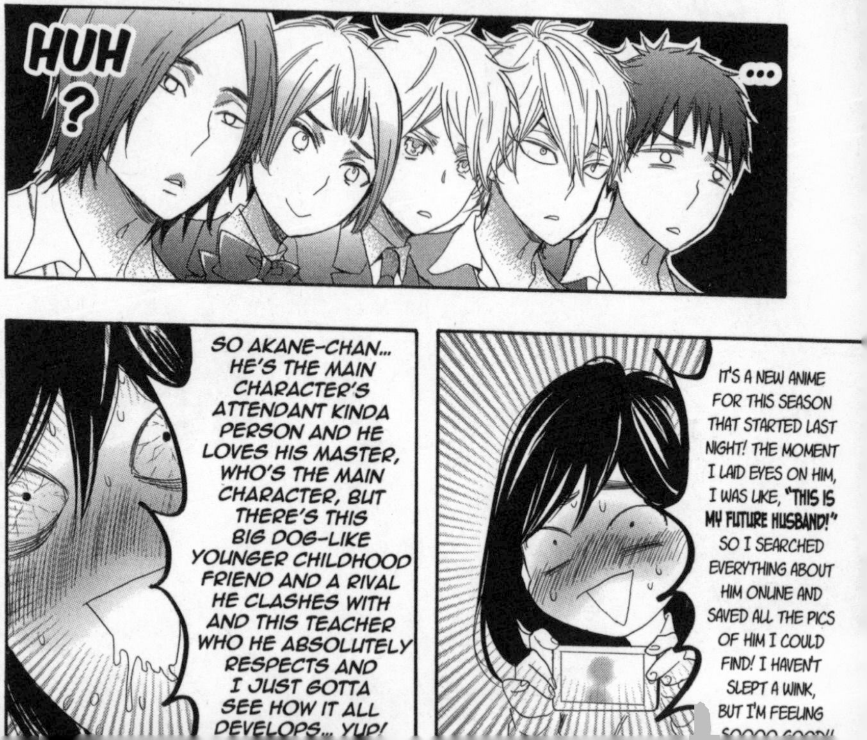
...
HUH ?
IT'S A NEW ANIME FOR THIS SEASON THAT STARTED LAST NIGHT! THE MOMENT I LAID EYES ON HIM, I WAS LIKE, "THIS IS MY FUTURE HUSBAND!" SO I SEARCHED EVERYTHING ABOUT HIM ONLINE AND SAVED ALL THE PICS OF HIM I COULD FIND! I HAVEN'T SLEPT A WINK, BUT I'M FEELING
SO AKANE-CHAN... HE'S THE MAIN CHARACTER'S ATTENDANT KINDA PERSON AND HE LOVES HIS MASTER, WHO'S THE MAIN CHARACTER, BUT THERE'S THIS BIG DOG-LIKE YOUNGER CHILDHOOD FRIEND AND A RIVAL HE CLASHES WITH AND THIS TEACHER WHO HE ABSOLUTELY RESPECTS AND I JUST GOTTA SEE HOW IT ALL DEVELOPS... YUP!

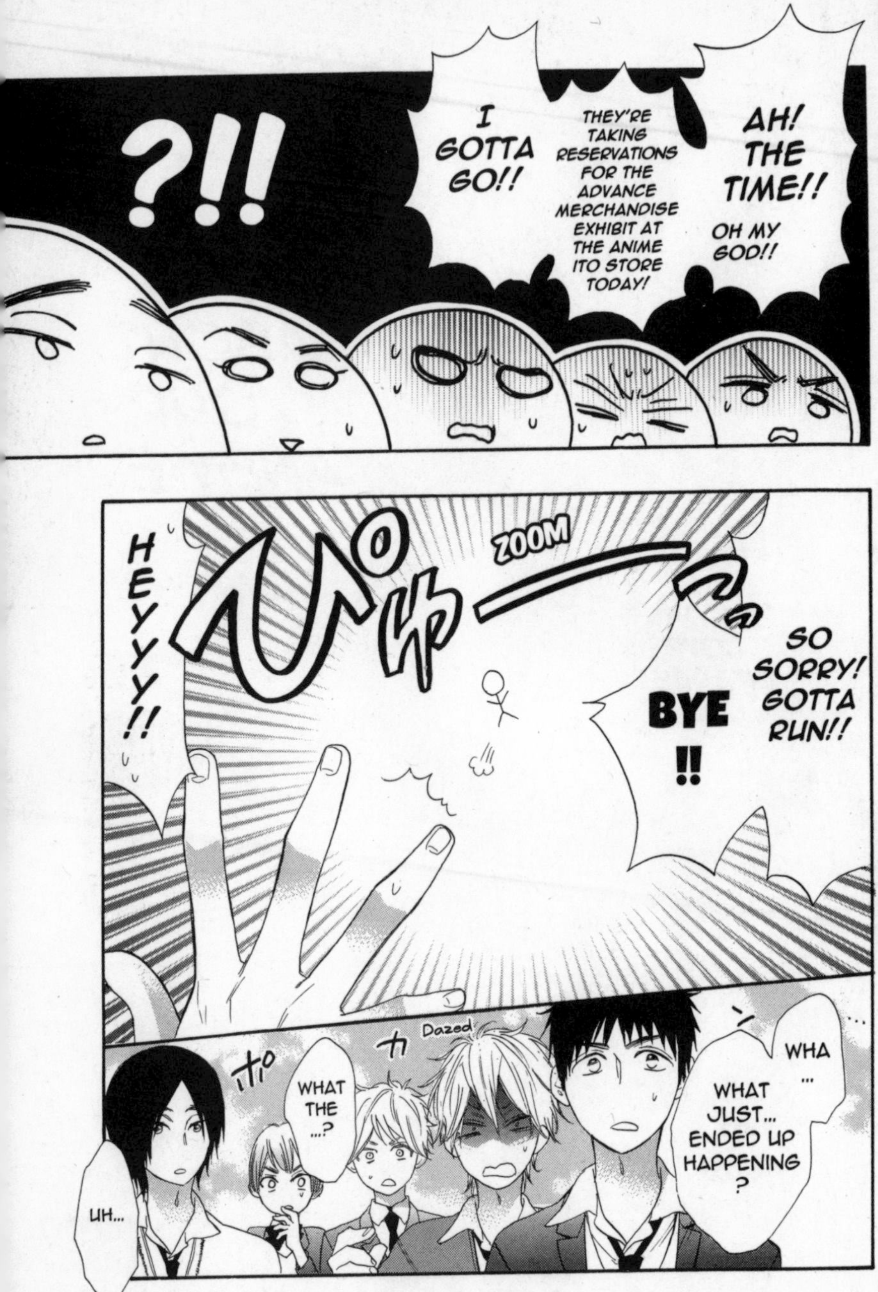
AH! THE TIME!!
OH MY GOD!!
THEY'RE TAKING RESERVATIONS FOR THE ADVANCE MERCHANDISE EXHIBIT AT THE ANIME ITO STORE TODAY!
I GOTTA GO!!
?!!
SO SORRY! GOTTA RUN!!
BYE !!
ZOOM
ぴゅーっ
HEYYY!!
WHA ...
WHAT JUST... ENDED UP HAPPENING ?
Dazed
WHAT THE ...?
UH...

WHAT ABOUT YOUR ANSWER?!

WAIT, SERINUMA-SAN!!

SENPAIIII! IS "KATCHU☆LOVE" INTERESTING?

I haven't seen it yet!

Haha! SERINUMA-SAN SEEMS LIKE SHE'S HAVING FUN. THAT'S GOOD.

IT'S NOT GOOD!!

#23 THE FUJOSHI DISPUTE

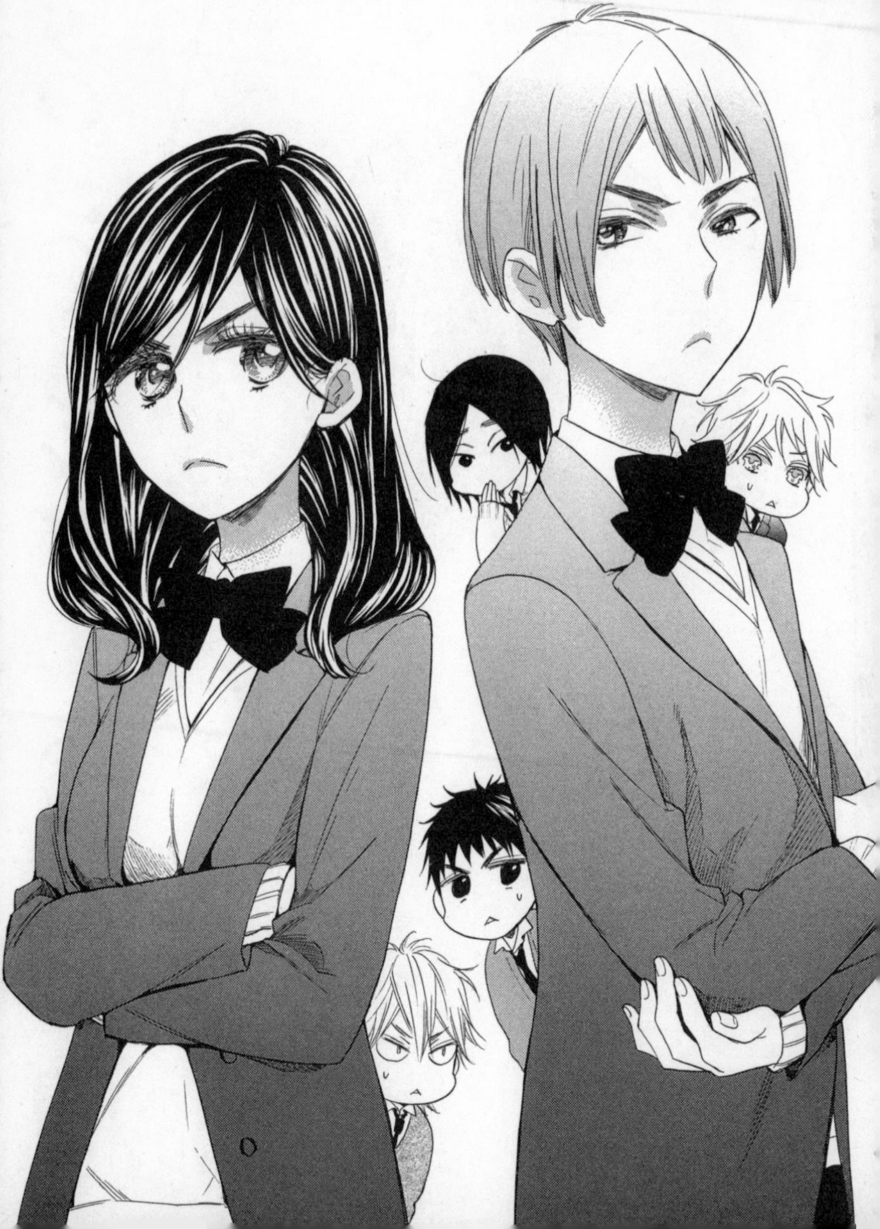

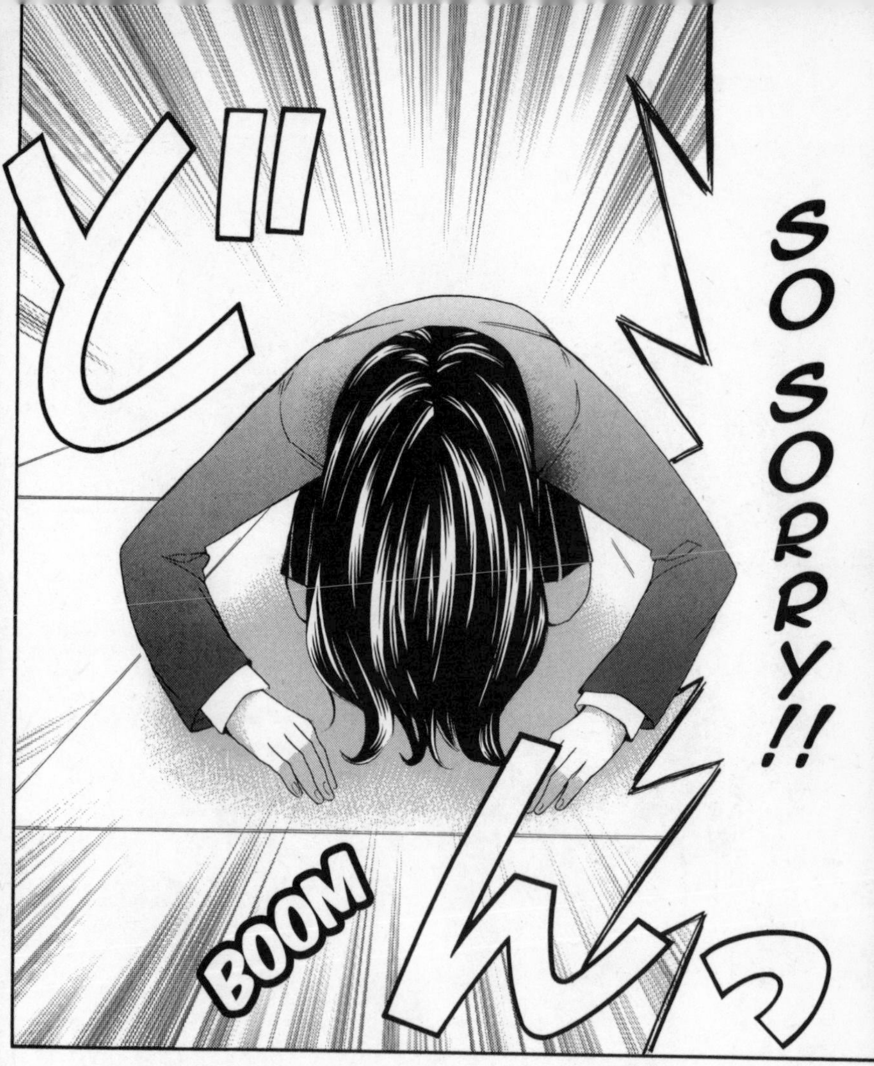
SO SORRY!!
どーんっ
BOOM

KiSS HiM, NOT ME!

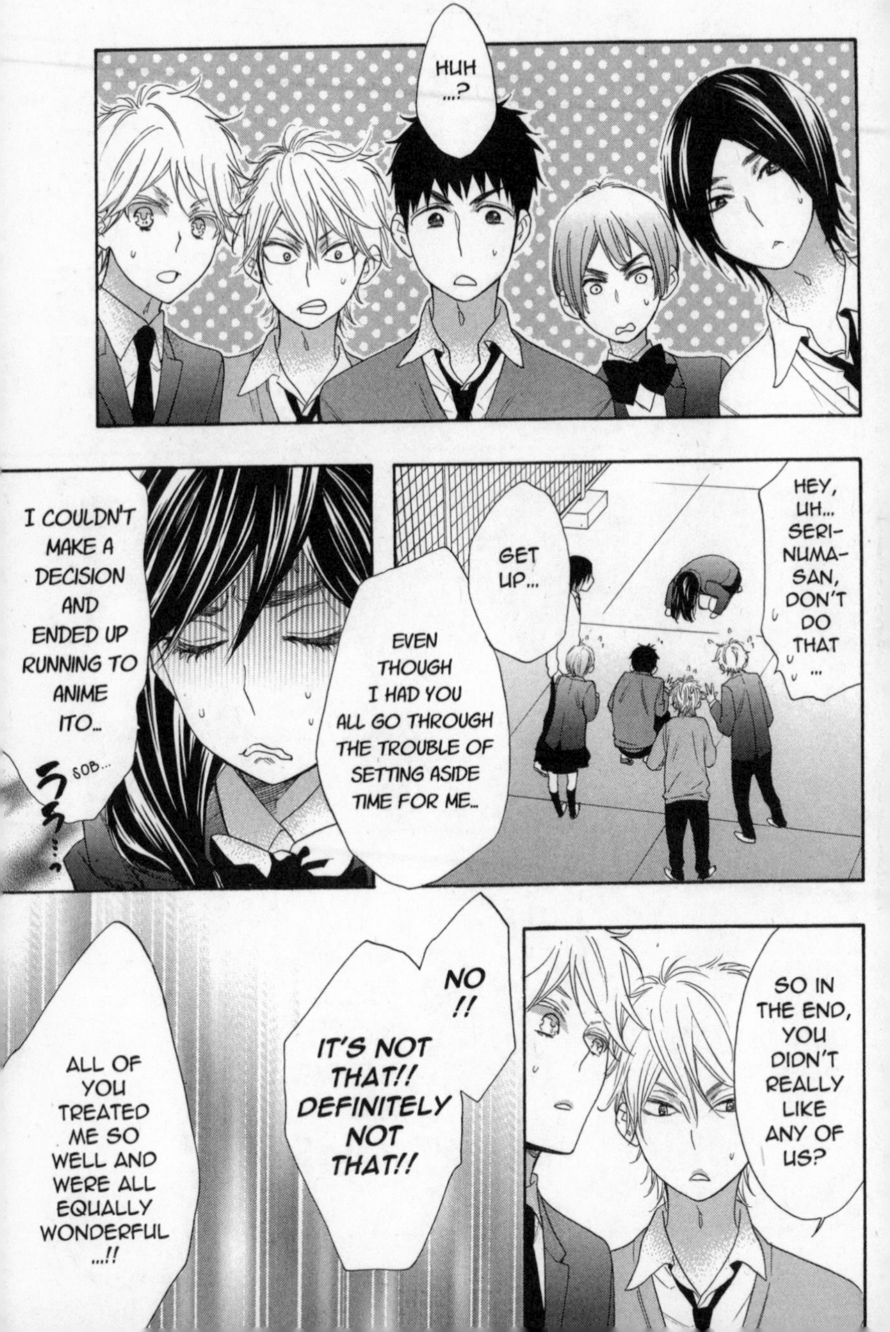
HUH ...?
HEY, UH... SERI-NUMA-SAN, DON'T DO THAT ...
GET UP...
EVEN THOUGH I HAD YOU ALL GO THROUGH THE TROUBLE OF SETTING ASIDE TIME FOR ME...
I COULDN'T MAKE A DECISION AND ENDED UP RUNNING TO ANIME ITO...
SOB...
SO IN THE END, YOU DIDN'T REALLY LIKE ANY OF US?
NO!!
IT'S NOT THAT!! DEFINITELY NOT THAT!!
ALL OF YOU TREATED ME SO WELL AND WERE ALL EQUALLY WONDERFUL ...!!

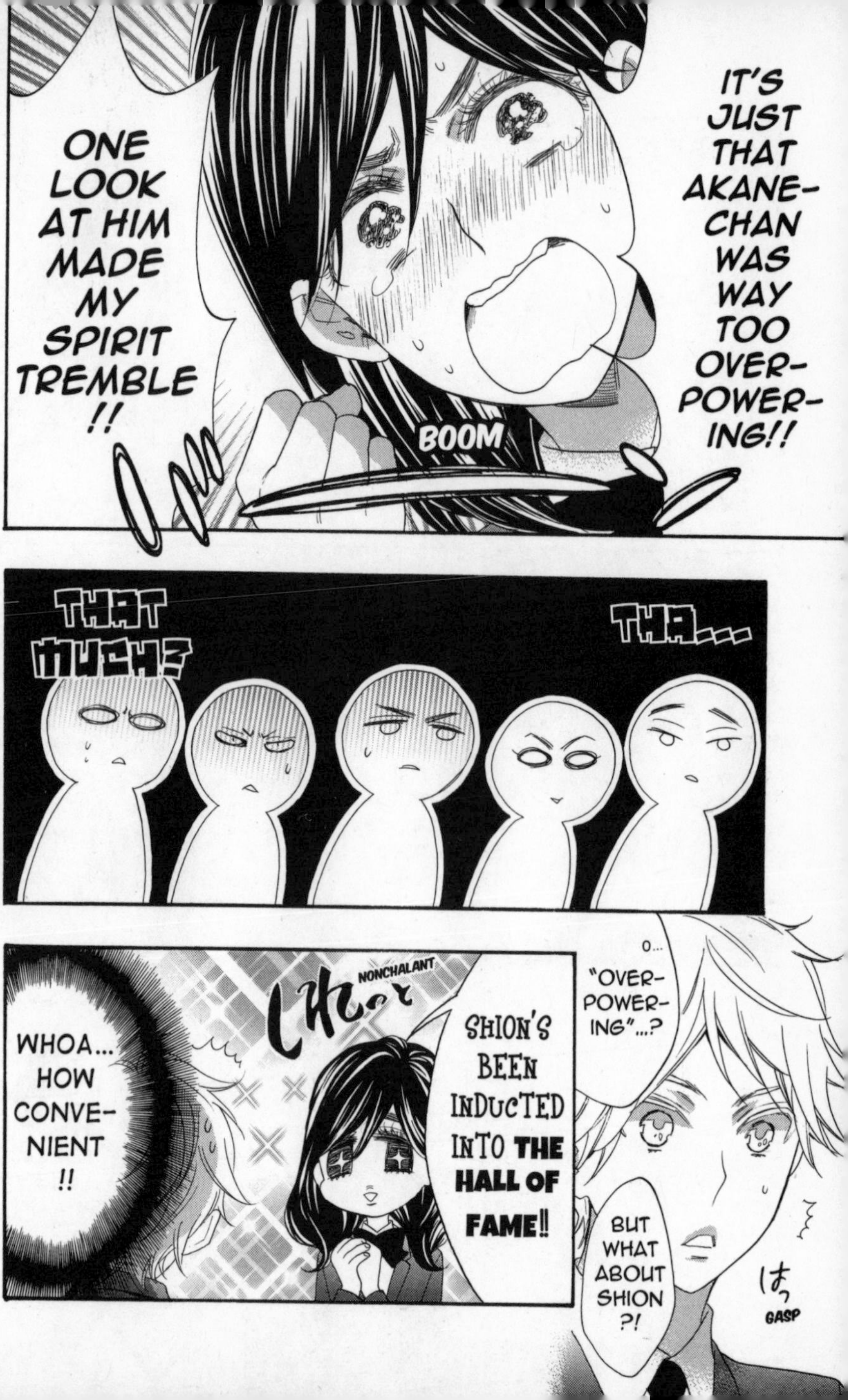
IT'S JUST THAT AKANE-CHAN WAS WAY TOO OVER-POWERING!!
ONE LOOK AT HIM MADE MY SPIRIT TREMBLE!!
BOOM
THA...
THAT MUCH?
O... "OVER-POWERING"...?
はっ
GASP
BUT WHAT ABOUT SHION?!
しれっと
NONCHALANT
SHION'S BEEN INDUCTED INTO THE HALL OF FAME!!
WHOA... HOW CONVENIENT!!

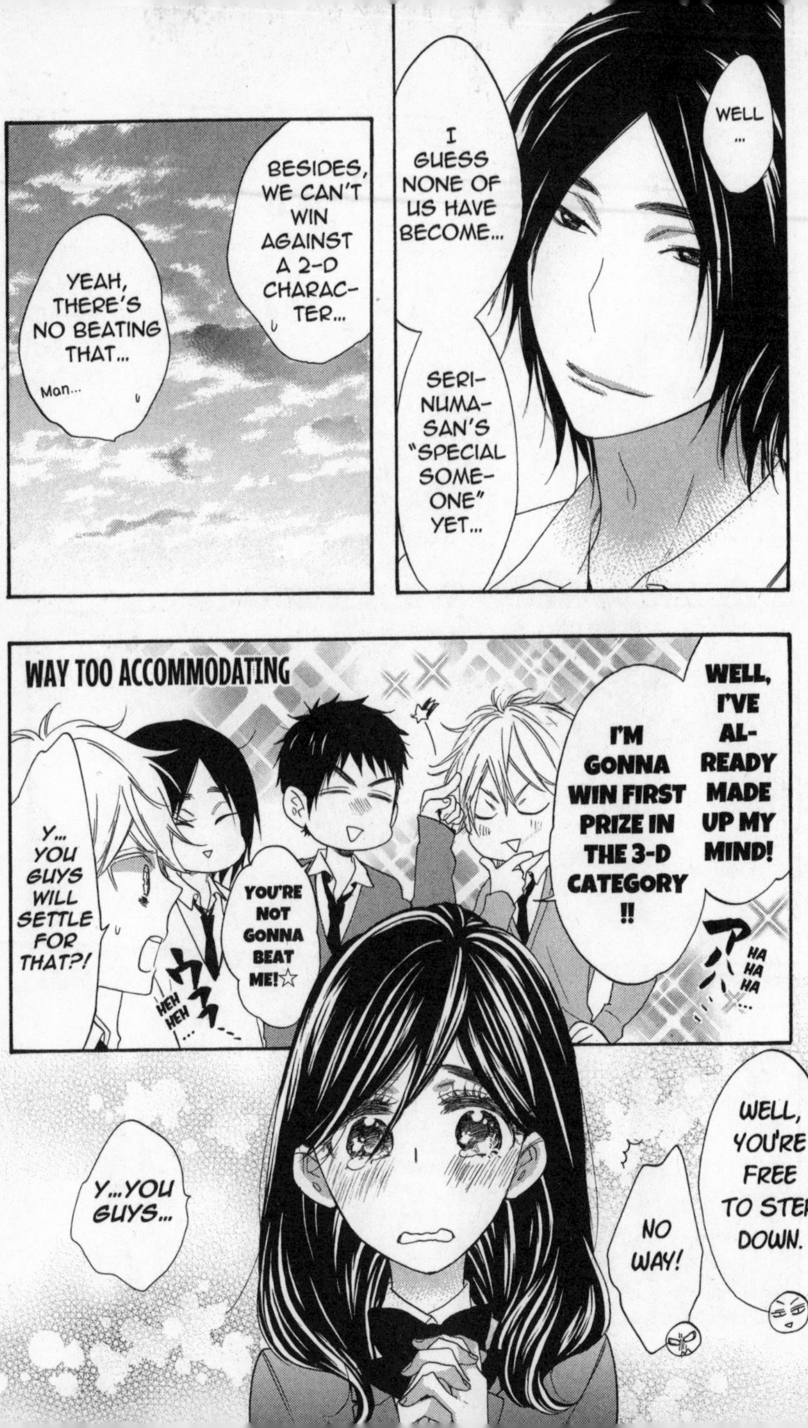
WELL...
I GUESS NONE OF US HAVE BECOME...
SERINUMA-SAN'S "SPECIAL SOMEONE" YET...
BESIDES, WE CAN'T WIN AGAINST A 2-D CHARACTER...
YEAH, THERE'S NO BEATING THAT...
Man...
WAY TOO ACCOMMODATING
WELL, I'VE ALREADY MADE UP MY MIND!
I'M GONNA WIN FIRST PRIZE IN THE 3-D CATEGORY!!
HA HA HA HA...
YOU'RE NOT GONNA BEAT ME!☆
HEH HEH...
Y... YOU GUYS WILL SETTLE FOR THAT?!
WELL, YOU'RE FREE TO STEP DOWN.
NO WAY!
Y...YOU GUYS...

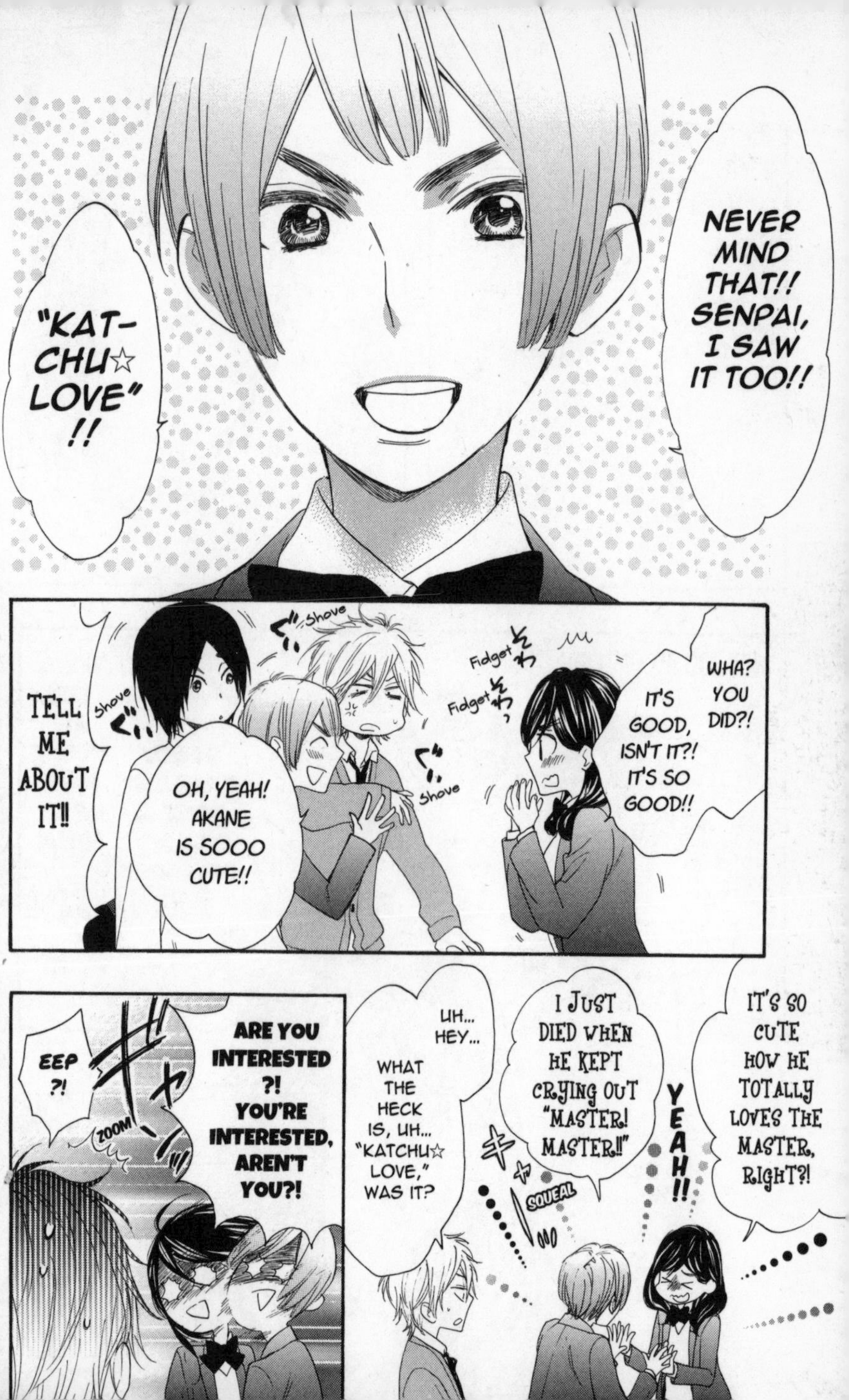
NEVER MIND THAT!! SENPAI, I SAW IT TOO!!
"KAT-CHU☆ LOVE"!!
WHA? YOU DID?!
IT'S GOOD, ISN'T IT?! IT'S SO GOOD!!
Fidget Fidget
Shove
Shove
Shove
OH, YEAH! AKANE IS SOOO CUTE!!
TELL ME ABOUT IT!!
IT'S SO CUTE HOW HE TOTALLY LOVES THE MASTER, RIGHT?!
YEAH!!
I JUST DIED WHEN HE KEPT CRYING OUT "MASTER! MASTER!!"
SQUEAL
UH... HEY...
WHAT THE HECK IS, UH... "KATCHU☆ LOVE," WAS IT?
ARE YOU INTERESTED?! YOU'RE INTERESTED, AREN'T YOU?!
ZOOM
EEP?!

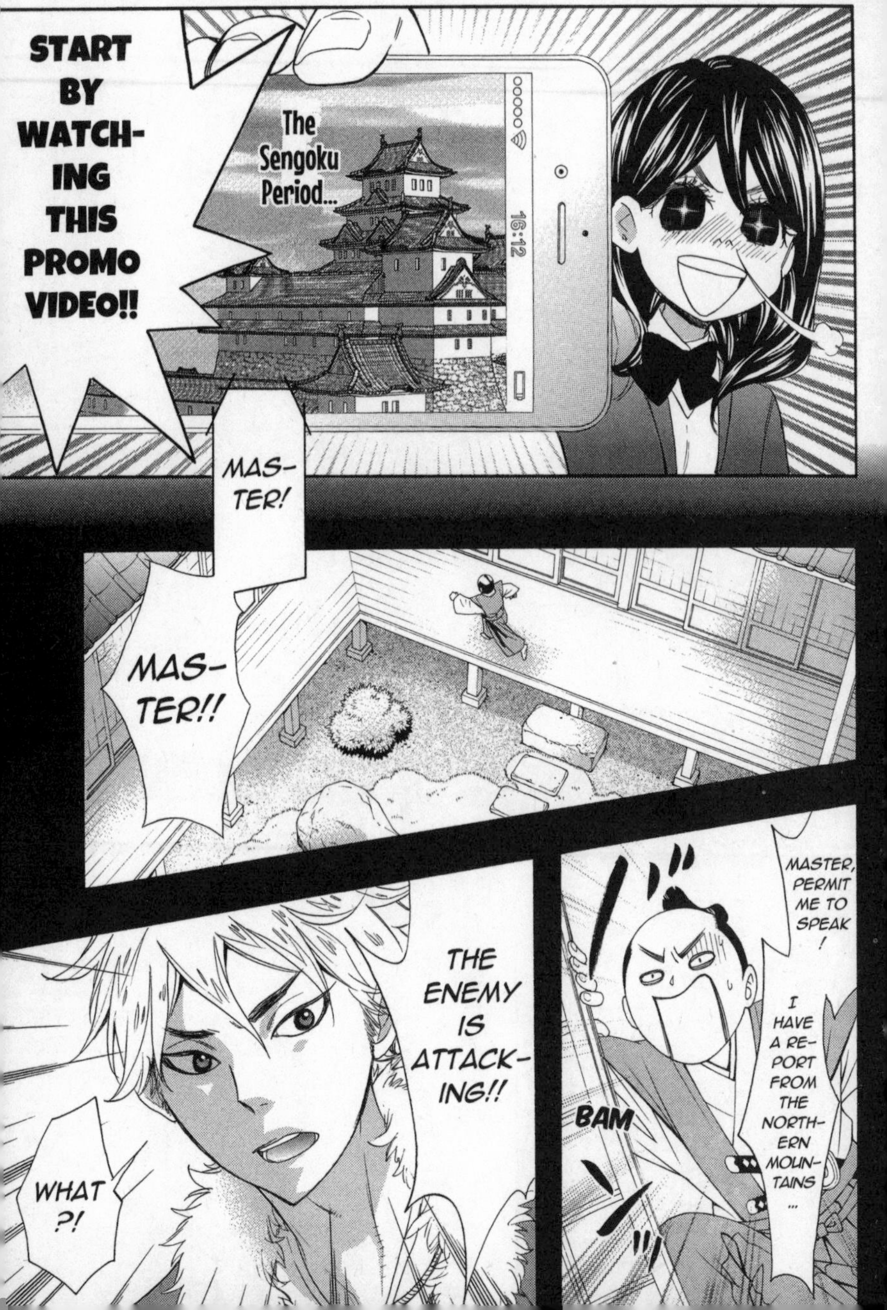
START BY WATCHING THIS PROMO VIDEO!!
The Sengoku Period...
16:12
MASTER!
MASTER!!
BAM
MASTER, PERMIT ME TO SPEAK!
I HAVE A REPORT FROM THE NORTHERN MOUNTAINS...
THE ENEMY IS ATTACKING!!
WHAT?!

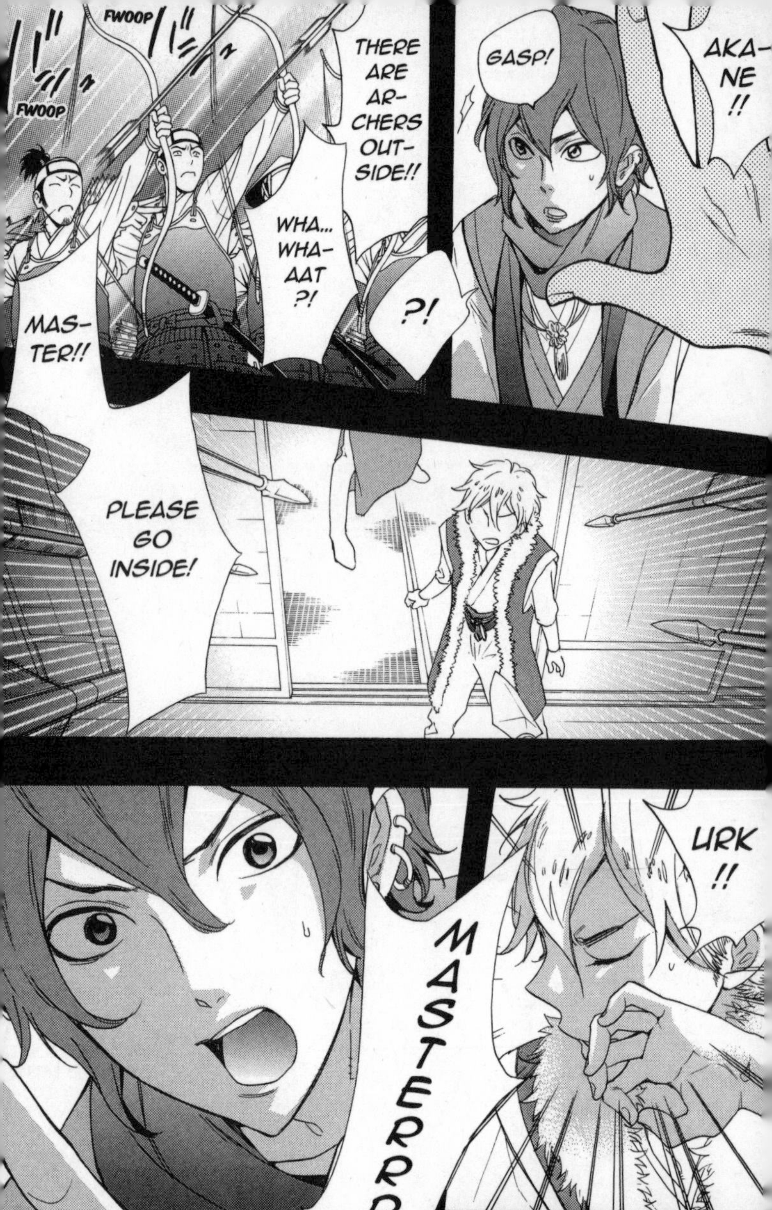
AKA-NE!!
GASP!
FWOOP
THERE ARE AR-CHERS OUT-SIDE!!
FWOOP
WHA... WHA-AAT?!
?!
MAS-TER!!
PLEASE GO INSIDE!
URK!!
MASTERRR

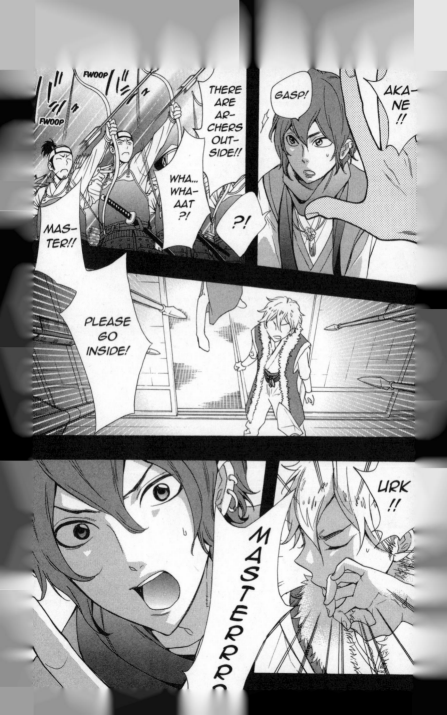

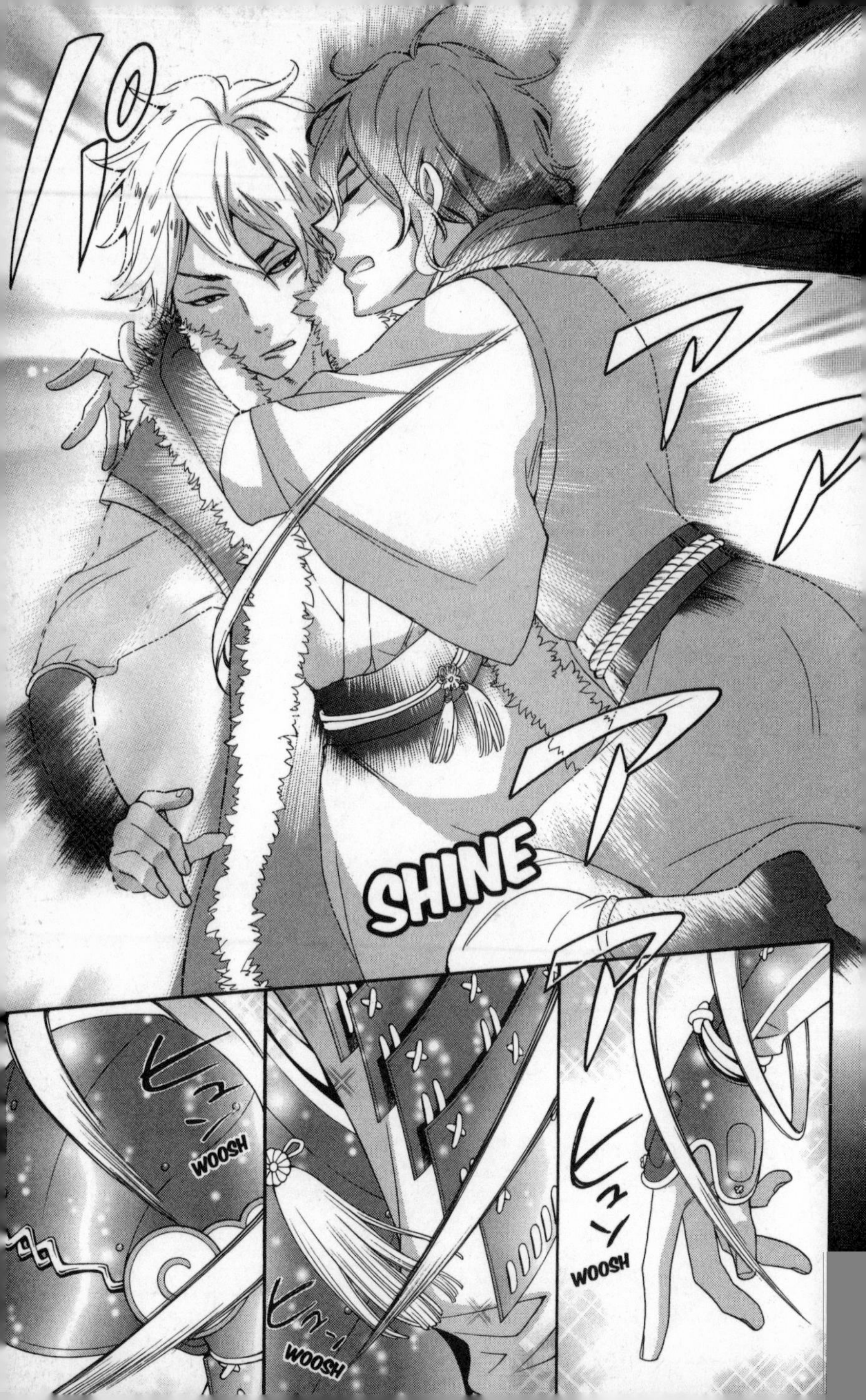
SHINE
WOOSH
WOOSH
WOOSH

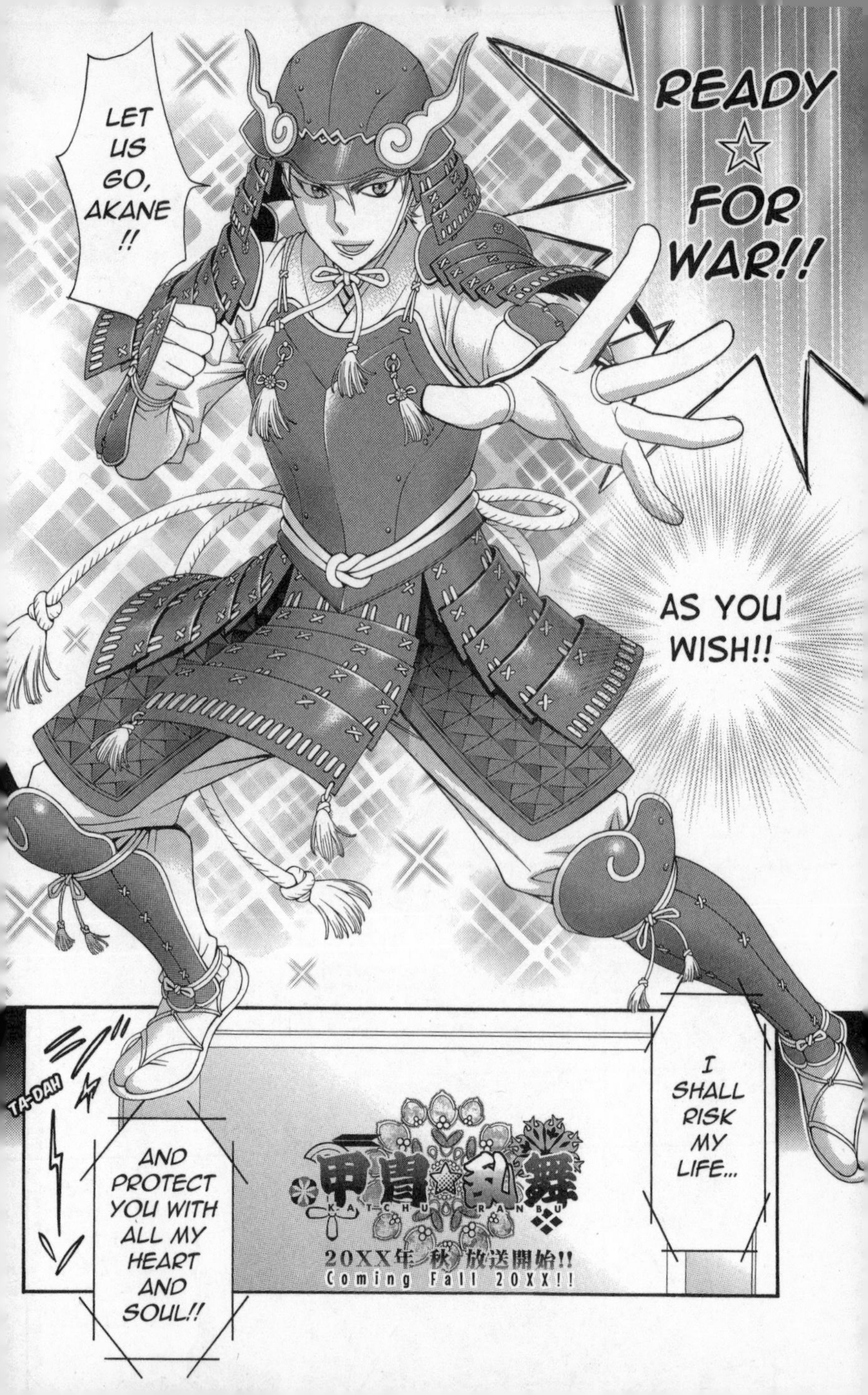
READY ☆ FOR WAR!!
LET US GO, AKANE!!
AS YOU WISH!!
I SHALL RISK MY LIFE...
甲冑☆乱舞
KATCHU RANBU
20XX年 秋 放送開始!!
Coming Fall 20XX!!
AND PROTECT YOU WITH ALL MY HEART AND SOUL!!
TA-DAH

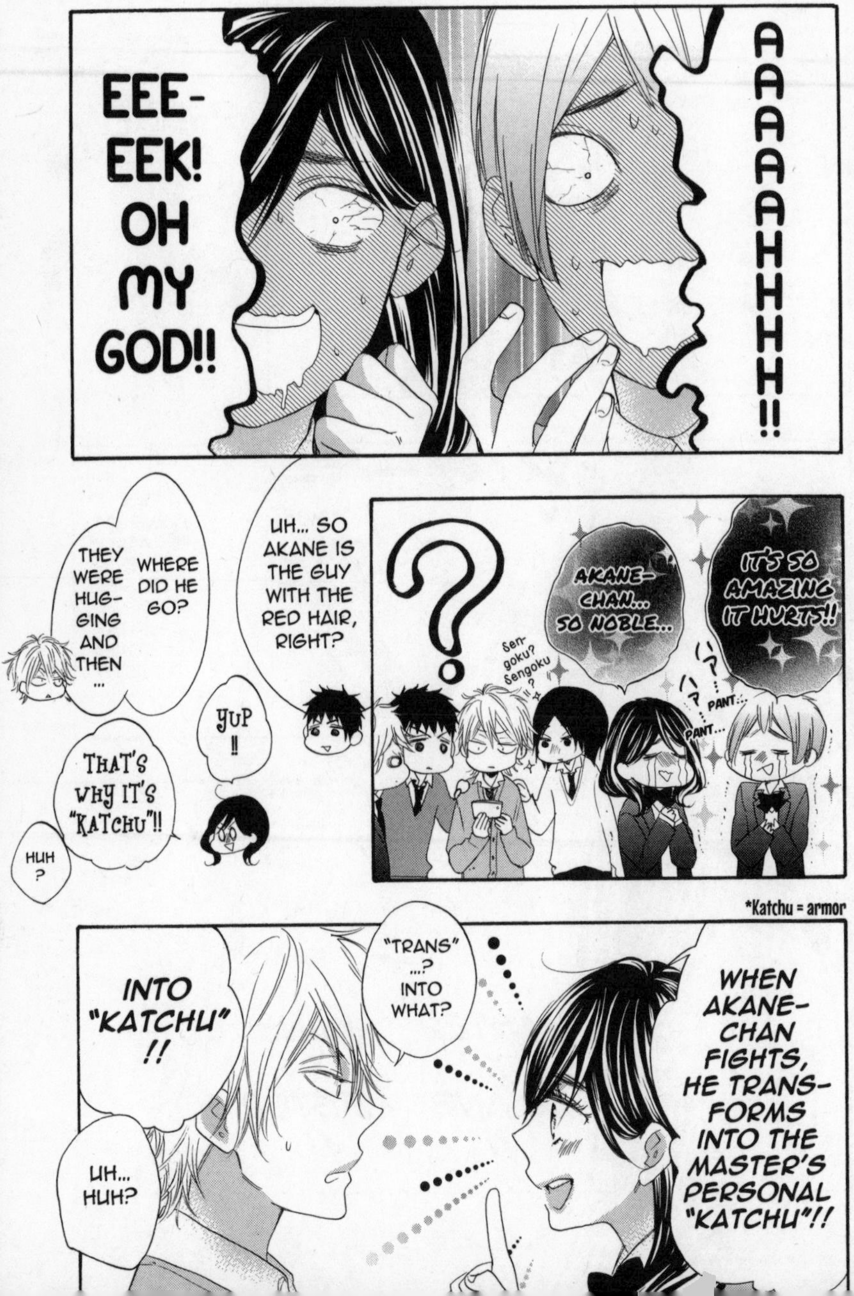
AAAAAAHHHHH!!
EEE-EEK! OH MY GOD!!
IT'S SO AMAZING IT HURTS!!
AKANE-CHAN... SO NOBLE...
PANT... PANT...
Sengoku? Sengoku?
UH... SO AKANE IS THE GUY WITH THE RED HAIR, RIGHT?
YUP!!
WHERE DID HE GO?
THEY WERE HUGGING AND THEN...
THAT'S WHY IT'S "KATCHU"!!
HUH?
*Katchu = armor
WHEN AKANE-CHAN FIGHTS, HE TRANSFORMS INTO THE MASTER'S PERSONAL "KATCHU"!!
"TRANS"...? INTO WHAT?
INTO "KATCHU"!!
UH... HUH?

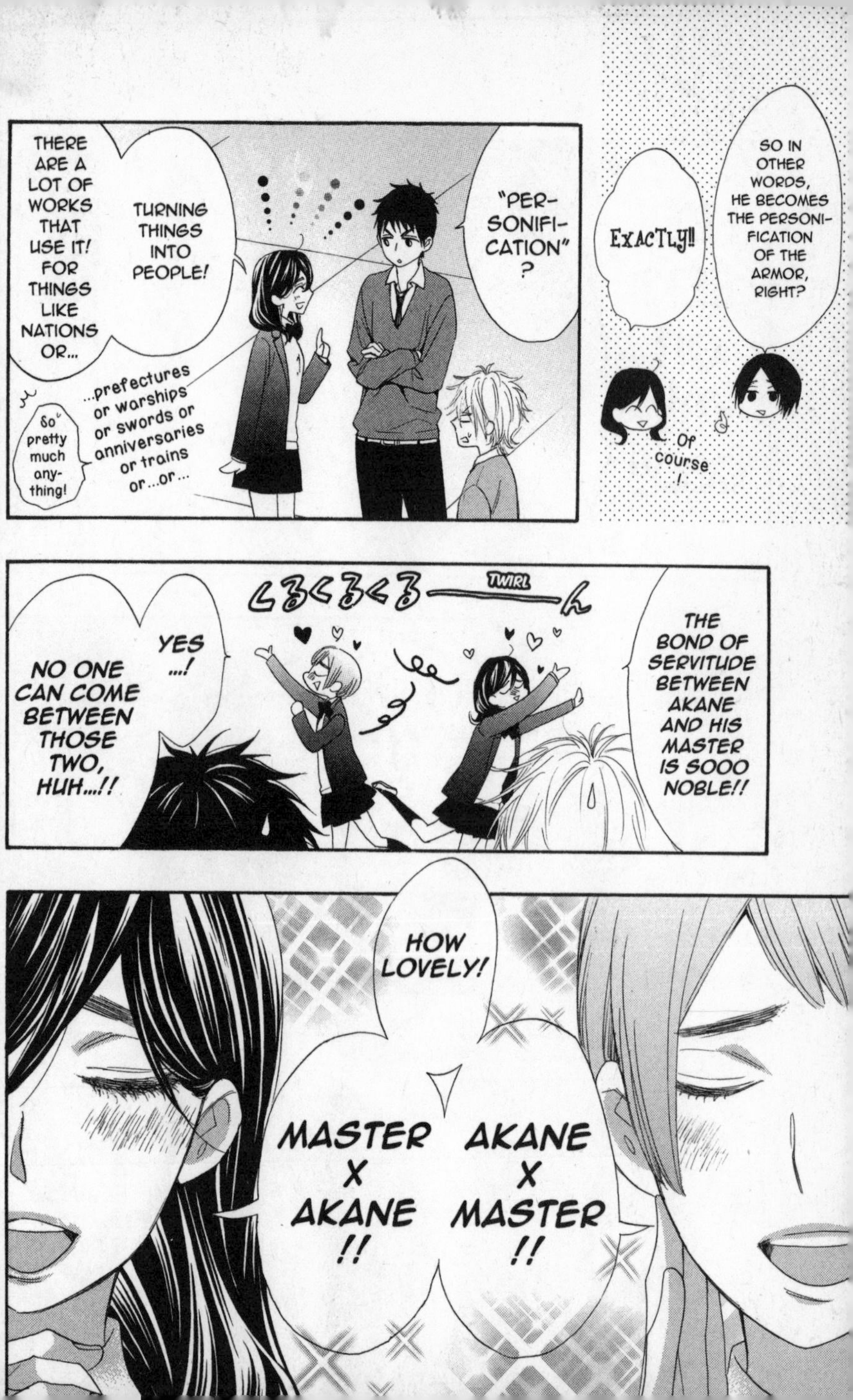
SO IN OTHER WORDS, HE BECOMES THE PERSONIFICATION OF THE ARMOR, RIGHT?
EXACTLY!!
Of course!
"PERSONIFICATION"?
TURNING THINGS INTO PEOPLE!
THERE ARE A LOT OF WORKS THAT USE IT! FOR THINGS LIKE NATIONS OR...
...prefectures or warships or swords or anniversaries or trains or...or...
So pretty much anything!
THE BOND OF SERVITUDE BETWEEN AKANE AND HIS MASTER IS SOOO NOBLE!!
TWIRL
YES ...!
NO ONE CAN COME BETWEEN THOSE TWO, HUH...!!
HOW LOVELY!
AKANE X MASTER !!
MASTER X AKANE !!

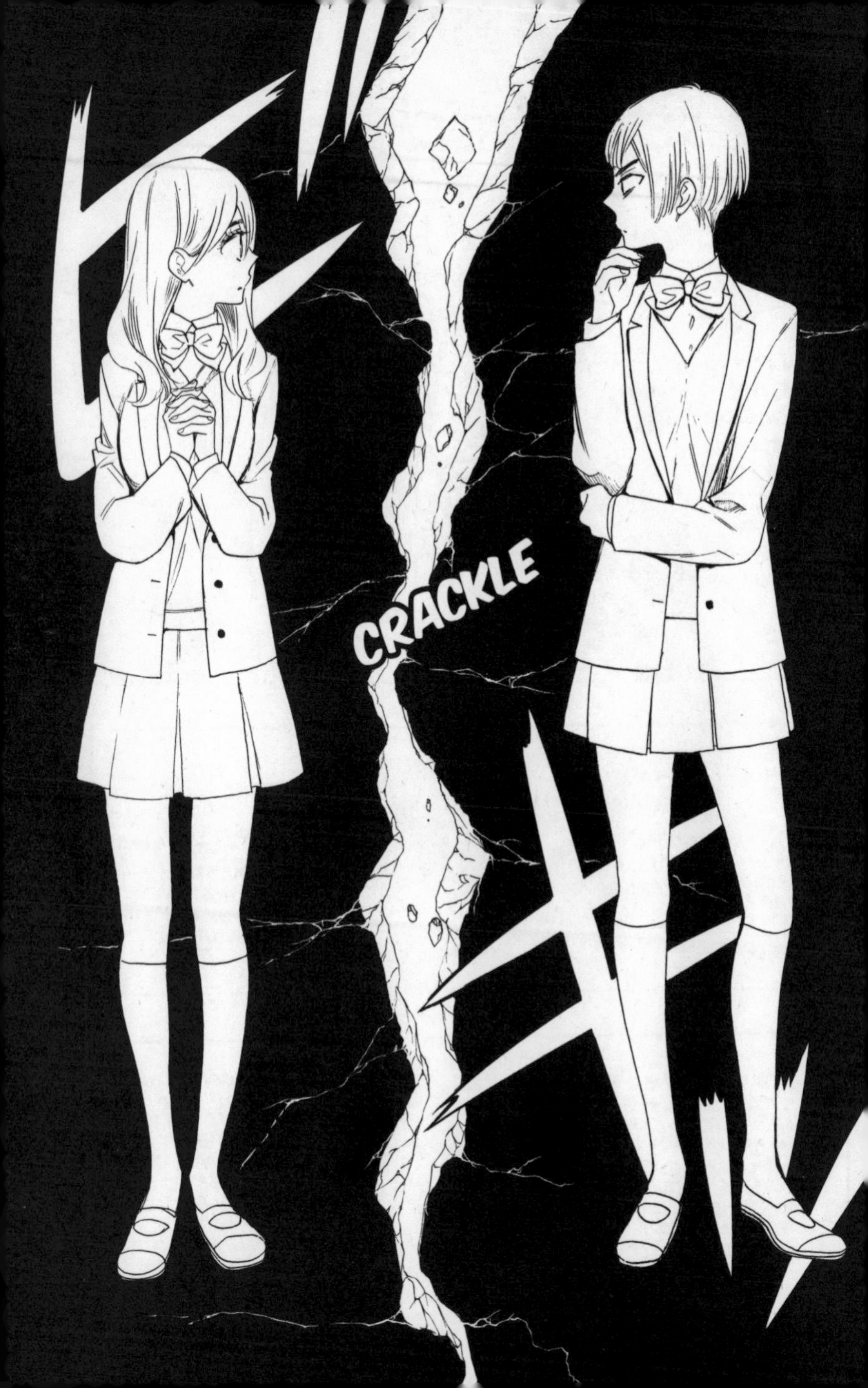
CRACKLE

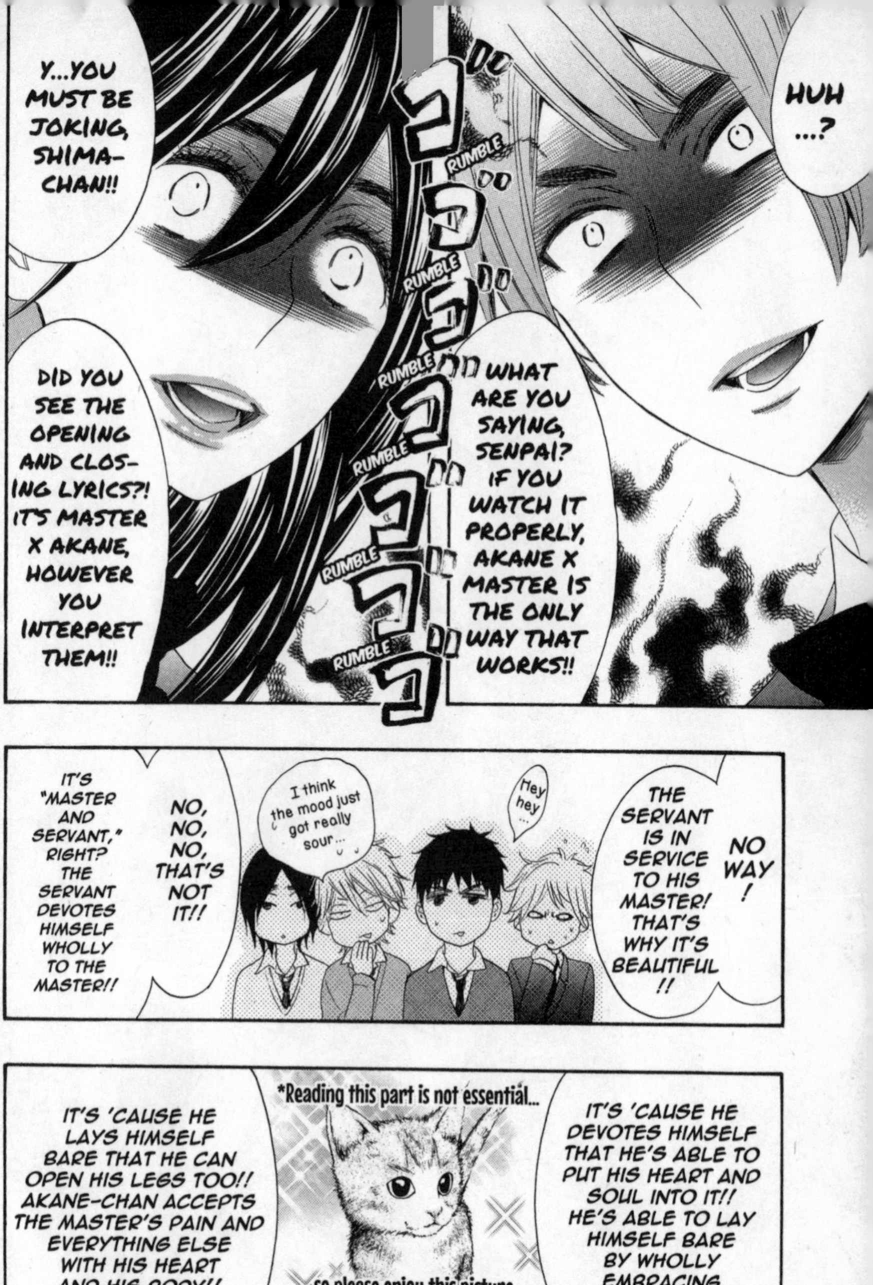
HUH ...?
RUMBLE RUMBLE RUMBLE RUMBLE RUMBLE RUMBLE
WHAT ARE YOU SAYING, SENPAI? IF YOU WATCH IT PROPERLY, AKANE X MASTER IS THE ONLY WAY THAT WORKS!!
Y...YOU MUST BE JOKING, SHIMA-CHAN!!
DID YOU SEE THE OPENING AND CLOSING LYRICS?! IT'S MASTER X AKANE, HOWEVER YOU INTERPRET THEM!!
NO WAY!
THE SERVANT IS IN SERVICE TO HIS MASTER! THAT'S WHY IT'S BEAUTIFUL!!
Hey hey...
I think the mood just got really sour...
NO, NO, NO, THAT'S NOT IT!!
IT'S "MASTER AND SERVANT," RIGHT? THE SERVANT DEVOTES HIMSELF WHOLLY TO THE MASTER!!
IT'S 'CAUSE HE DEVOTES HIMSELF THAT HE'S ABLE TO PUT HIS HEART AND SOUL INTO IT!! HE'S ABLE TO LAY HIMSELF BARE BY WHOLLY EMBRACING THE MASTER!!
*Reading this part is not essential...
...so please enjoy this picture of a cute cat.
IT'S 'CAUSE HE LAYS HIMSELF BARE THAT HE CAN OPEN HIS LEGS TOO!! AKANE-CHAN ACCEPTS THE MASTER'S PAIN AND EVERYTHING ELSE WITH HIS HEART AND HIS BODY!!

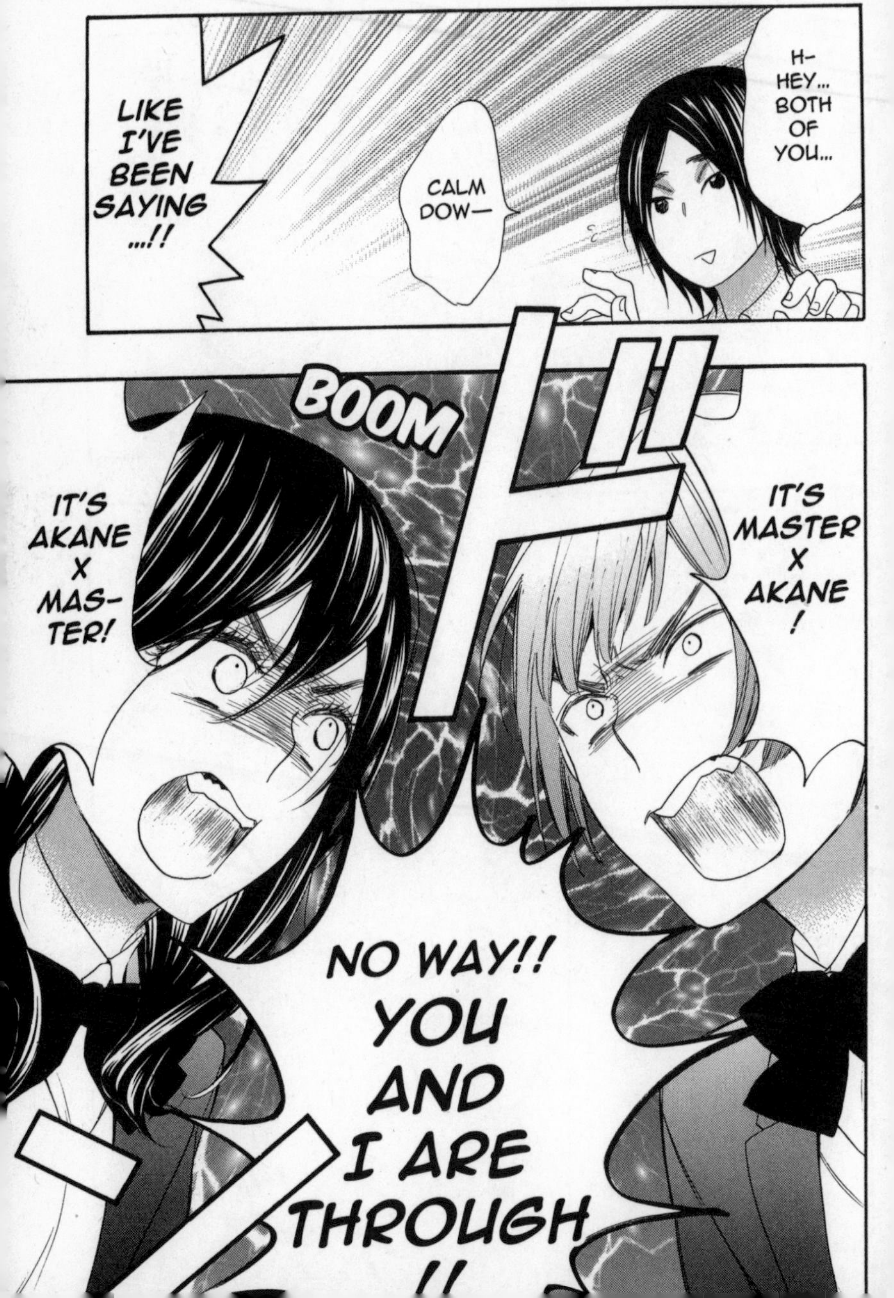
H- HEY... BOTH OF YOU...
CALM DOW—
LIKE I'VE BEEN SAYING ...!!
BOOM
IT'S MASTER X AKANE!
IT'S AKANE X MAS-TER!
NO WAY!! YOU AND I ARE THROUGH !!

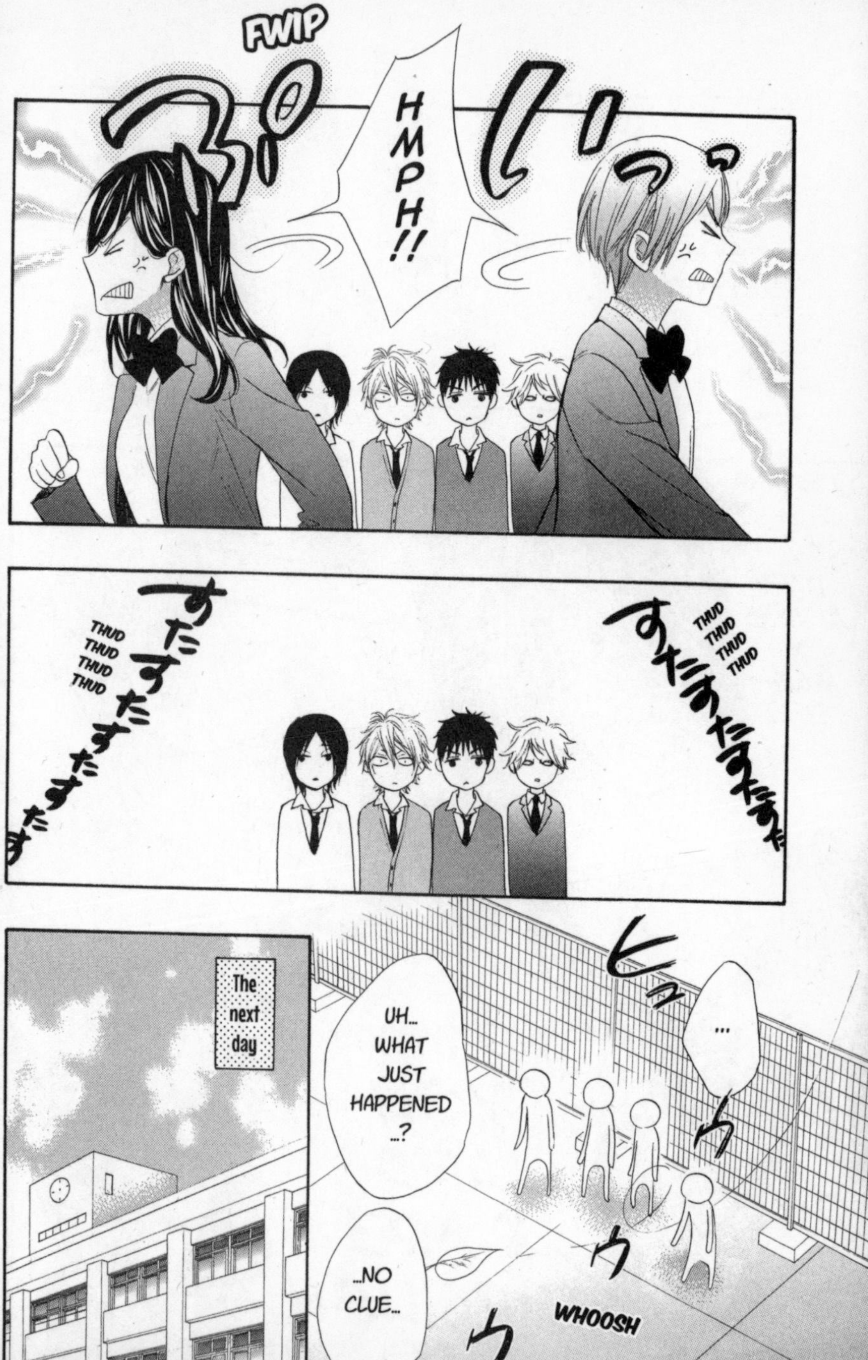
FWIP
HMPH!!
THUD THUD THUD THUD
THUD THUD THUD THUD
...
WHOOSH
UH... WHAT JUST HAPPENED ...?
...NO CLUE...
The next day

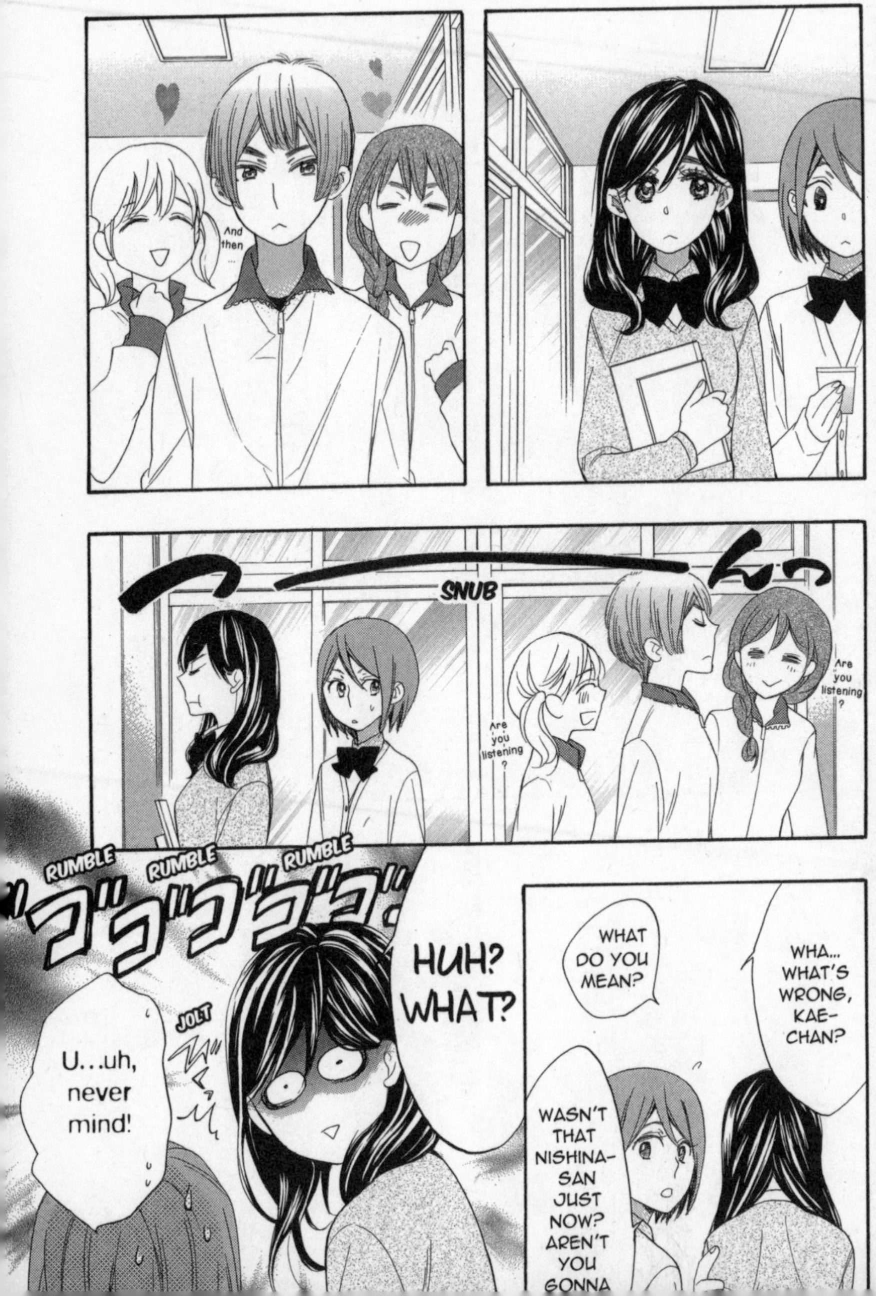
And then ...
SNUB
Are you listening?
Are you listening?
WHA... WHAT'S WRONG, KAE-CHAN?
WHAT DO YOU MEAN?
WASN'T THAT NISHINA-SAN JUST NOW? AREN'T YOU GONNA
RUMBLE RUMBLE RUMBLE
HUH? WHAT?
JOLT
U...uh, never mind!

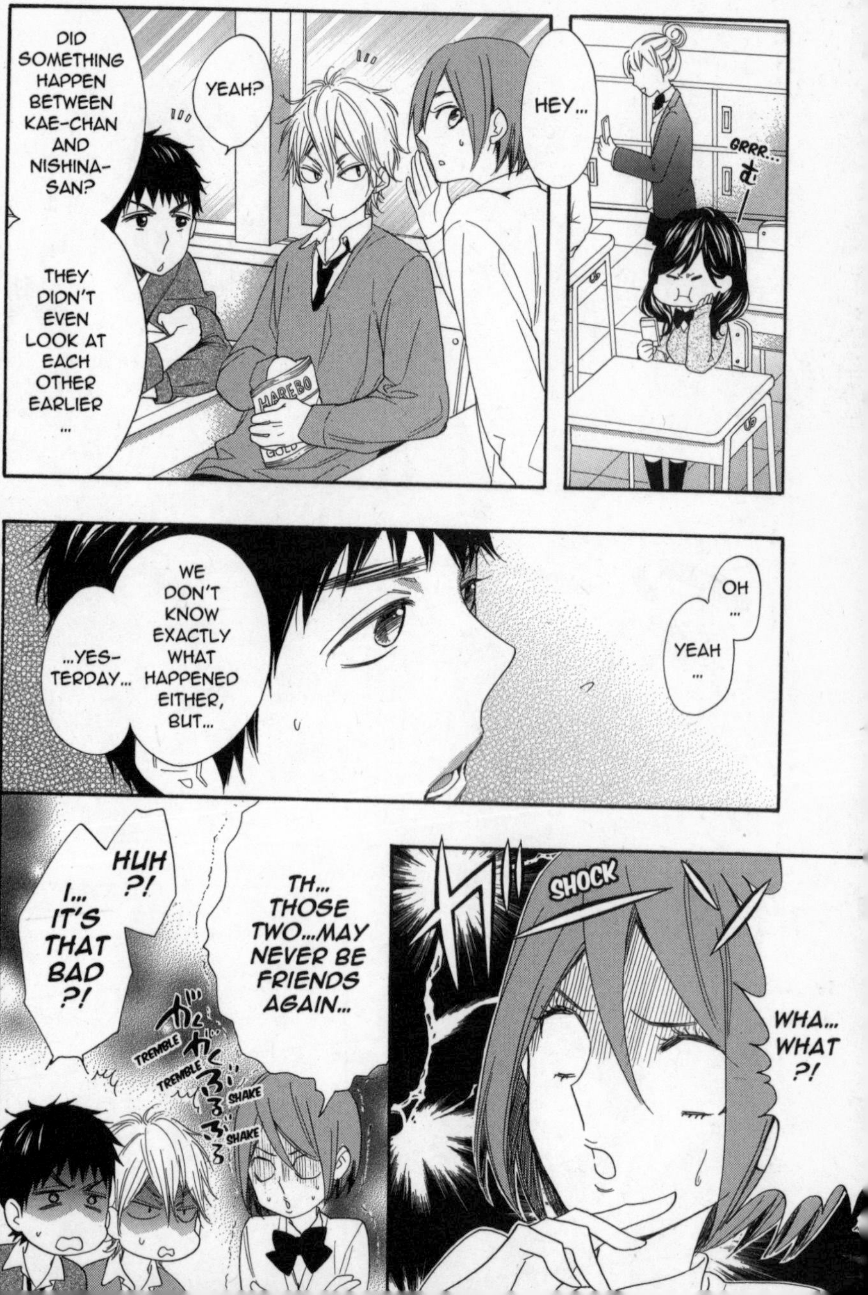
HEY...
GRRR...
YEAH?
DID SOMETHING HAPPEN BETWEEN KAE-CHAN AND NISHINA-SAN?
THEY DIDN'T EVEN LOOK AT EACH OTHER EARLIER...
HAREBO
GOLD
OH... YEAH...
WE DON'T KNOW EXACTLY WHAT HAPPENED EITHER, BUT...
...YESTERDAY...
SHOCK
WHA... WHAT?!
TH... THOSE TWO...MAY NEVER BE FRIENDS AGAIN...
HUH?!
I... IT'S THAT BAD?!
TREMBLE
TREMBLE
SHAKE
SHAKE

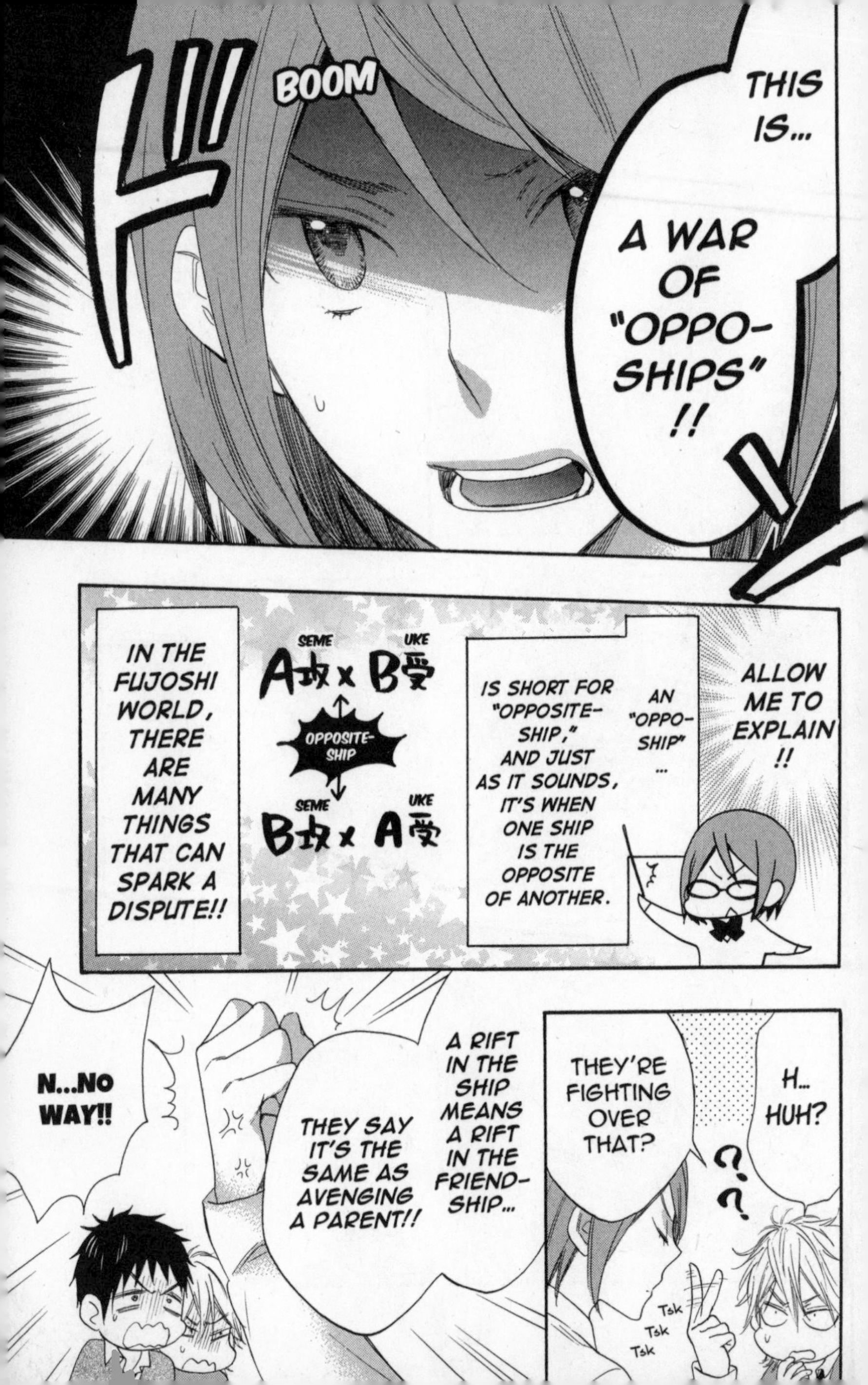
BOOM
THIS IS... A WAR OF "OPPO-SHIPS"!!
ALLOW ME TO EXPLAIN!!
AN "OPPO-SHIP"...
IS SHORT FOR "OPPOSITE-SHIP," AND JUST AS IT SOUNDS, IT'S WHEN ONE SHIP IS THE OPPOSITE OF ANOTHER.
SEME UKE
A攻 x B受
OPPOSITE-SHIP
SEME UKE
B攻 x A受
IN THE FUJOSHI WORLD, THERE ARE MANY THINGS THAT CAN SPARK A DISPUTE!!
H... HUH?
THEY'RE FIGHTING OVER THAT?
Tsk
Tsk
Tsk
A RIFT IN THE SHIP MEANS A RIFT IN THE FRIEND-SHIP...
THEY SAY IT'S THE SAME AS AVENGING A PARENT!!
N...NO WAY!!

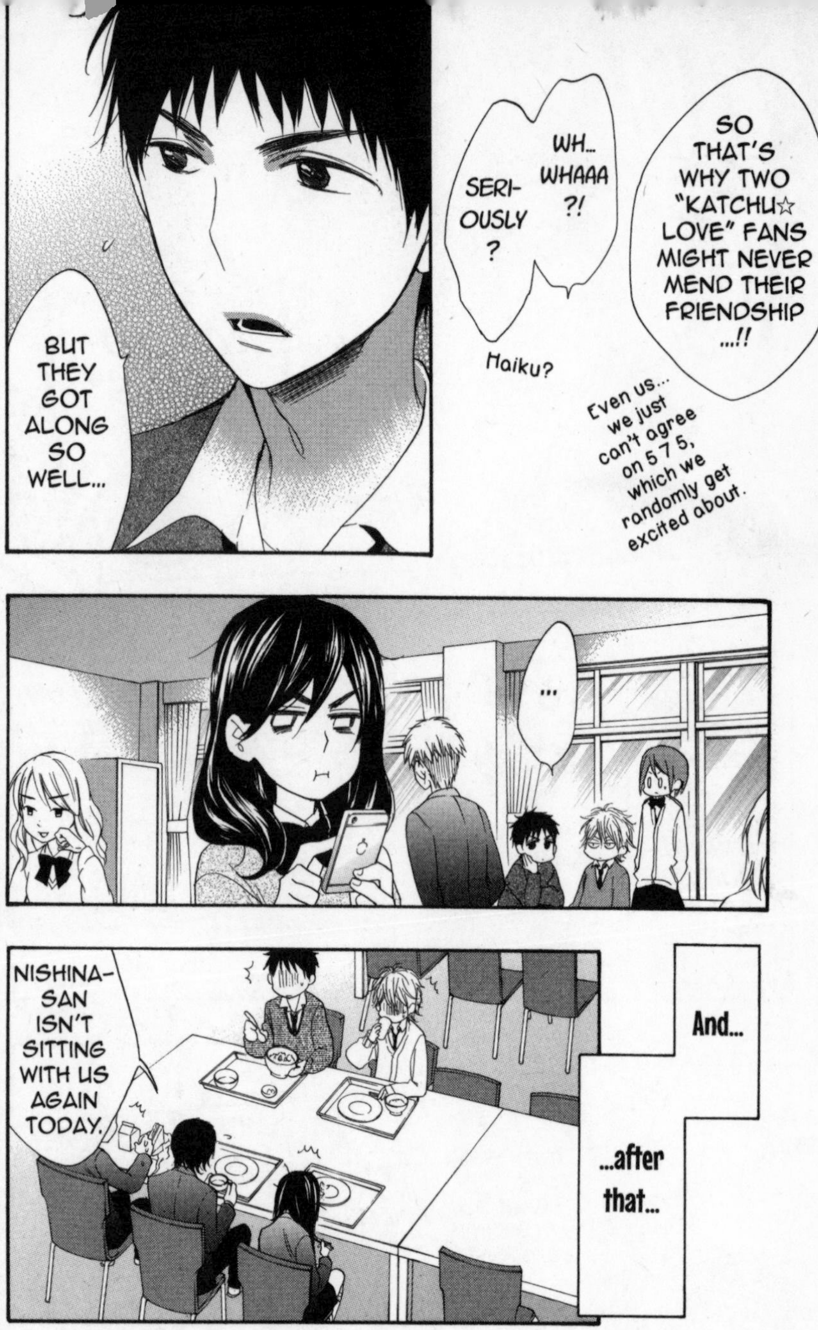
SO THAT'S WHY TWO "KATCHU☆LOVE" FANS MIGHT NEVER MEND THEIR FRIENDSHIP ...!!
WH... WHAAA?!
SERI-OUSLY?
Haiku?
Even us... we just can't agree on 5 7 5, which we randomly get excited about.
BUT THEY GOT ALONG SO WELL...
...
And...
...after that...
NISHINA-SAN ISN'T SITTING WITH US AGAIN TODAY.

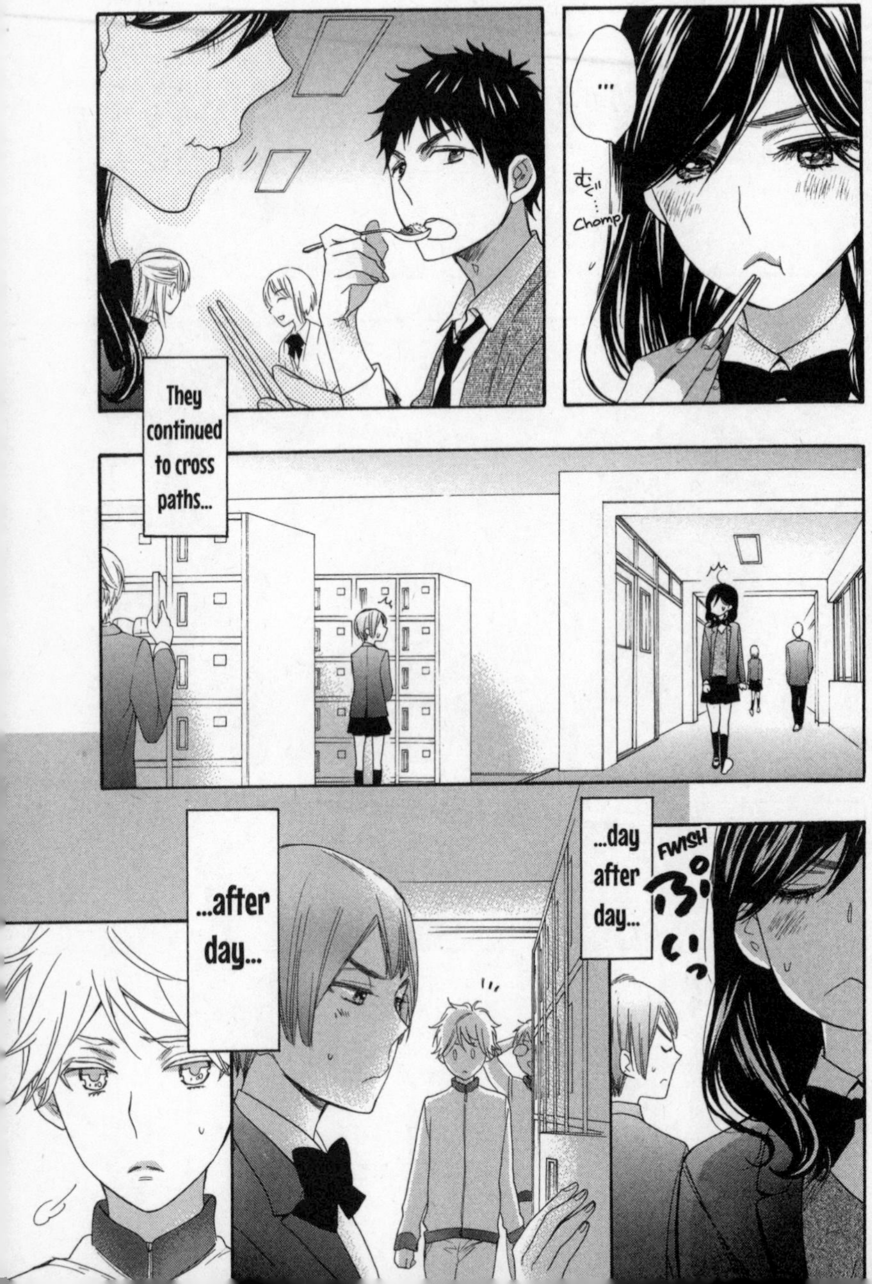
...
むぐ…
Chomp
They continued to cross paths...
...day after day...
FWISH
ぷいっ
...after day...

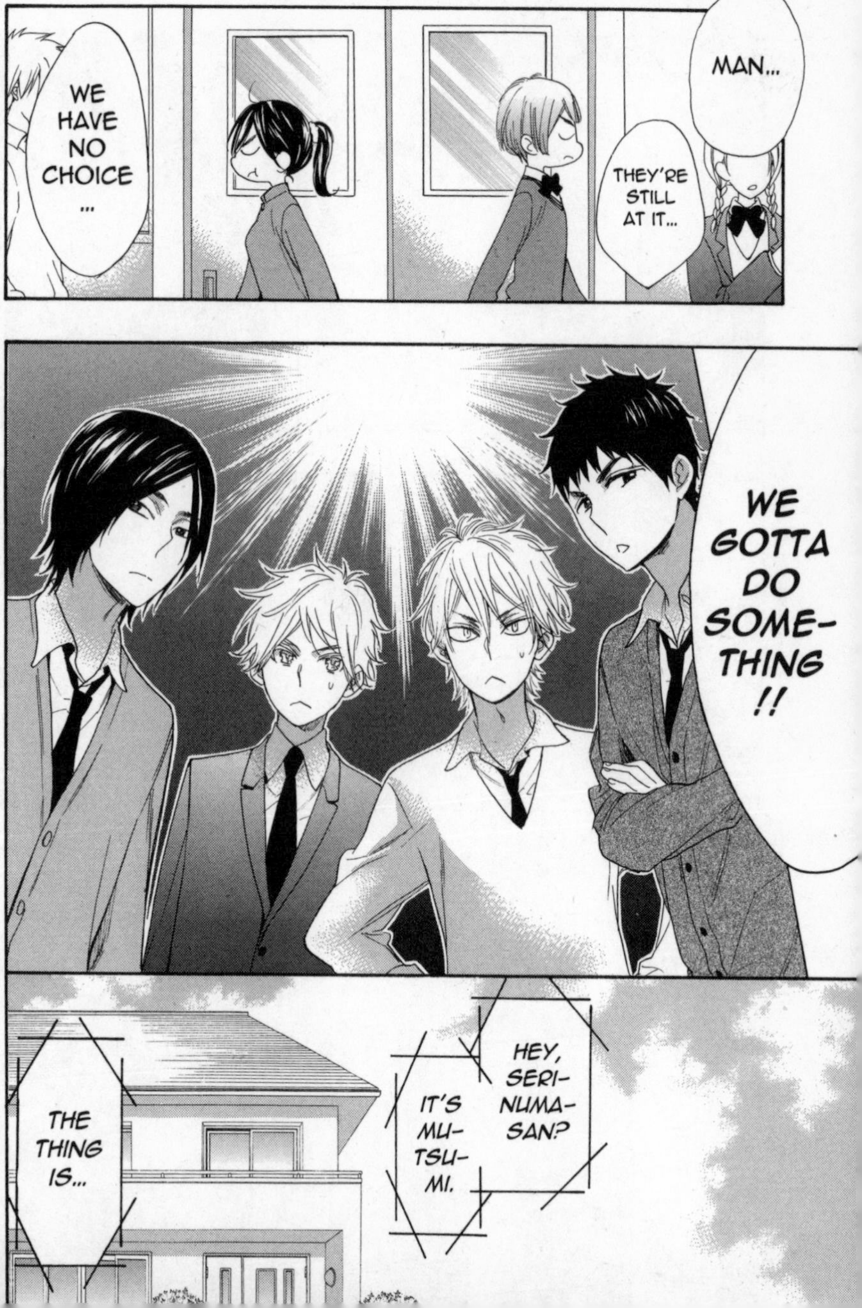
MAN...
THEY'RE STILL AT IT...
WE HAVE NO CHOICE ...
WE GOTTA DO SOME-THING !!
HEY, SERI-NUMA-SAN?
IT'S MU-TSU-MI.
THE THING IS...

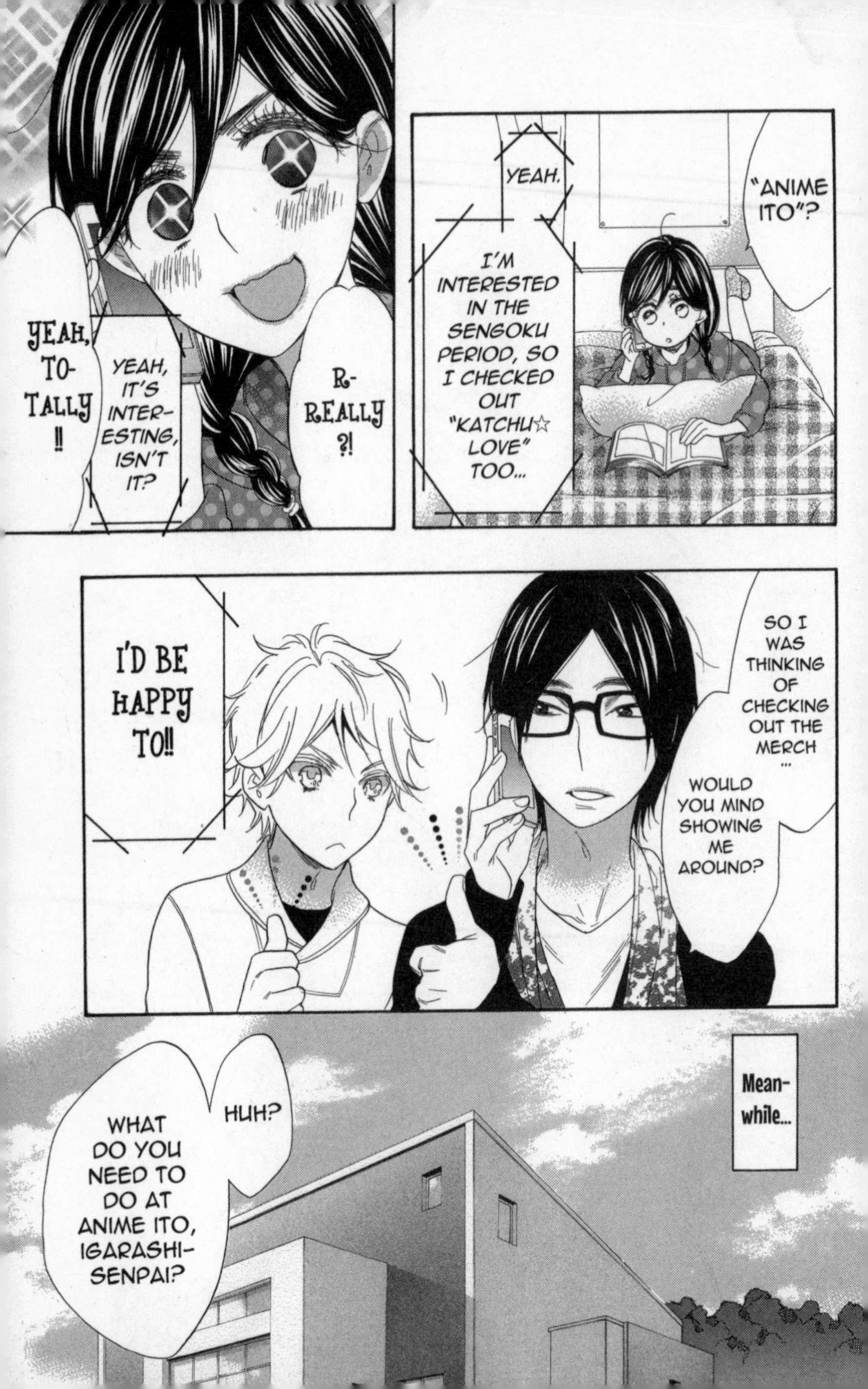
"ANIME ITO"?
YEAH.
I'M INTERESTED IN THE SENGOKU PERIOD, SO I CHECKED OUT "KATCHU☆LOVE" TOO...
R-REALLY?!
YEAH, IT'S INTERESTING, ISN'T IT?
YEAH, TOTALLY!!
SO I WAS THINKING OF CHECKING OUT THE MERCH...
WOULD YOU MIND SHOWING ME AROUND?
I'D BE HAPPY TO!!
Meanwhile...
HUH?
WHAT DO YOU NEED TO DO AT ANIME ITO, IGARASHI-SENPAI?

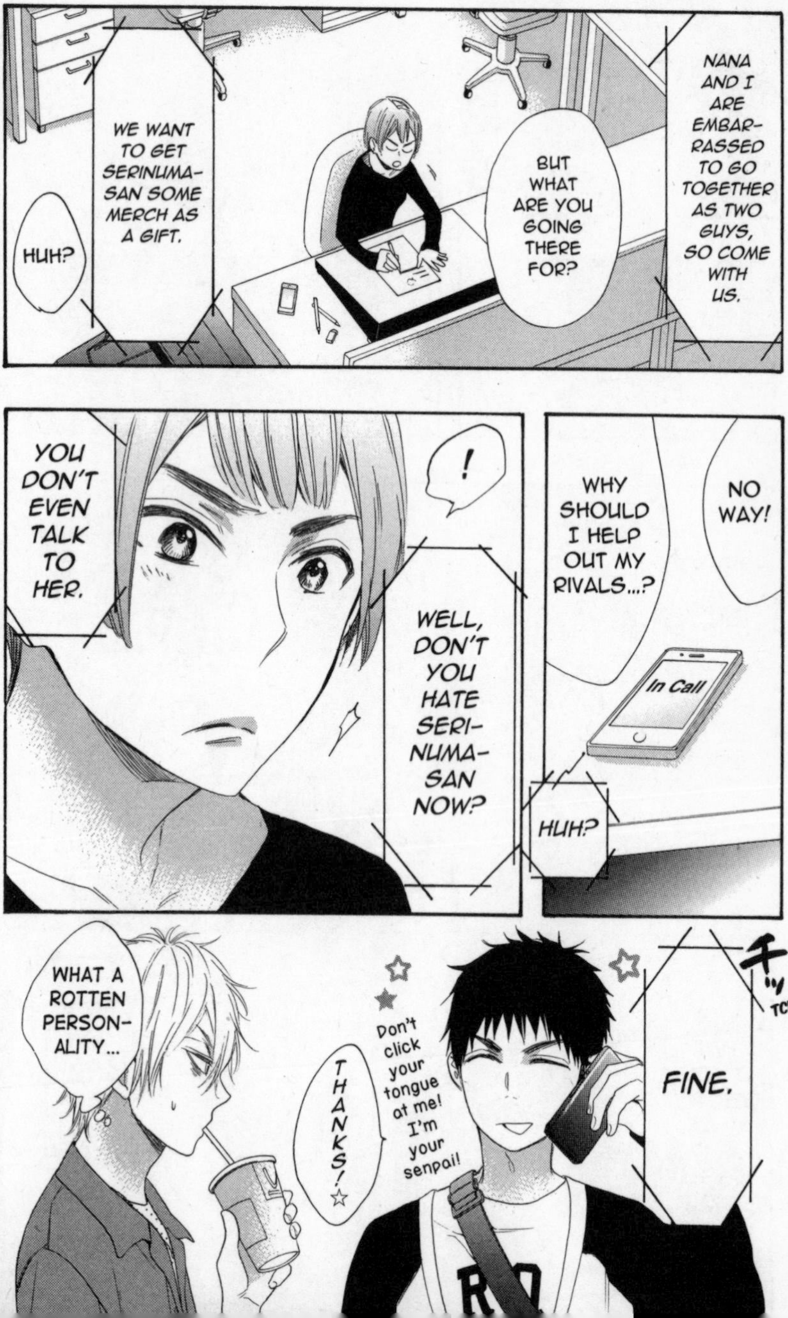

NANA AND I ARE EMBARRASSED TO GO TOGETHER AS TWO GUYS, SO COME WITH US.
BUT WHAT ARE YOU GOING THERE FOR?
WE WANT TO GET SERINUMA-SAN SOME MERCH AS A GIFT.
HUH?
NO WAY!
WHY SHOULD I HELP OUT MY RIVALS...?
In Call
HUH?
!
WELL, DON'T YOU HATE SERINUMA-SAN NOW?
YOU DON'T EVEN TALK TO HER.
チッ
TCH!
FINE.
Don't click your tongue at me! I'm your senpai!
THANKS!☆
WHAT A ROTTEN PERSONALITY...

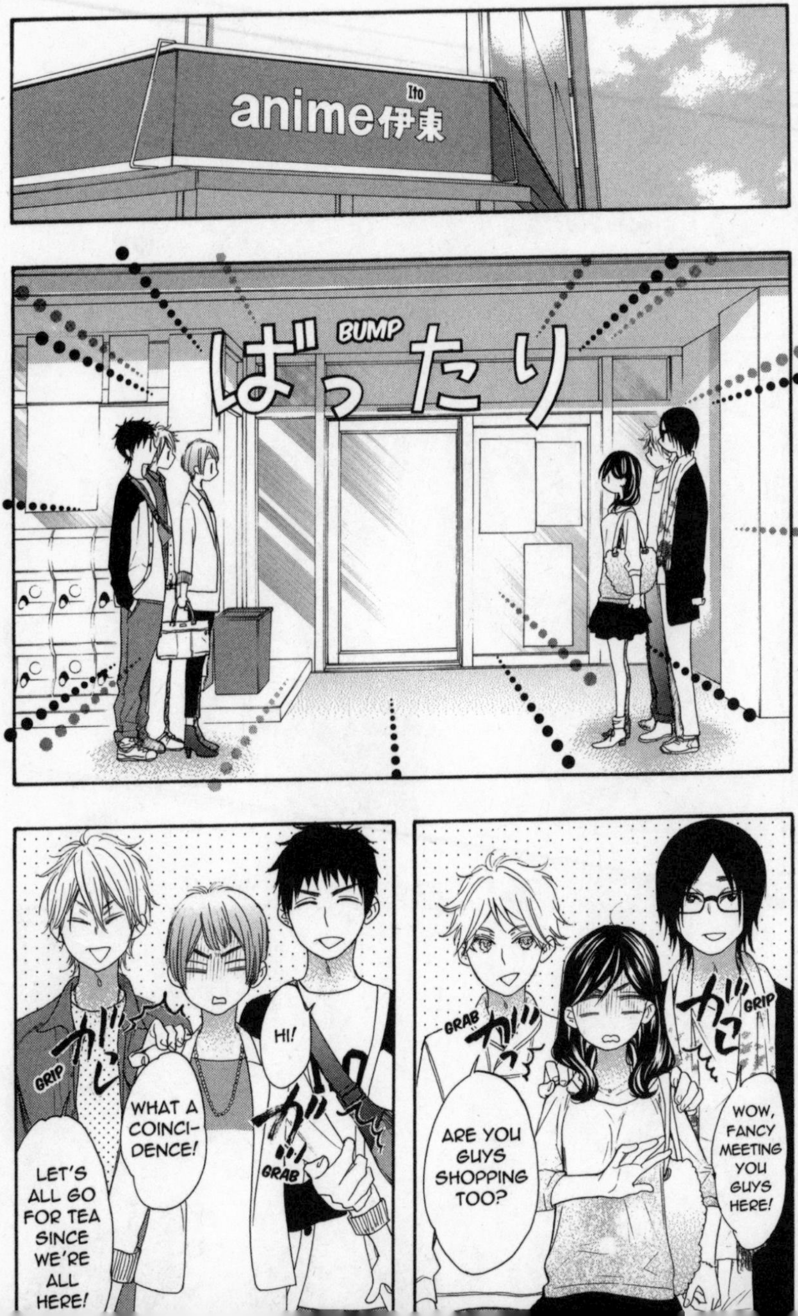
Ito
anime伊東
BUMP
ばったり
GRIP
WOW, FANCY MEETING YOU GUYS HERE!
GRAB
ARE YOU GUYS SHOPPING TOO?
HI!
GRAB
WHAT A COINCIDENCE!
GRIP
LET'S ALL GO FOR TEA SINCE WE'RE ALL HERE!

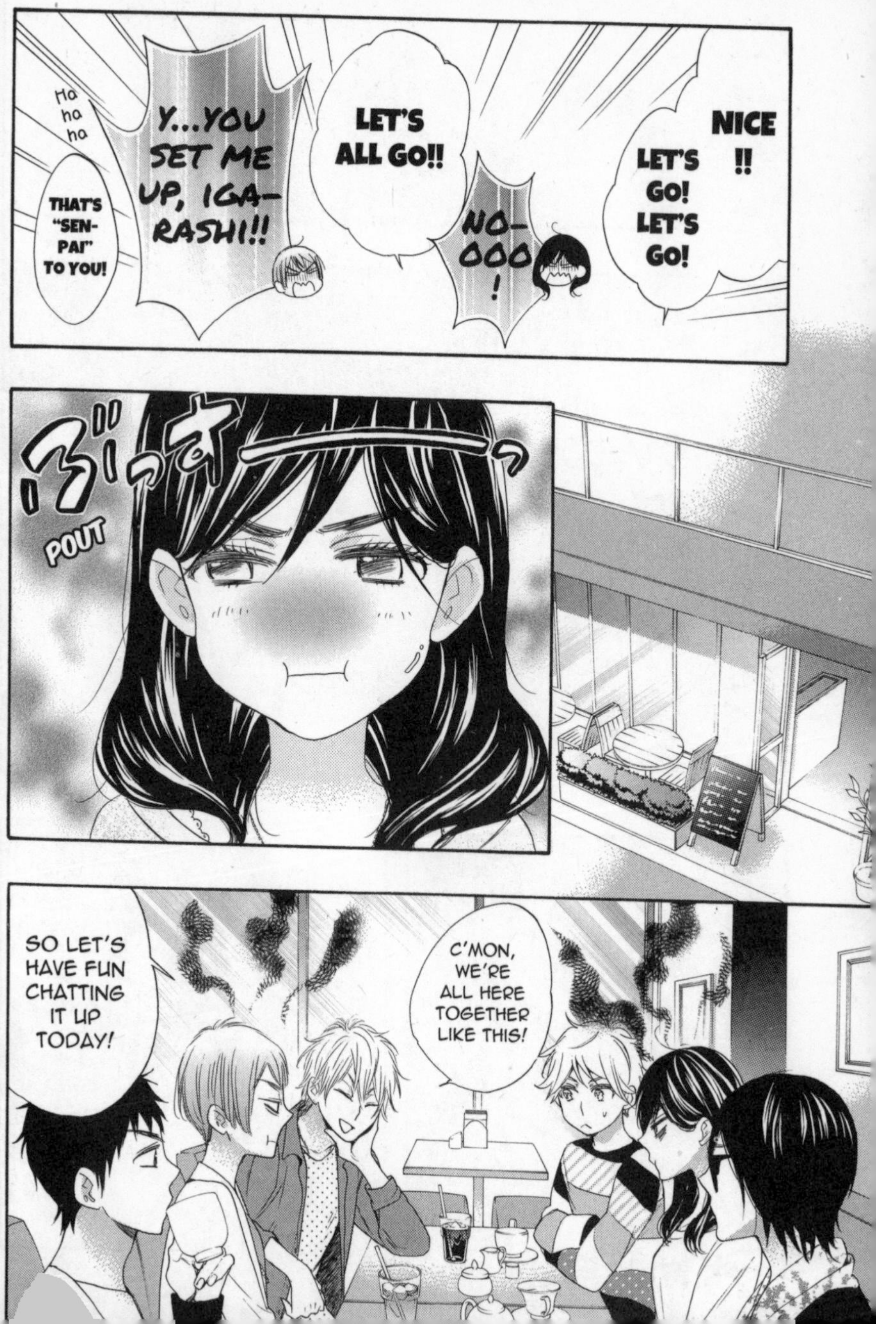
NICE!!
LET'S GO! LET'S GO!
NO-OOOO!
LET'S ALL GO!!
Y...YOU SET ME UP, IGA-RASHI!!
Ha ha ha
THAT'S "SEN-PAI" TO YOU!
POUT
C'MON, WE'RE ALL HERE TOGETHER LIKE THIS!
SO LET'S HAVE FUN CHATTING IT UP TODAY!

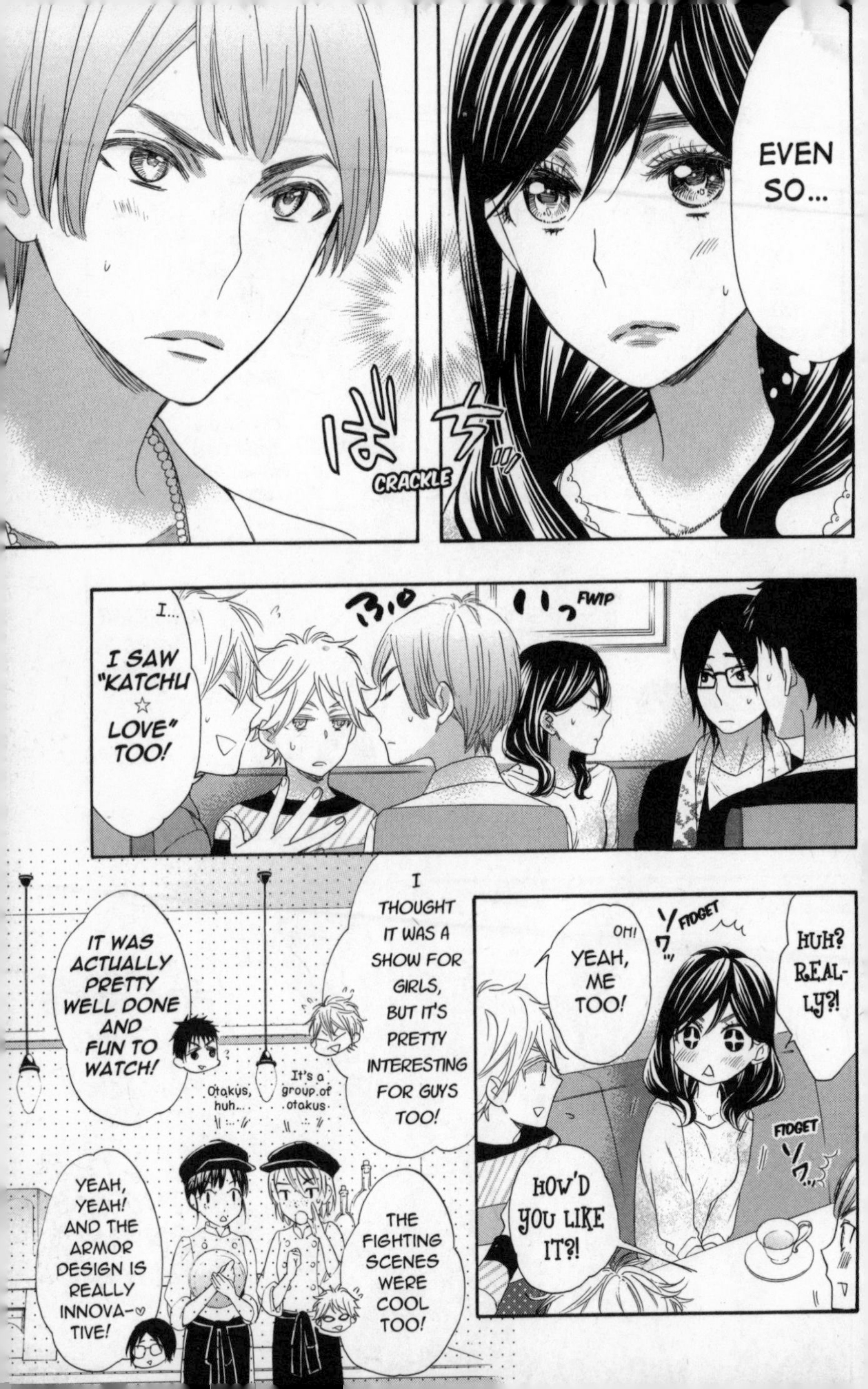
EVEN SO...
CRACKLE
FWIP
I...
I SAW "KATCHU☆LOVE" TOO!
HUH? REAL-LY?!
OH! YEAH, ME TOO!
FIDGET
HOW'D YOU LIKE IT?!
FIDGET
I THOUGHT IT WAS A SHOW FOR GIRLS, BUT IT'S PRETTY INTERESTING FOR GUYS TOO!
IT WAS ACTUALLY PRETTY WELL DONE AND FUN TO WATCH!
It's a group of otakus
Otakus, huh...
THE FIGHTING SCENES WERE COOL TOO!
YEAH, YEAH! AND THE ARMOR DESIGN IS REALLY INNOVA-TIVE!♡

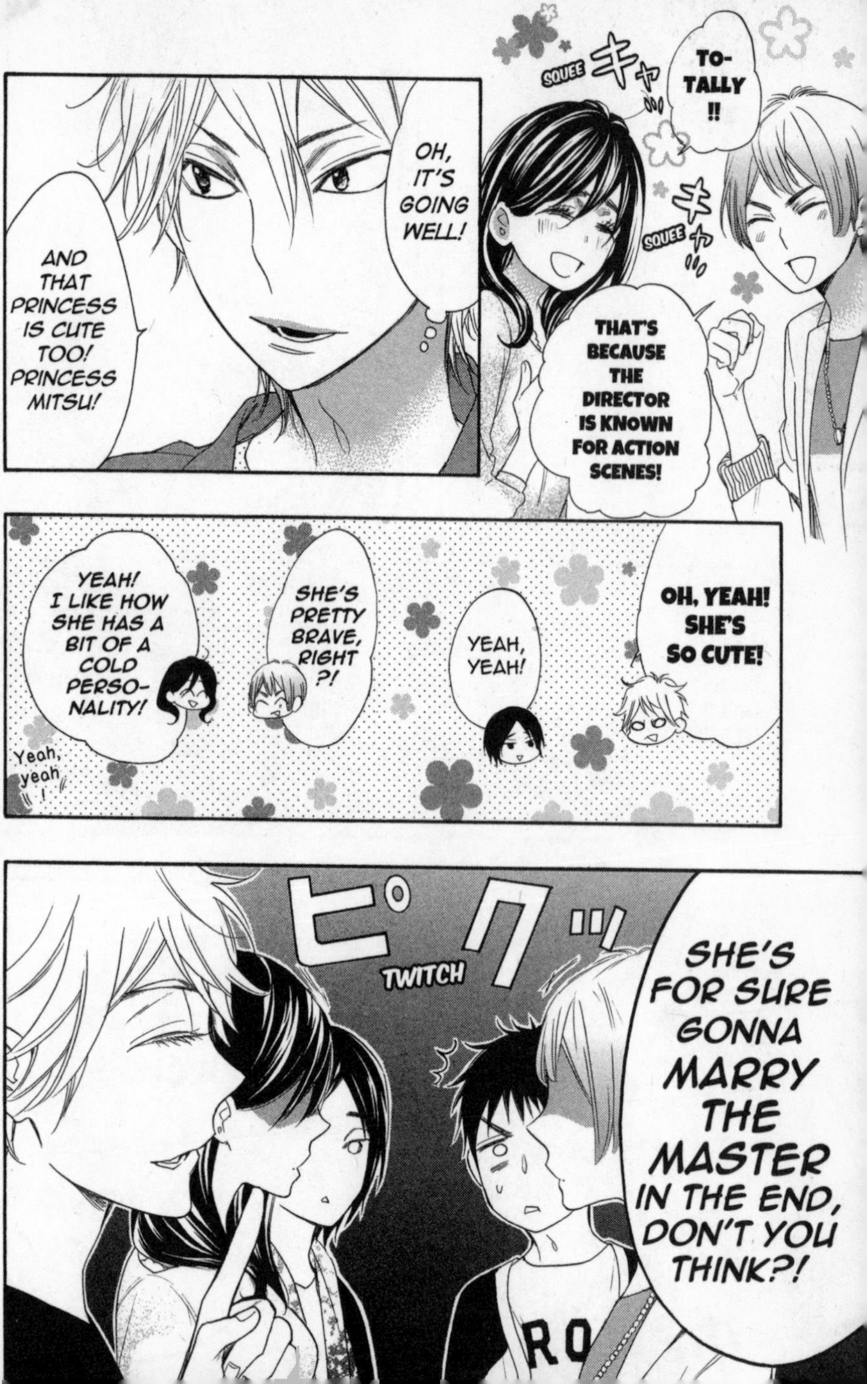
TO-TALLY!!
SQUEE
SQUEE
THAT'S BECAUSE THE DIRECTOR IS KNOWN FOR ACTION SCENES!
OH, IT'S GOING WELL!
AND THAT PRINCESS IS CUTE TOO! PRINCESS MITSU!
OH, YEAH! SHE'S SO CUTE!
YEAH, YEAH!
SHE'S PRETTY BRAVE, RIGHT?!
YEAH! I LIKE HOW SHE HAS A BIT OF A COLD PERSONALITY!
Yeah, yeah!
SHE'S FOR SURE GONNA MARRY THE MASTER IN THE END, DON'T YOU THINK?!
TWITCH

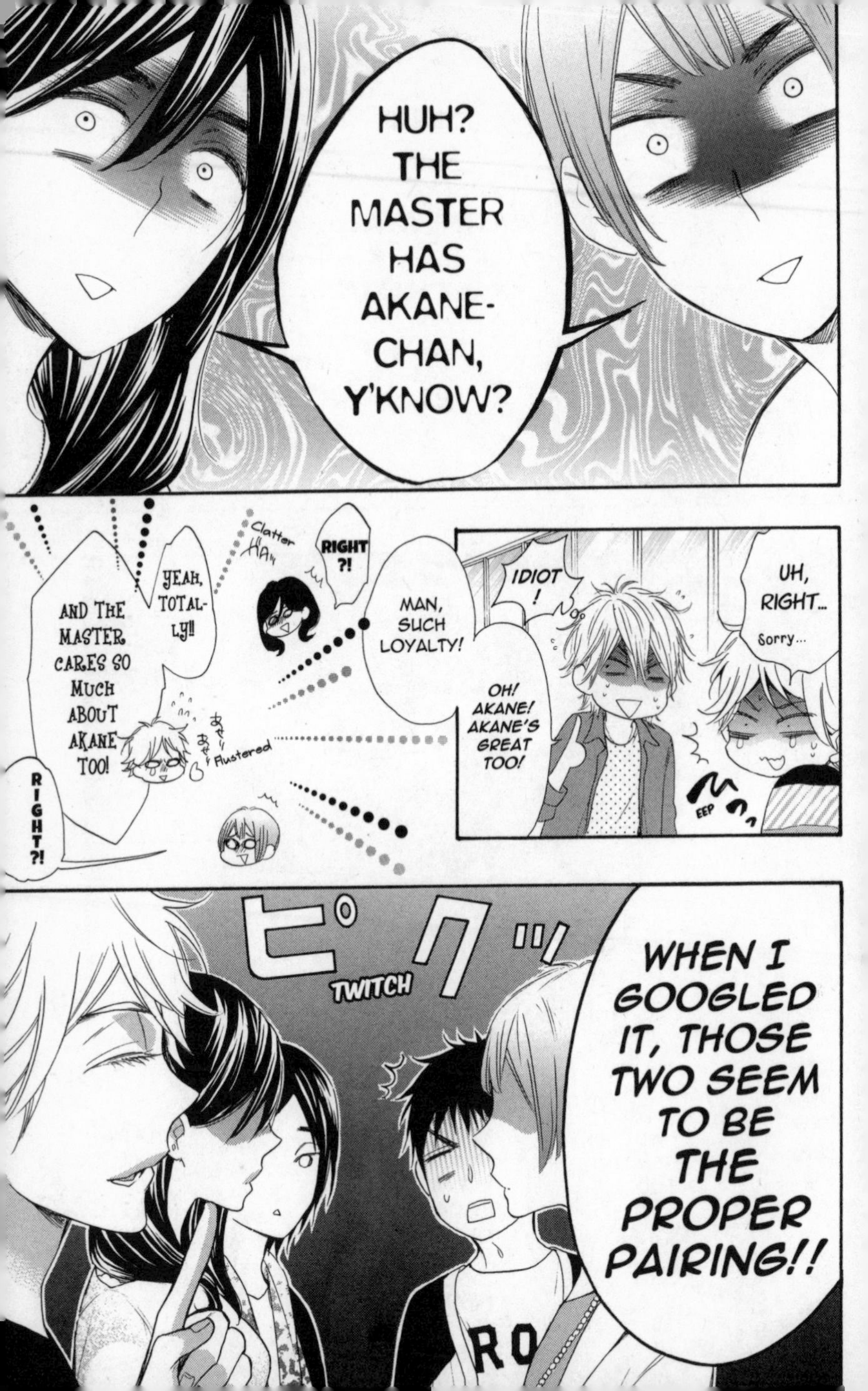
HUH? THE MASTER HAS AKANE-CHAN, Y'KNOW?
UH, RIGHT...
Sorry...
IDIOT!
EEP
MAN, SUCH LOYALTY!
OH! AKANE! AKANE'S GREAT TOO!
RIGHT?!
Clatter
YEAH, TOTALLY!!
AND THE MASTER CARES SO MUCH ABOUT AKANE TOO!
Flustered
RIGHT?!
WHEN I GOOGLED IT, THOSE TWO SEEM TO BE THE PROPER PAIRING!!
ピクッ
TWITCH
RO

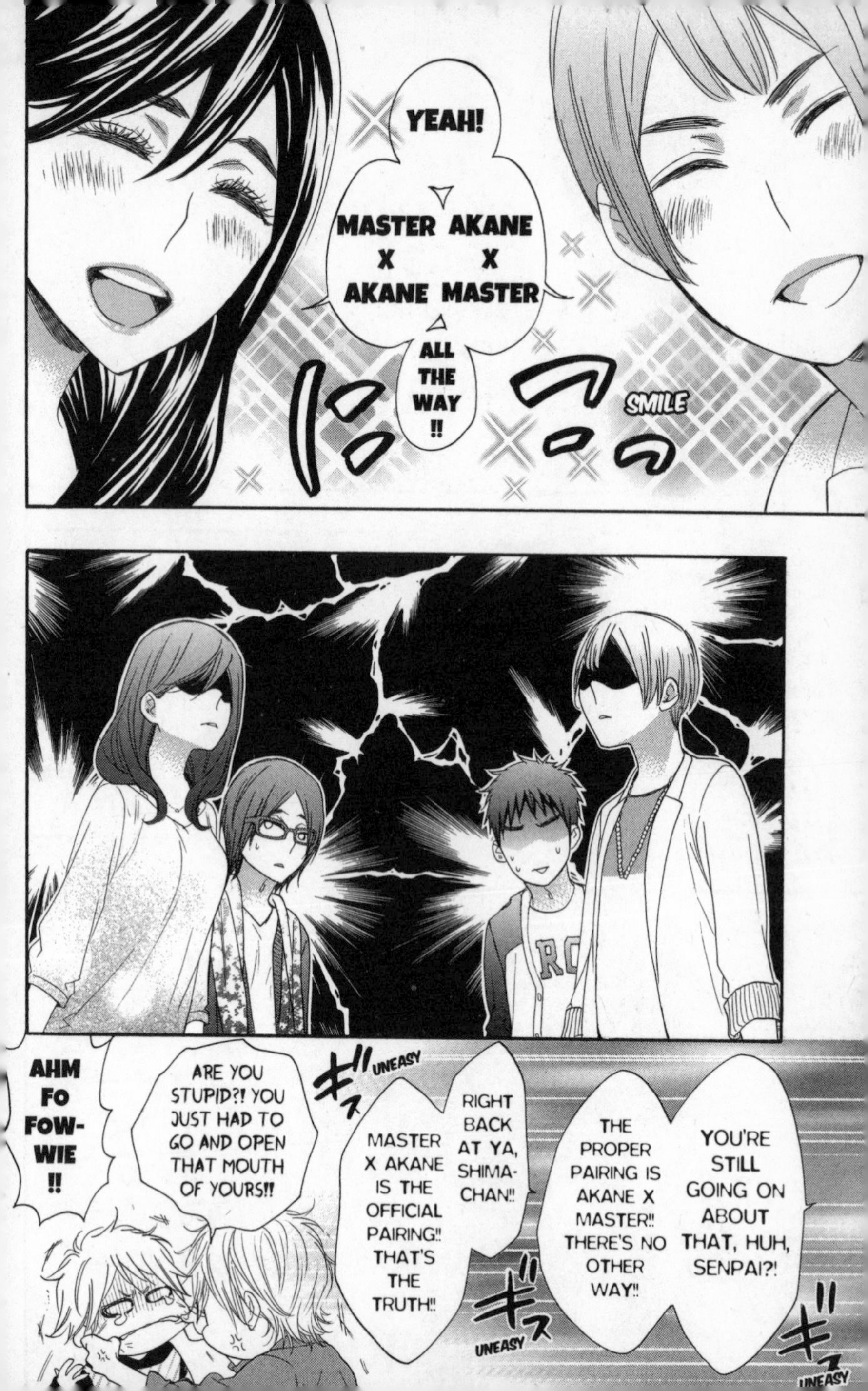
YEAH!
▽
MASTER X AKANE
AKANE X MASTER
△
ALL THE WAY!!
SMILE
YOU'RE STILL GOING ON ABOUT THAT, HUH, SENPAI?!
UNEASY
THE PROPER PAIRING IS AKANE X MASTER!! THERE'S NO OTHER WAY!!
UNEASY
RIGHT BACK AT YA, SHIMA-CHAN!!
MASTER X AKANE IS THE OFFICIAL PAIRING!! THAT'S THE TRUTH!!
UNEASY
ARE YOU STUPID?! YOU JUST HAD TO GO AND OPEN THAT MOUTH OF YOURS!!
AHM FO FOW-WIE!!

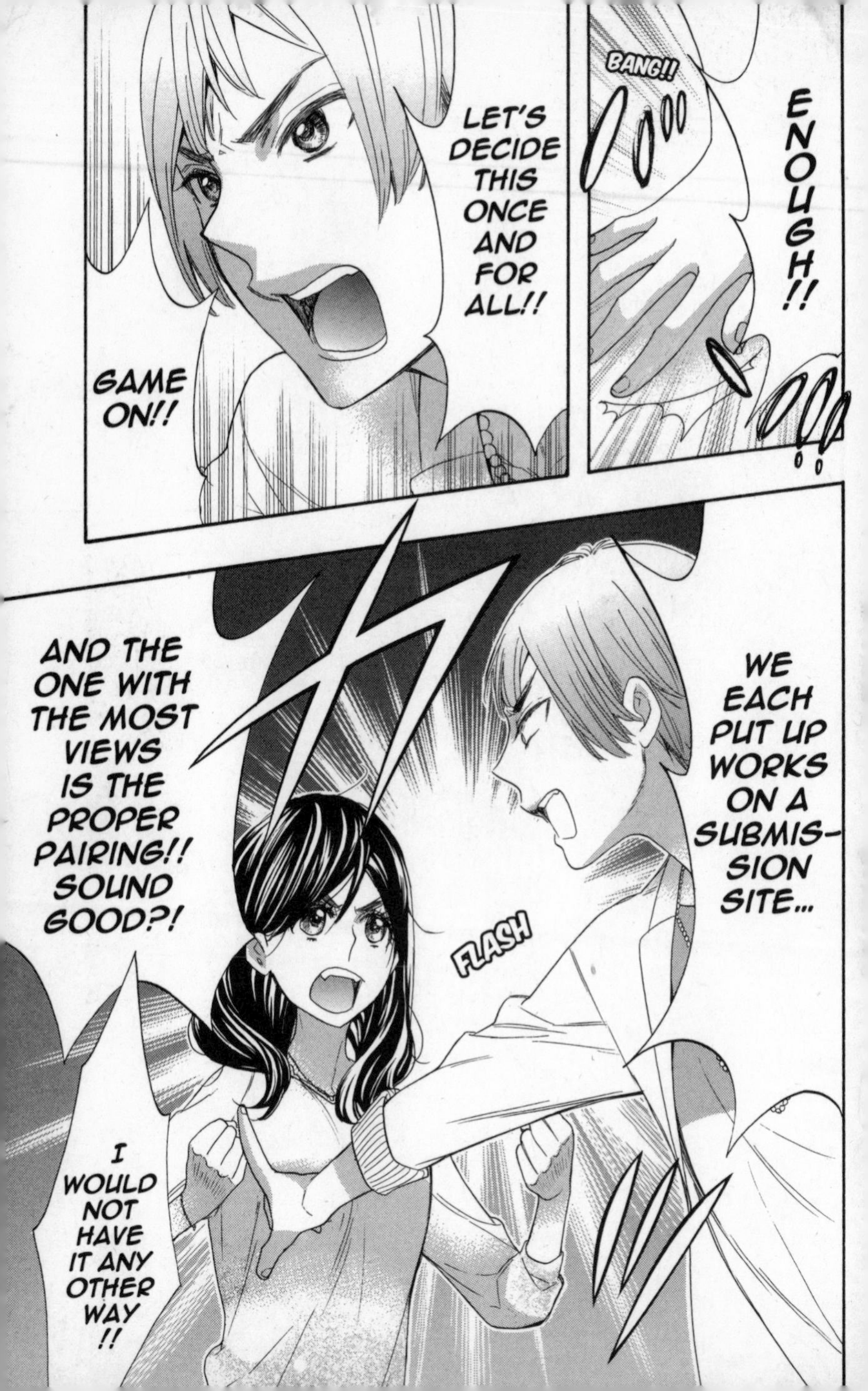
BANG!!
ENOUGH!!
LET'S DECIDE THIS ONCE AND FOR ALL!!
GAME ON!!
WE EACH PUT UP WORKS ON A SUBMISSION SITE...
FLASH
AND THE ONE WITH THE MOST VIEWS IS THE PROPER PAIRING!! SOUND GOOD?!
I WOULD NOT HAVE IT ANY OTHER WAY!!

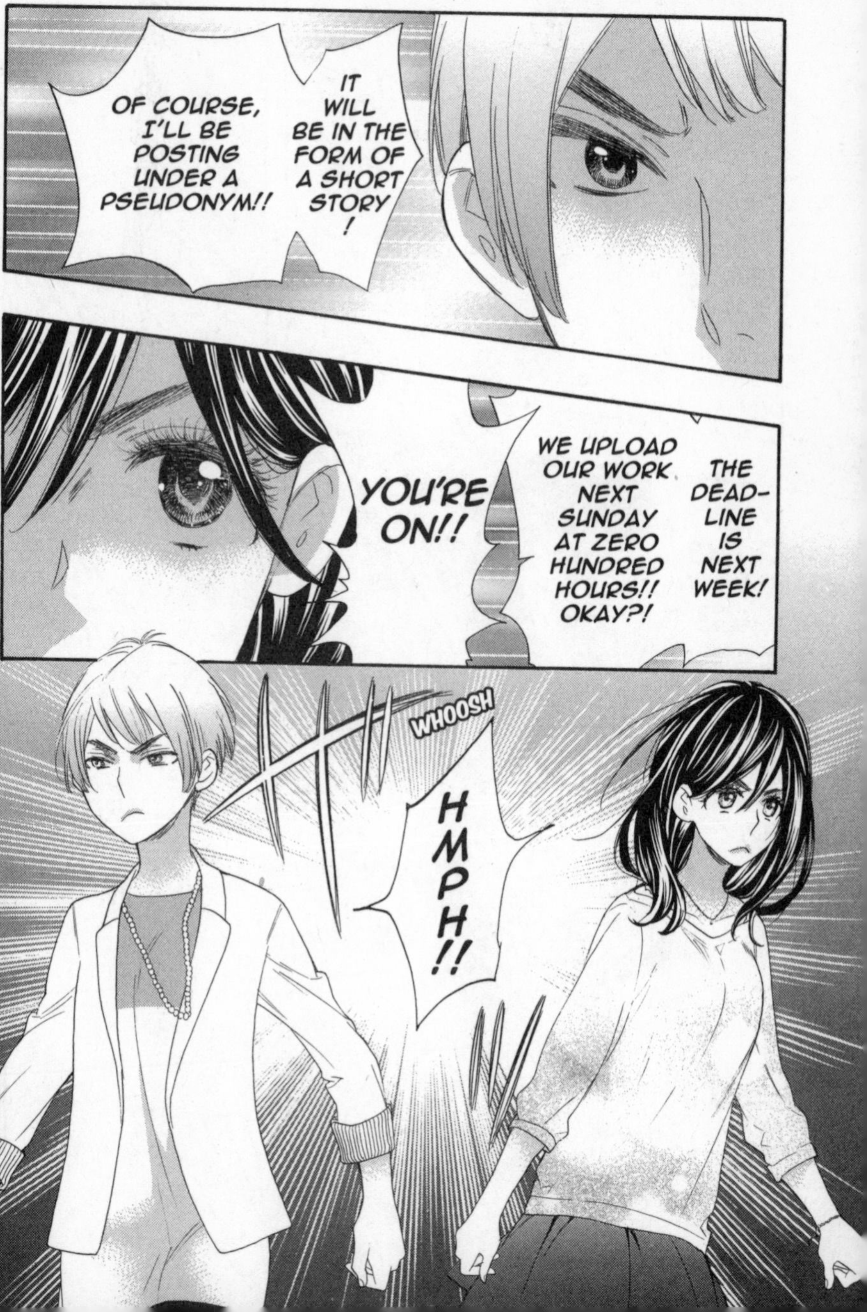
IT WILL BE IN THE FORM OF A SHORT STORY!
OF COURSE, I'LL BE POSTING UNDER A PSEUDONYM!!
THE DEAD-LINE IS NEXT WEEK!
WE UPLOAD OUR WORK NEXT SUNDAY AT ZERO HUNDRED HOURS!! OKAY?!
YOU'RE ON!!
WHOOSH
HMPH!!

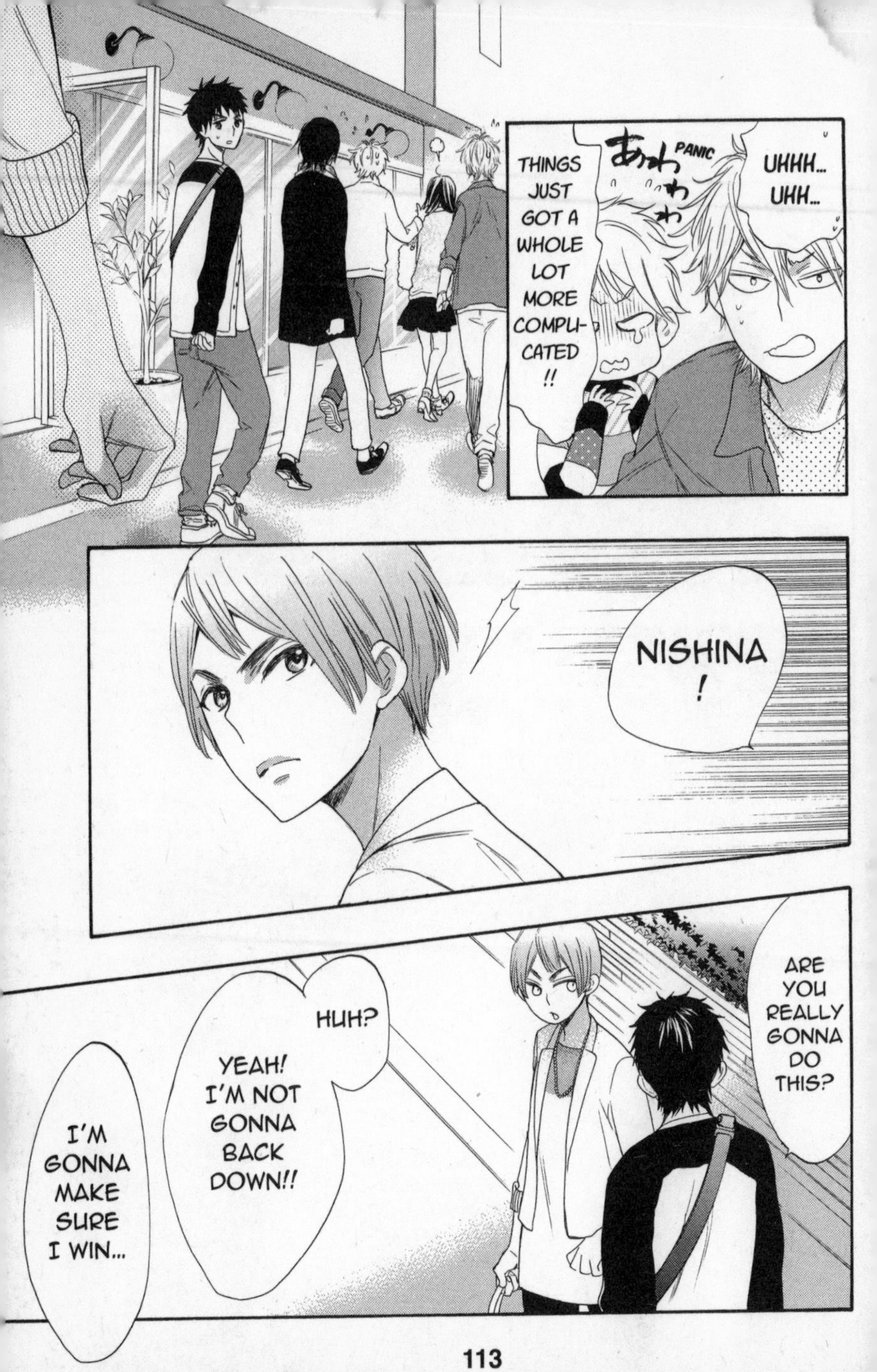
UHHH... UHH...
あわわわ PANIC
THINGS JUST GOT A WHOLE LOT MORE COMPLICATED!!
NISHINA!
ARE YOU REALLY GONNA DO THIS?
HUH?
YEAH! I'M NOT GONNA BACK DOWN!!
I'M GONNA MAKE SURE I WIN...

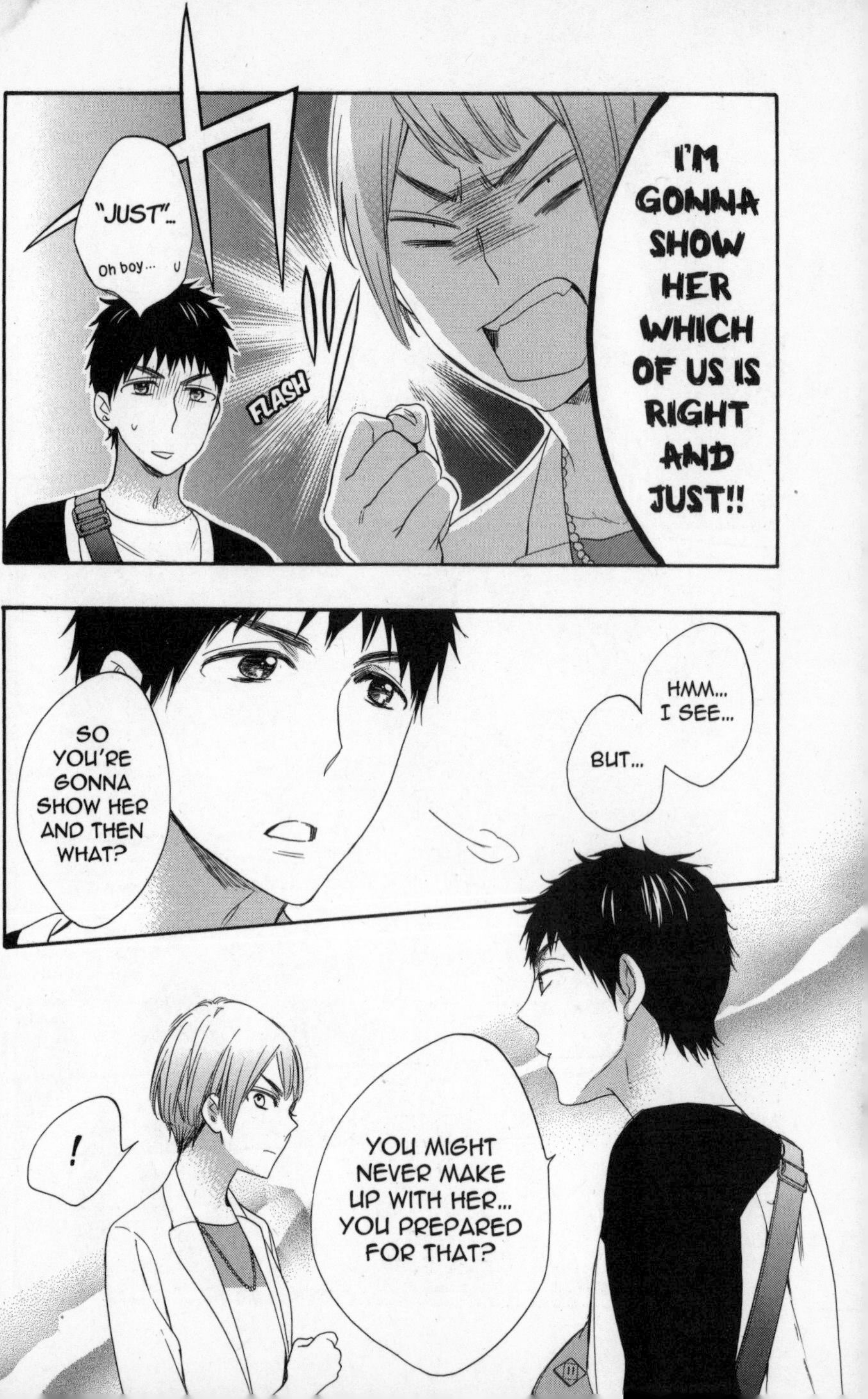
I'M GONNA SHOW HER WHICH OF US IS RIGHT AND JUST!!
FLASH
"JUST"...
Oh boy...
HMM... I SEE...
BUT...
SO YOU'RE GONNA SHOW HER AND THEN WHAT?
YOU MIGHT NEVER MAKE UP WITH HER... YOU PREPARED FOR THAT?
!

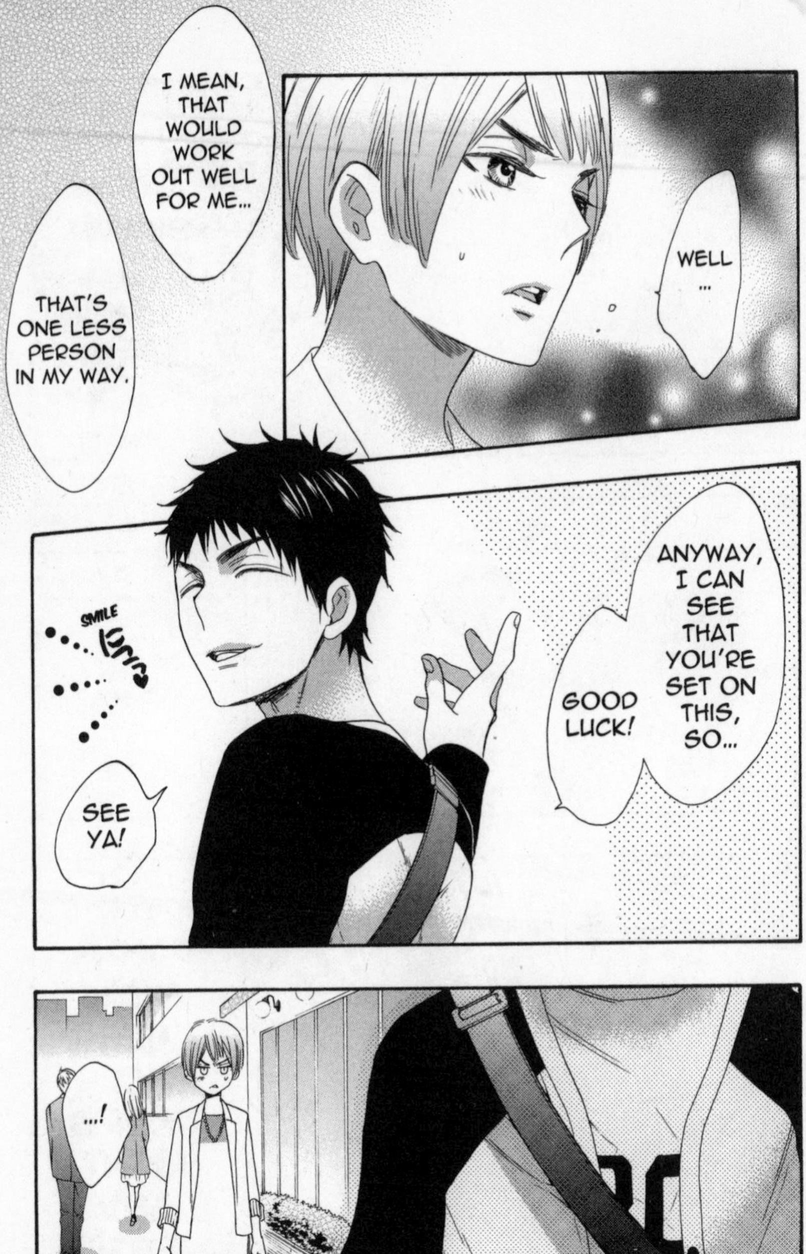
WELL ...
I MEAN, THAT WOULD WORK OUT WELL FOR ME...
THAT'S ONE LESS PERSON IN MY WAY.
ANYWAY, I CAN SEE THAT YOU'RE SET ON THIS, SO...
GOOD LUCK!
SMILE
SEE YA!
...!

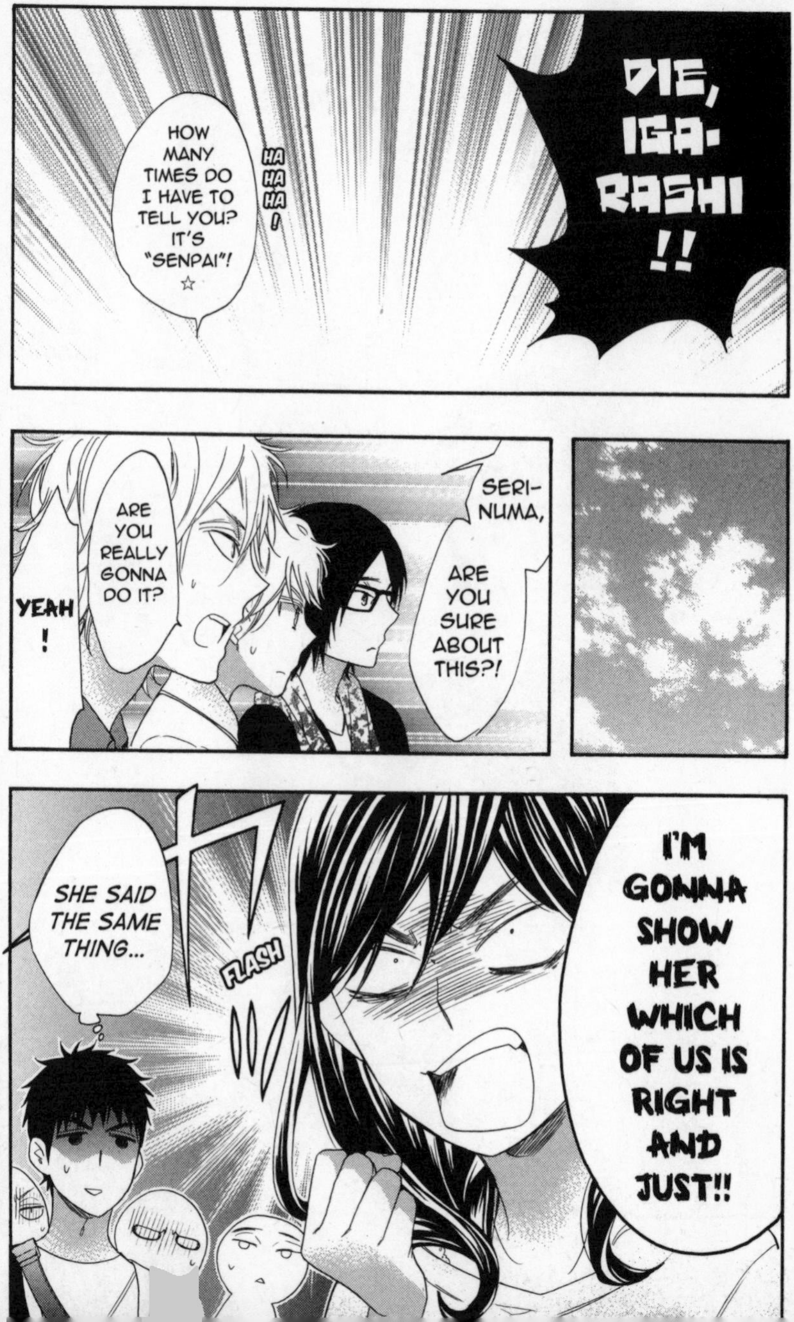
DIE, IGA-RASHI!!
HOW MANY TIMES DO I HAVE TO TELL YOU? IT'S "SENPAI"! ☆
HA HA HA!
SERI-NUMA, ARE YOU SURE ABOUT THIS?!
ARE YOU REALLY GONNA DO IT?
YEAH!
I'M GONNA SHOW HER WHICH OF US IS RIGHT AND JUST!!
FLASH
SHE SAID THE SAME THING...

#24 SOMETHING PRECIOUS

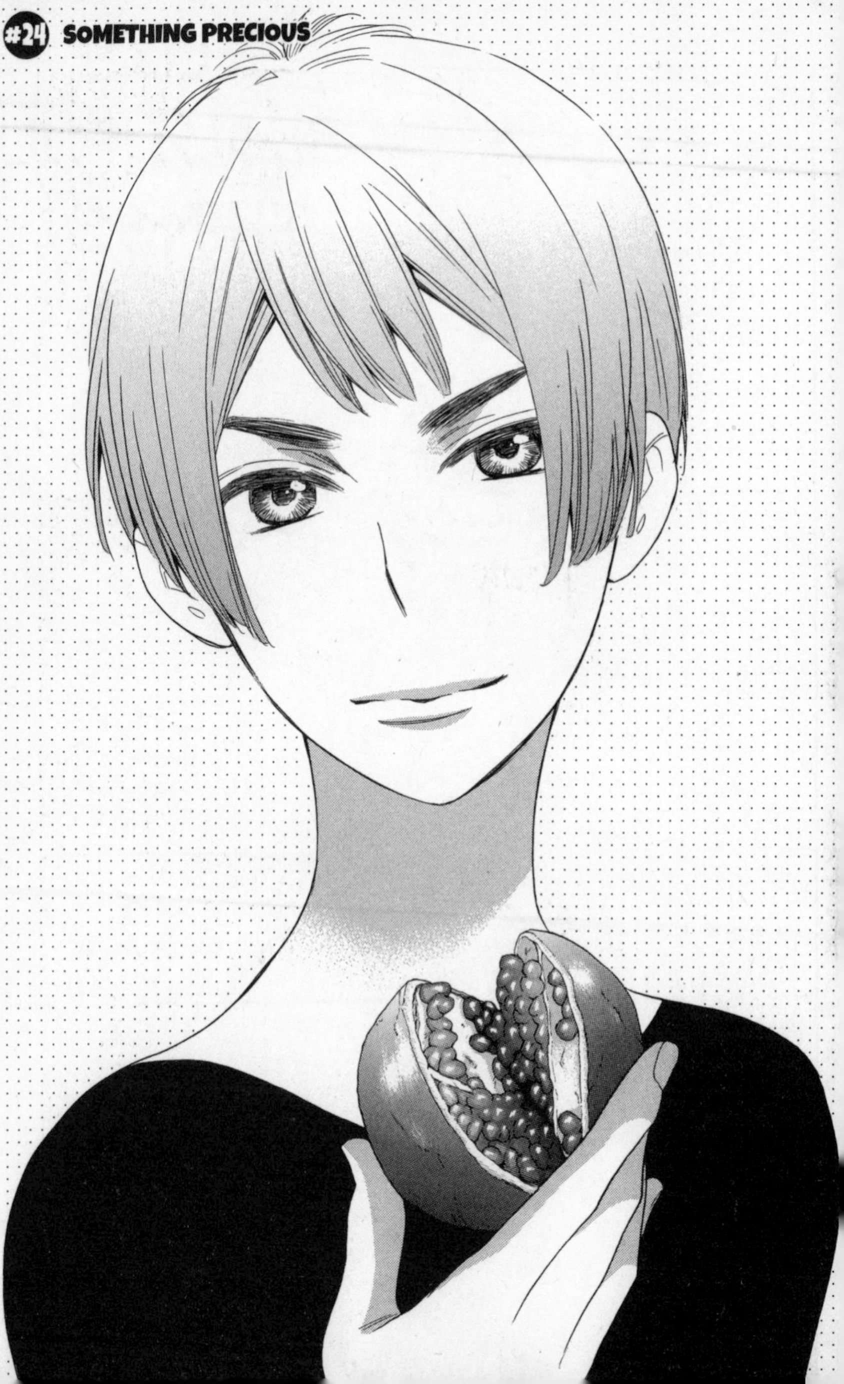

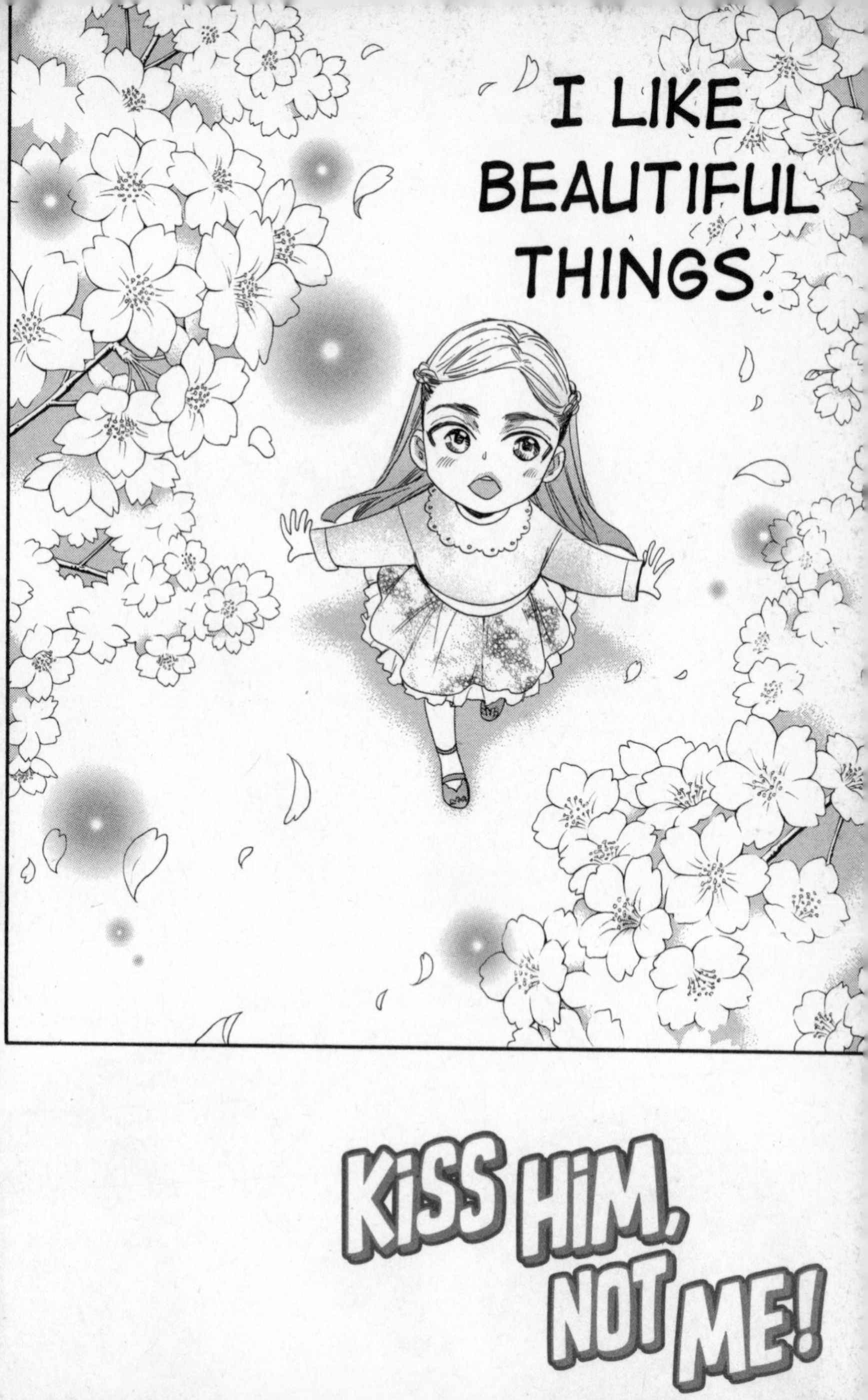
I LIKE BEAUTIFUL THINGS.

KiSS HiM, NOT ME!

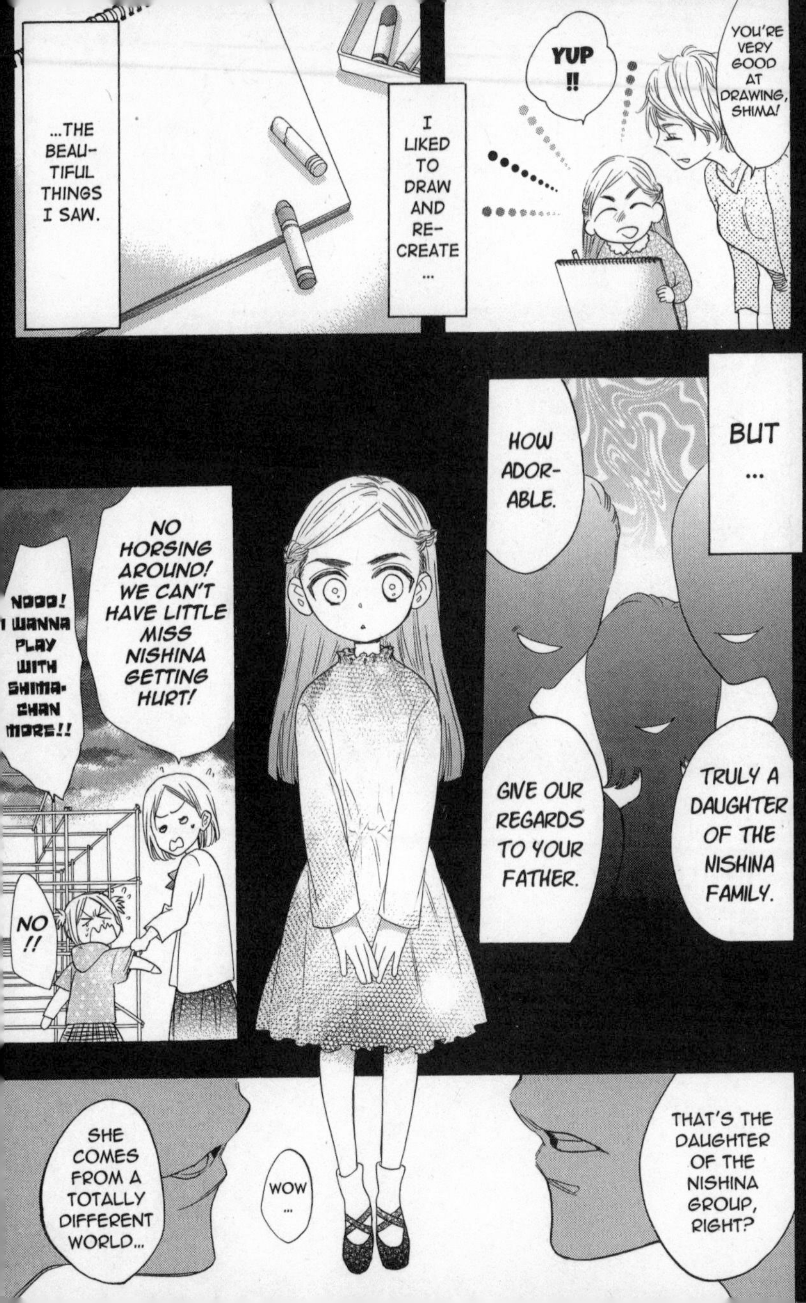
YOU'RE VERY GOOD AT DRAWING, SHIMA!
YUP !!
I LIKED TO DRAW AND RE-CREATE ...
...THE BEAUTIFUL THINGS I SAW.
BUT ...
HOW ADORABLE.
TRULY A DAUGHTER OF THE NISHINA FAMILY.
GIVE OUR REGARDS TO YOUR FATHER.
NO HORSING AROUND! WE CAN'T HAVE LITTLE MISS NISHINA GETTING HURT!
NOOO! I WANNA PLAY WITH SHIMA-CHAN MORE!!
NO !!
THAT'S THE DAUGHTER OF THE NISHINA GROUP, RIGHT?
WOW ...
SHE COMES FROM A TOTALLY DIFFERENT WORLD...

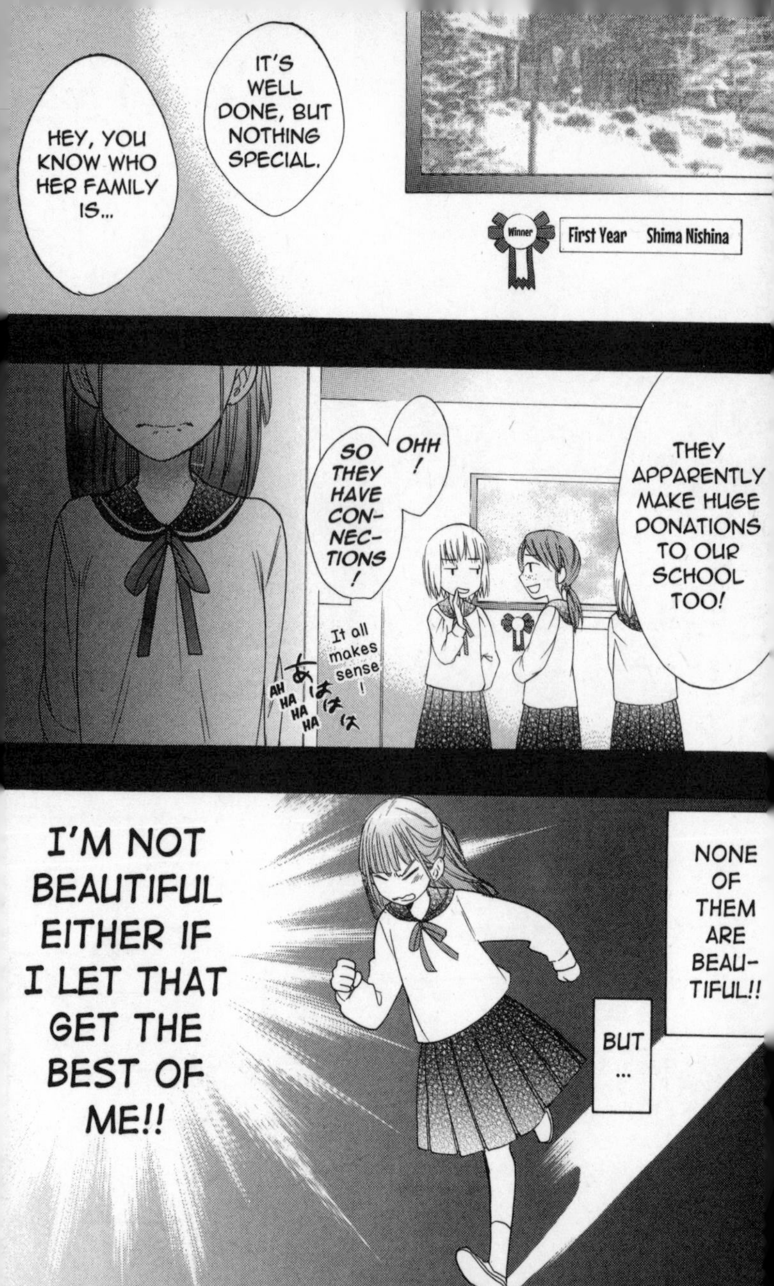
Winner
First Year Shima Nishina
IT'S WELL DONE, BUT NOTHING SPECIAL.
HEY, YOU KNOW WHO HER FAMILY IS...
THEY APPARENTLY MAKE HUGE DONATIONS TO OUR SCHOOL TOO!
OHH!
SO THEY HAVE CON-NEC-TIONS!
It all makes sense!
AH HA HA HA
あははは
NONE OF THEM ARE BEAU-TIFUL!!
BUT...
I'M NOT BEAUTIFUL EITHER IF I LET THAT GET THE BEST OF ME!!

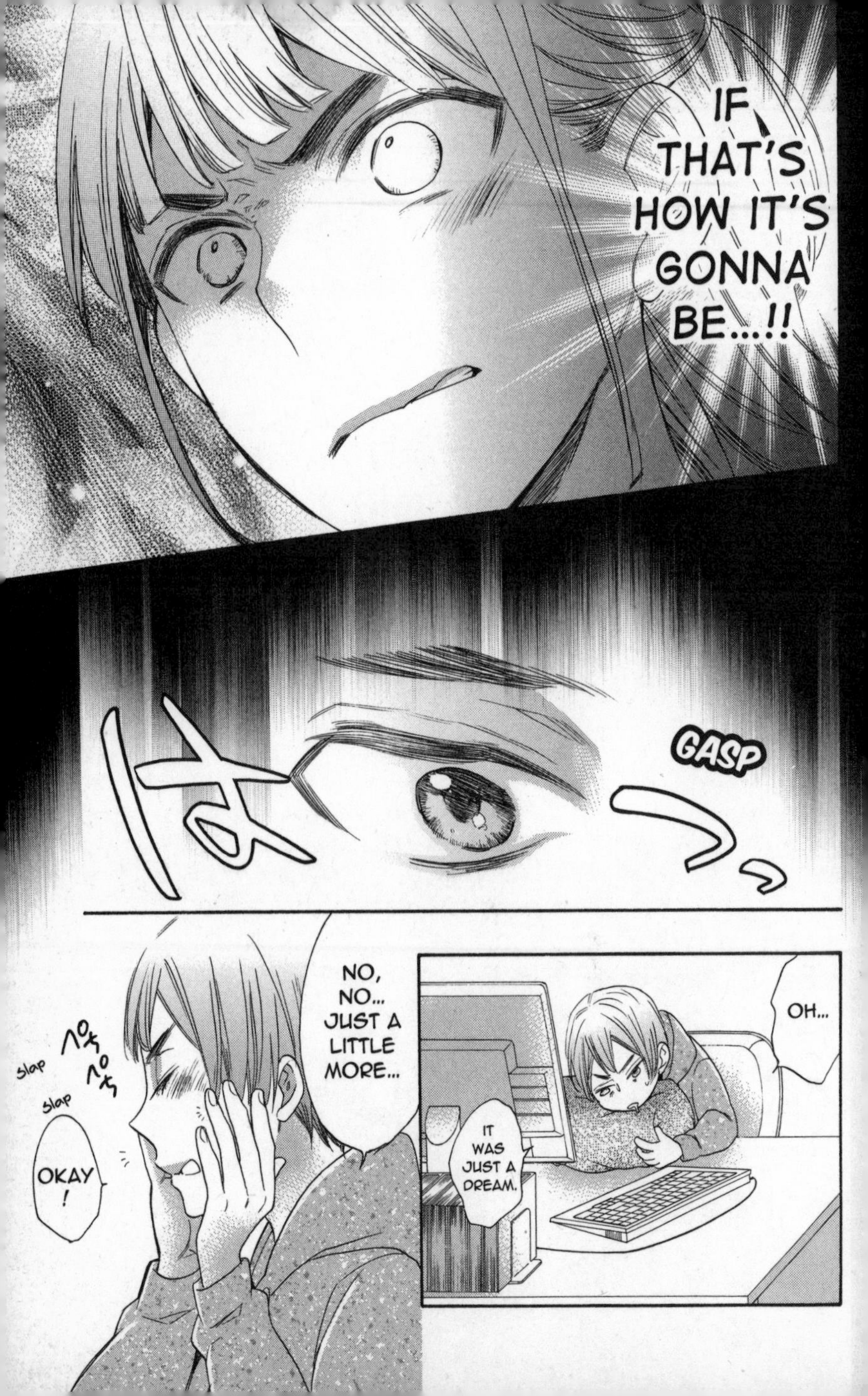
IF THAT'S HOW IT'S GONNA BE...!!
はっ
GASP
OH...
IT WAS JUST A DREAM.
NO, NO... JUST A LITTLE MORE...
ぺち ぺち
slap slap
OKAY!

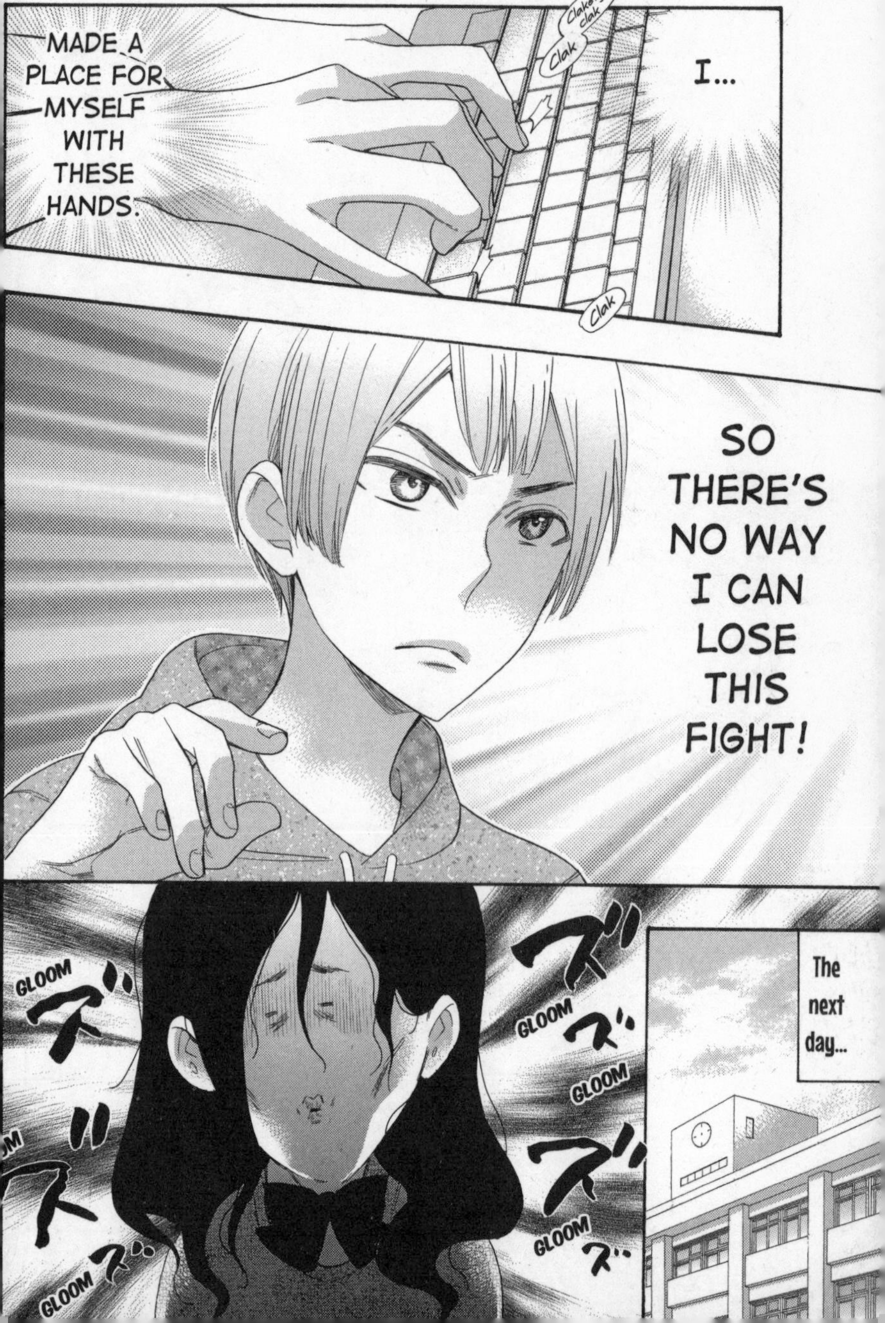
I...
Clakety-clak
Clak
MADE A PLACE FOR MYSELF WITH THESE HANDS.
Clak
SO THERE'S NO WAY I CAN LOSE THIS FIGHT!
The next day...
GLOOM
GLOOM
GLOOM
GLOOM
GLOOM
GLOOM

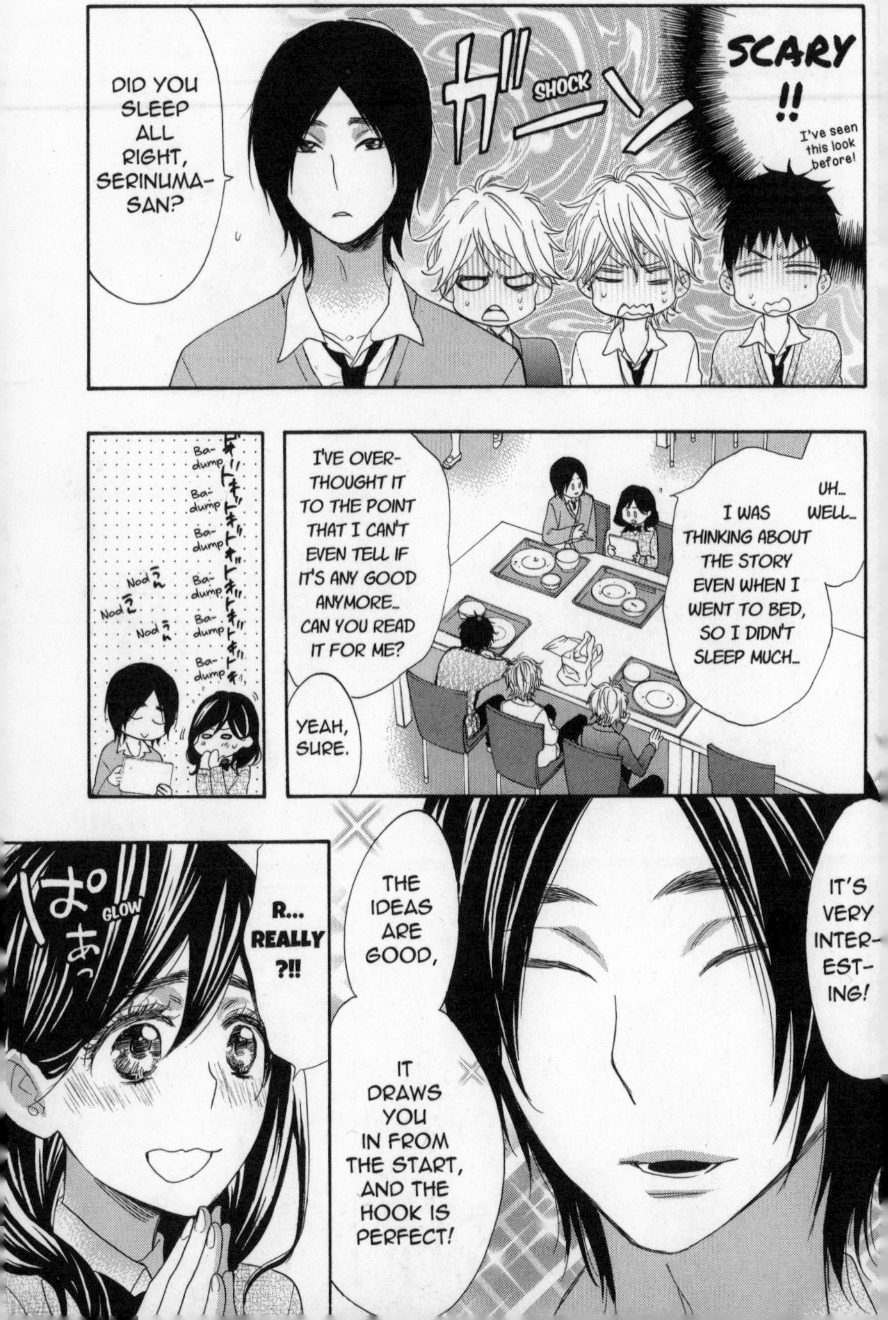
SCARY!!
I've seen this look before!
SHOCK
DID YOU SLEEP ALL RIGHT, SERINUMA-SAN?
UH... WELL... I WAS THINKING ABOUT THE STORY EVEN WHEN I WENT TO BED, SO I DIDN'T SLEEP MUCH...
I'VE OVER-THOUGHT IT TO THE POINT THAT I CAN'T EVEN TELL IF IT'S ANY GOOD ANYMORE... CAN YOU READ IT FOR ME?
YEAH, SURE.
Ba-dump
Ba-dump
Ba-dump
Ba-dump
Ba-dump
Ba-dump
Nod
Nod
Nod
IT'S VERY INTER-EST-ING!
THE IDEAS ARE GOOD,
IT DRAWS YOU IN FROM THE START, AND THE HOOK IS PERFECT!
R... REALLY?!!
GLOW

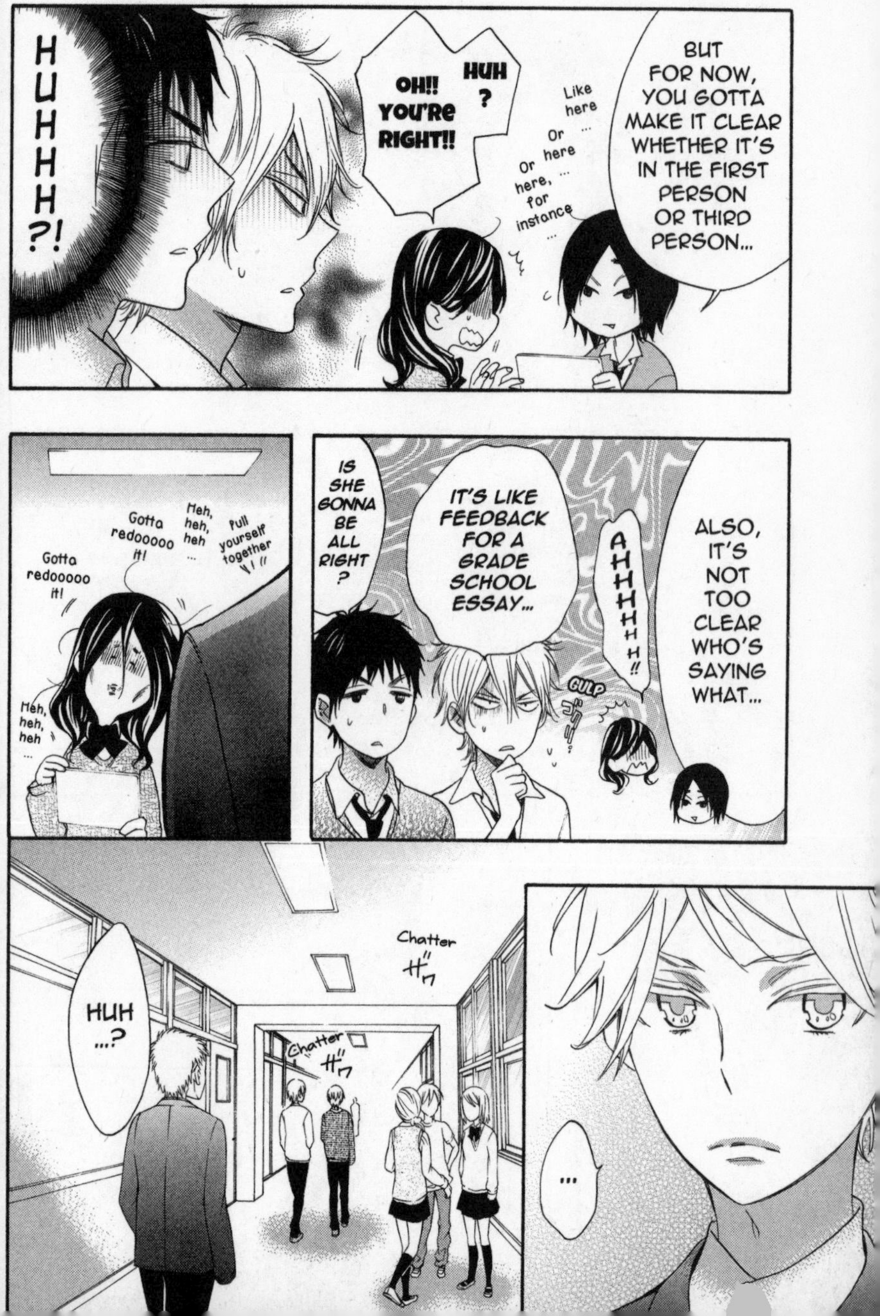
BUT FOR NOW, YOU GOTTA MAKE IT CLEAR WHETHER IT'S IN THE FIRST PERSON OR THIRD PERSON...
Like here ...
Or here ...
Or here, ... for instance ...
HUH ?
OH!! YOU'RE RIGHT!!
HUHHHH?!
ALSO, IT'S NOT TOO CLEAR WHO'S SAYING WHAT...
AHHHHHH!!
GULP
IT'S LIKE FEEDBACK FOR A GRADE SCHOOL ESSAY...
IS SHE GONNA BE ALL RIGHT ?
Pull yourself together
Heh, heh, heh ...
Gotta redoooooo it!
Gotta redoooooo it!
Heh, heh, heh ...
...
Chatter
Chatter
HUH ...?

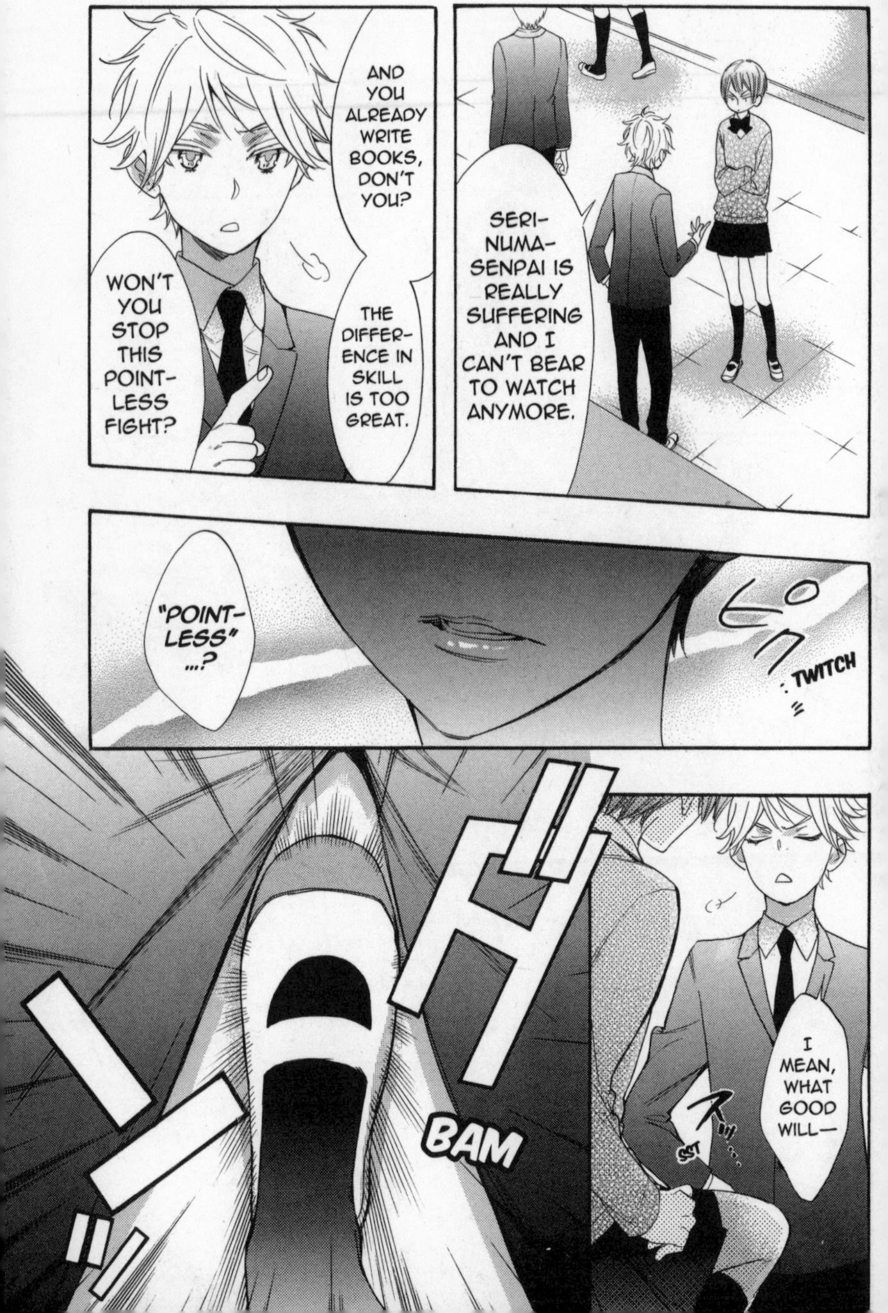
SERI-NUMA-SENPAI IS REALLY SUFFERING AND I CAN'T BEAR TO WATCH ANYMORE.
AND YOU ALREADY WRITE BOOKS, DON'T YOU?
THE DIFFERENCE IN SKILL IS TOO GREAT.
WON'T YOU STOP THIS POINTLESS FIGHT?
TWITCH
"POINTLESS" ...?
SST
I MEAN, WHAT GOOD WILL—
BAM

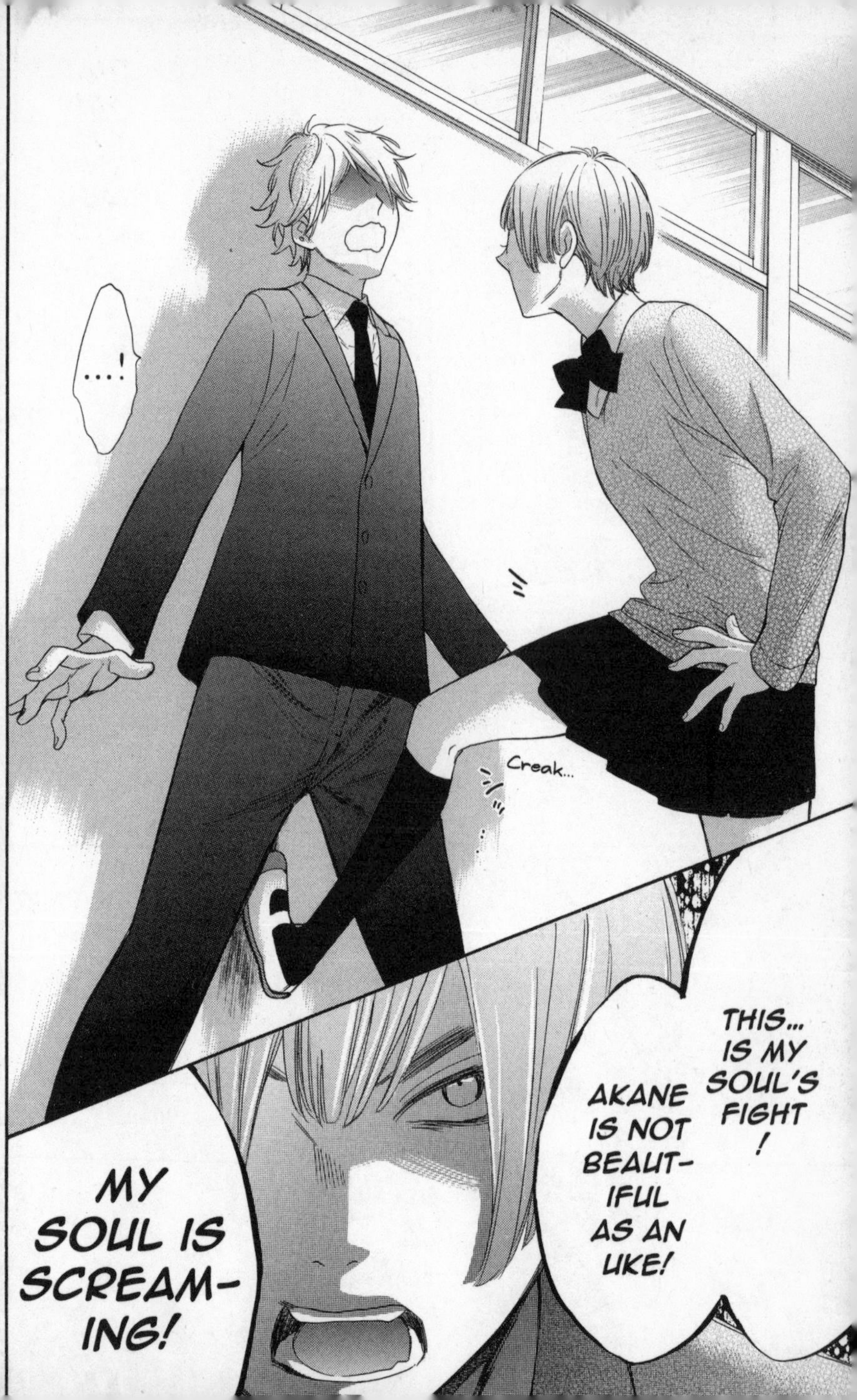
...!
Creak...
THIS... IS MY SOUL'S FIGHT!
AKANE IS NOT BEAUTIFUL AS AN UKE!
MY SOUL IS SCREAMING!

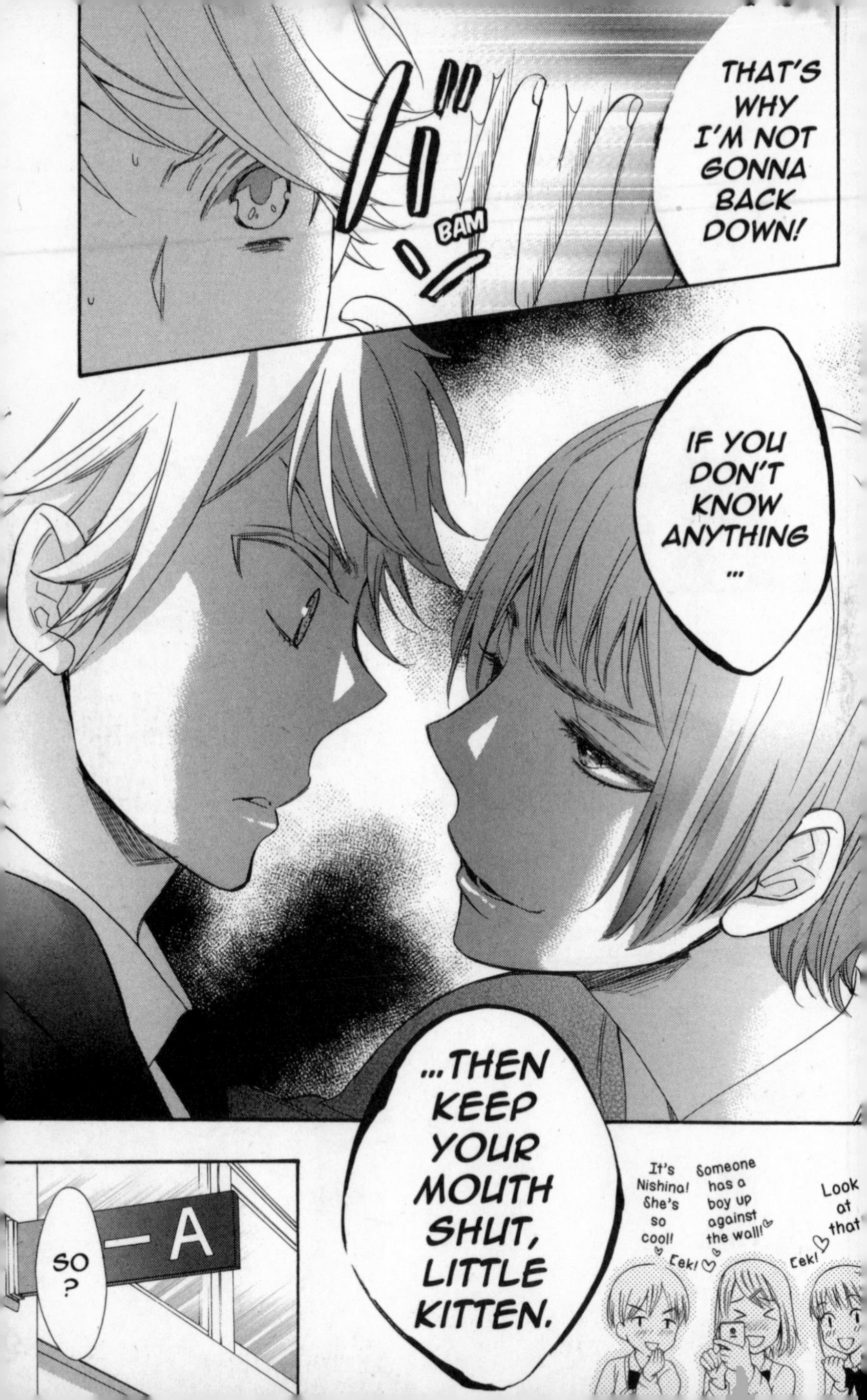
THAT'S WHY I'M NOT GONNA BACK DOWN!
BAM
IF YOU DON'T KNOW ANYTHING ...
...THEN KEEP YOUR MOUTH SHUT, LITTLE KITTEN.
Look at that
Eek!
Someone has a boy up against the wall!
Eek!
It's Nishina! She's so cool!
—A
SO ?

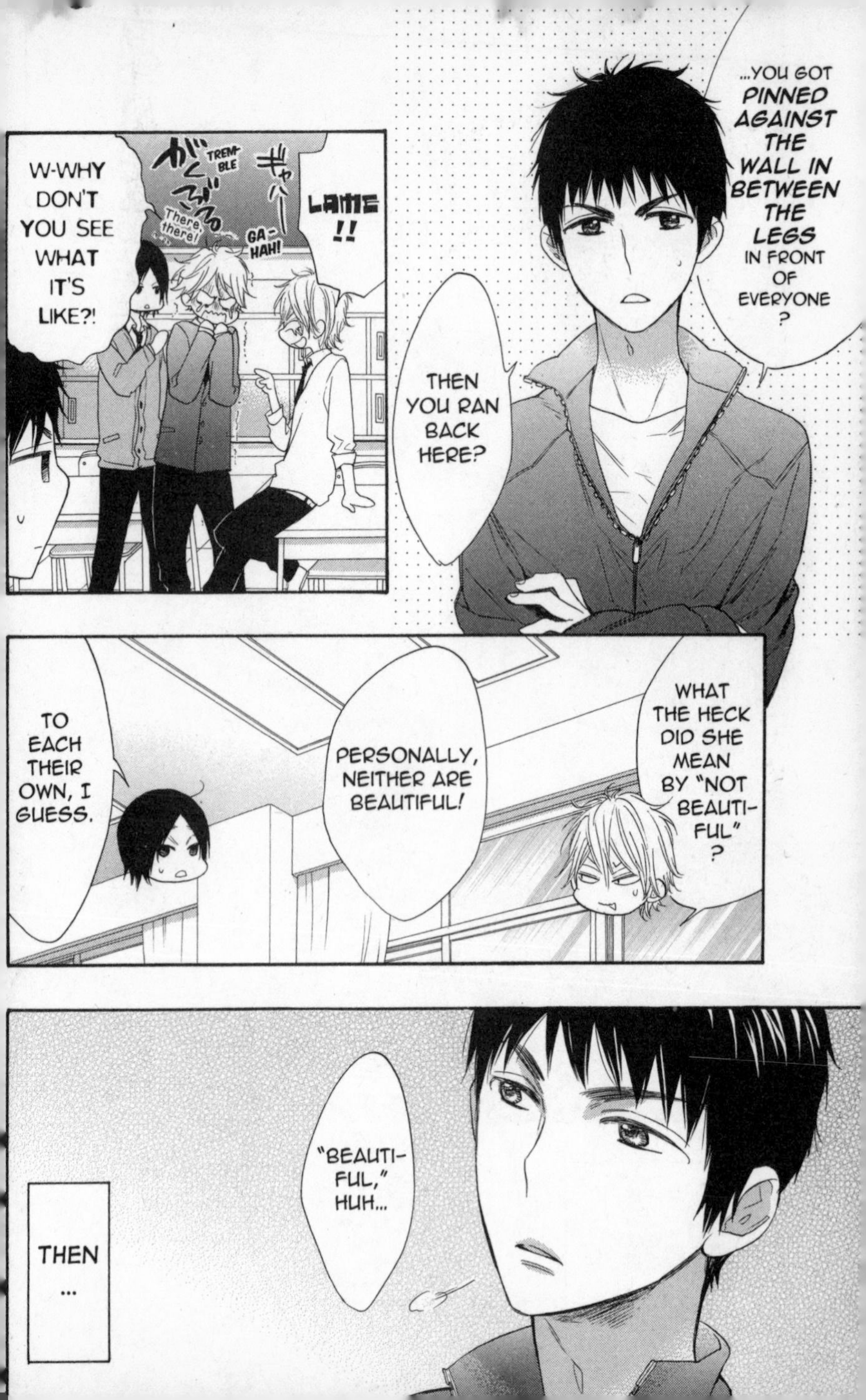
...YOU GOT PINNED AGAINST THE WALL IN BETWEEN THE LEGS IN FRONT OF EVERYONE?
THEN YOU RAN BACK HERE?
LAME!!
ギャハー
GA-HAH!
がくぶる
TREMBLE
There, there!
W-WHY DON'T YOU SEE WHAT IT'S LIKE?!
WHAT THE HECK DID SHE MEAN BY "NOT BEAUTIFUL"?
PERSONALLY, NEITHER ARE BEAUTIFUL!
TO EACH THEIR OWN, I GUESS.
"BEAUTIFUL," HUH...
THEN...

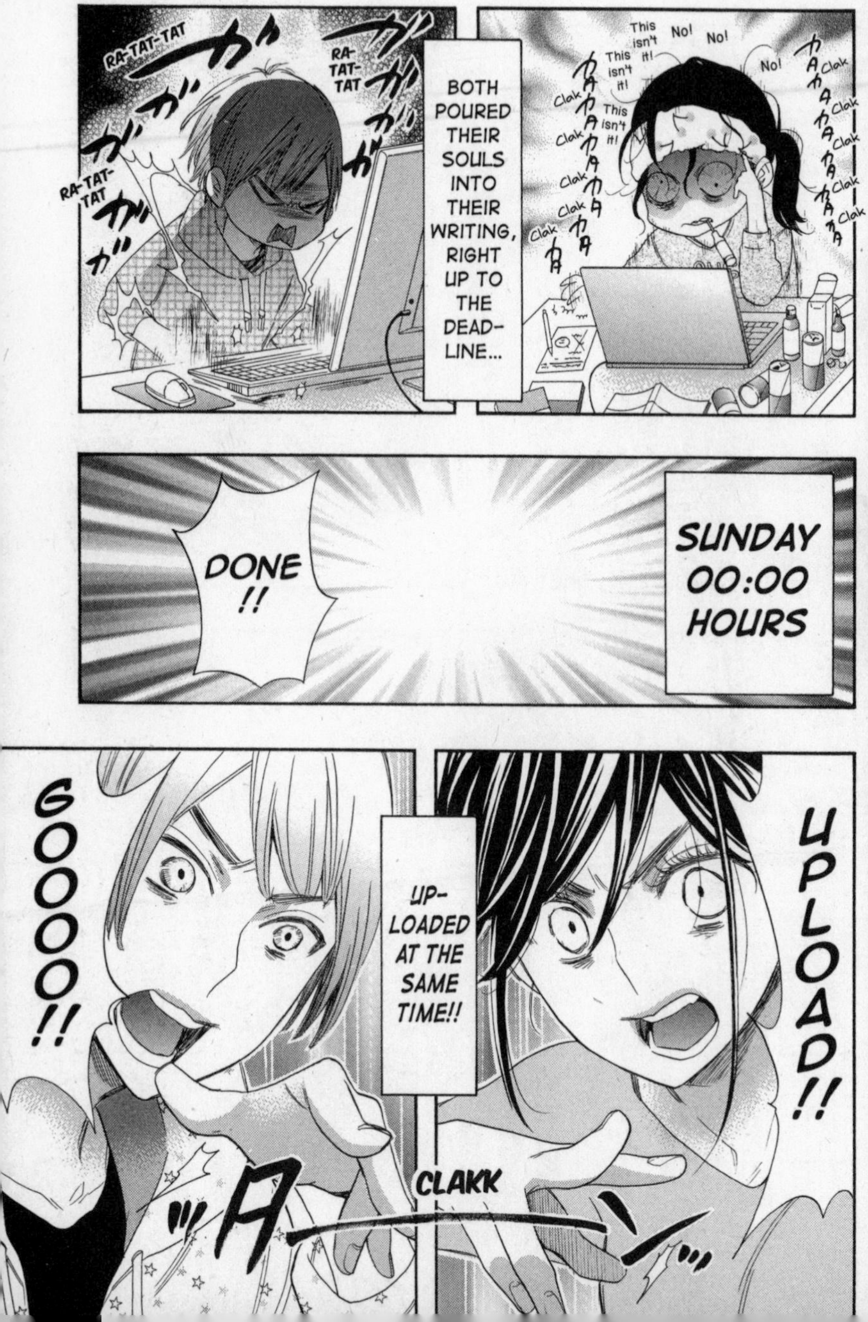
No!
No!
This isn't it!
No!
This isn't it!
This isn't it!
Clak
Clak
Clak
Clak
Clak
Clak
Clak
Clak
Clak
Clak
BOTH POURED THEIR SOULS INTO THEIR WRITING, RIGHT UP TO THE DEAD-LINE...
RA-TAT-TAT
RA-TAT-TAT
RA-TAT-TAT
SUNDAY 00:00 HOURS
DONE!!
UPLOAD!!
UP-LOADED AT THE SAME TIME!!
GOOOOO!!
CLAKK

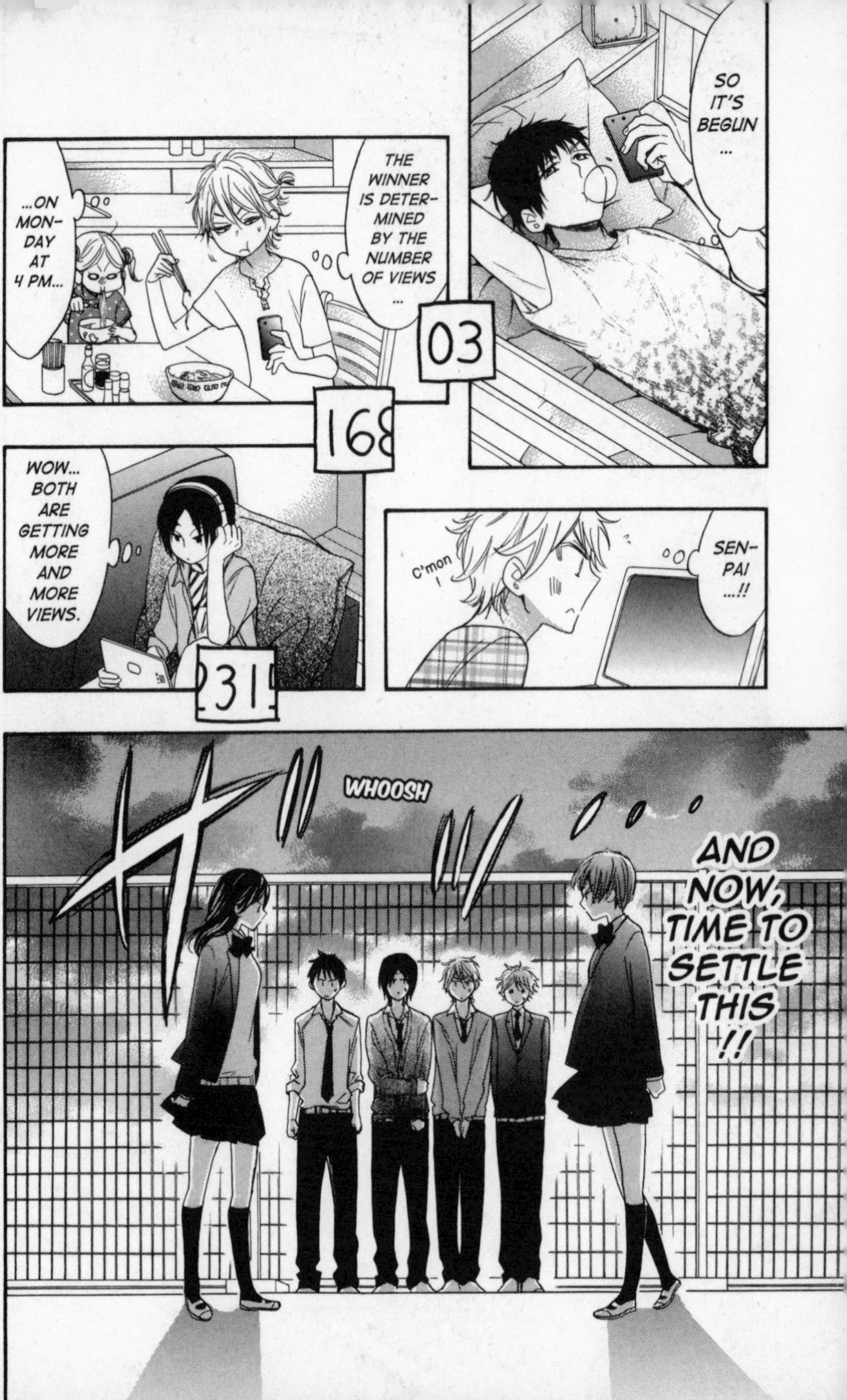
SO IT'S BEGUN ...
03
THE WINNER IS DETERMINED BY THE NUMBER OF VIEWS ...
...ON MONDAY AT 4 PM...
168
SENPAI ...!!
C'mon!
WOW... BOTH ARE GETTING MORE AND MORE VIEWS.
231
AND NOW, TIME TO SETTLE THIS!!
WHOOSH

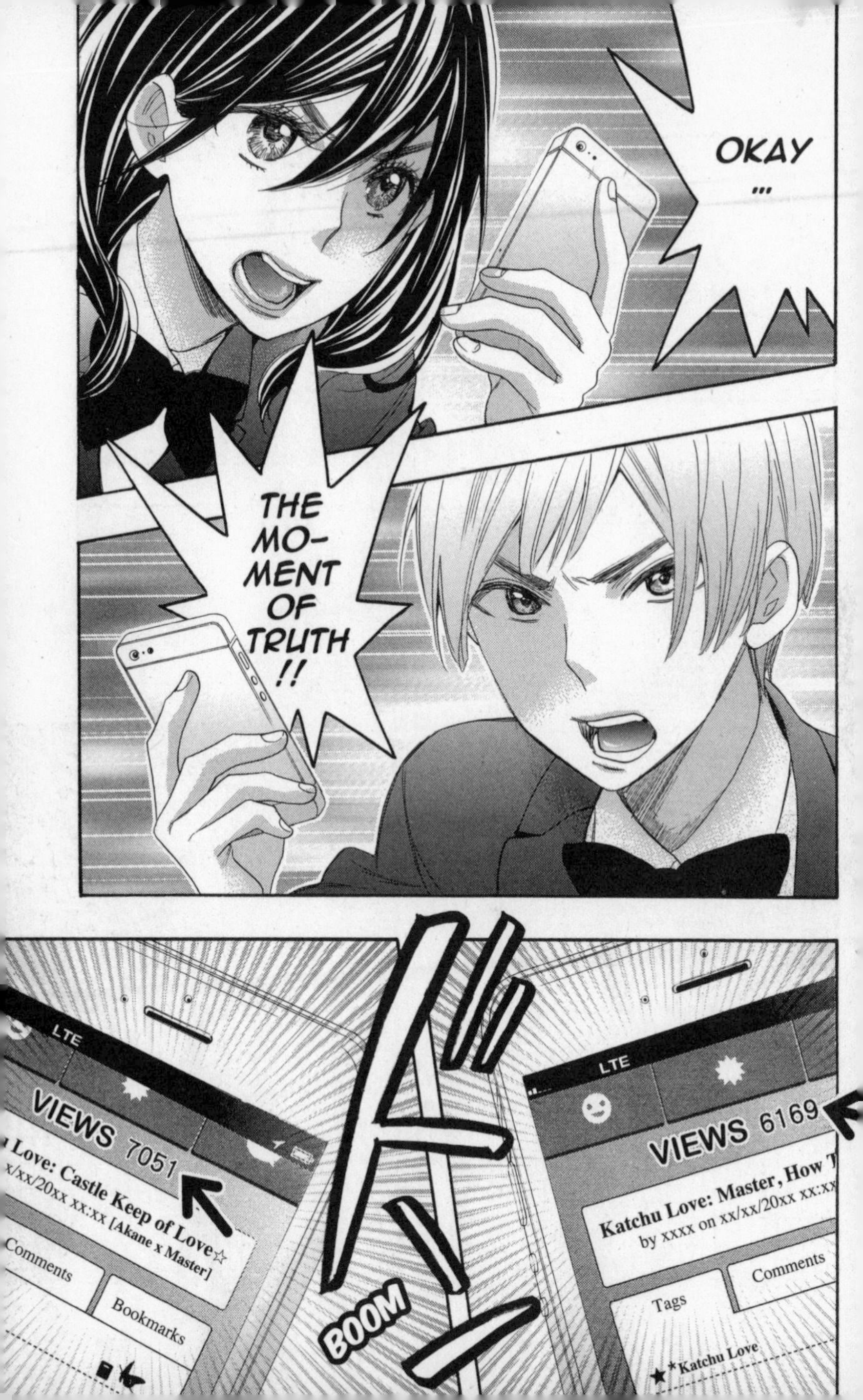
OKAY ...
THE MO-MENT OF TRUTH !!
LTE
VIEWS 6169
Katchu Love: Master, How T
by xxxx on xx/xx/20xx xx:xx
Comments
Tags
*Katchu Love
BOOM
LTE
VIEWS 7051
Love: Castle Keep of Love☆
x/xx/20xx xx:xx [Akane x Master]
Comments
Bookmarks

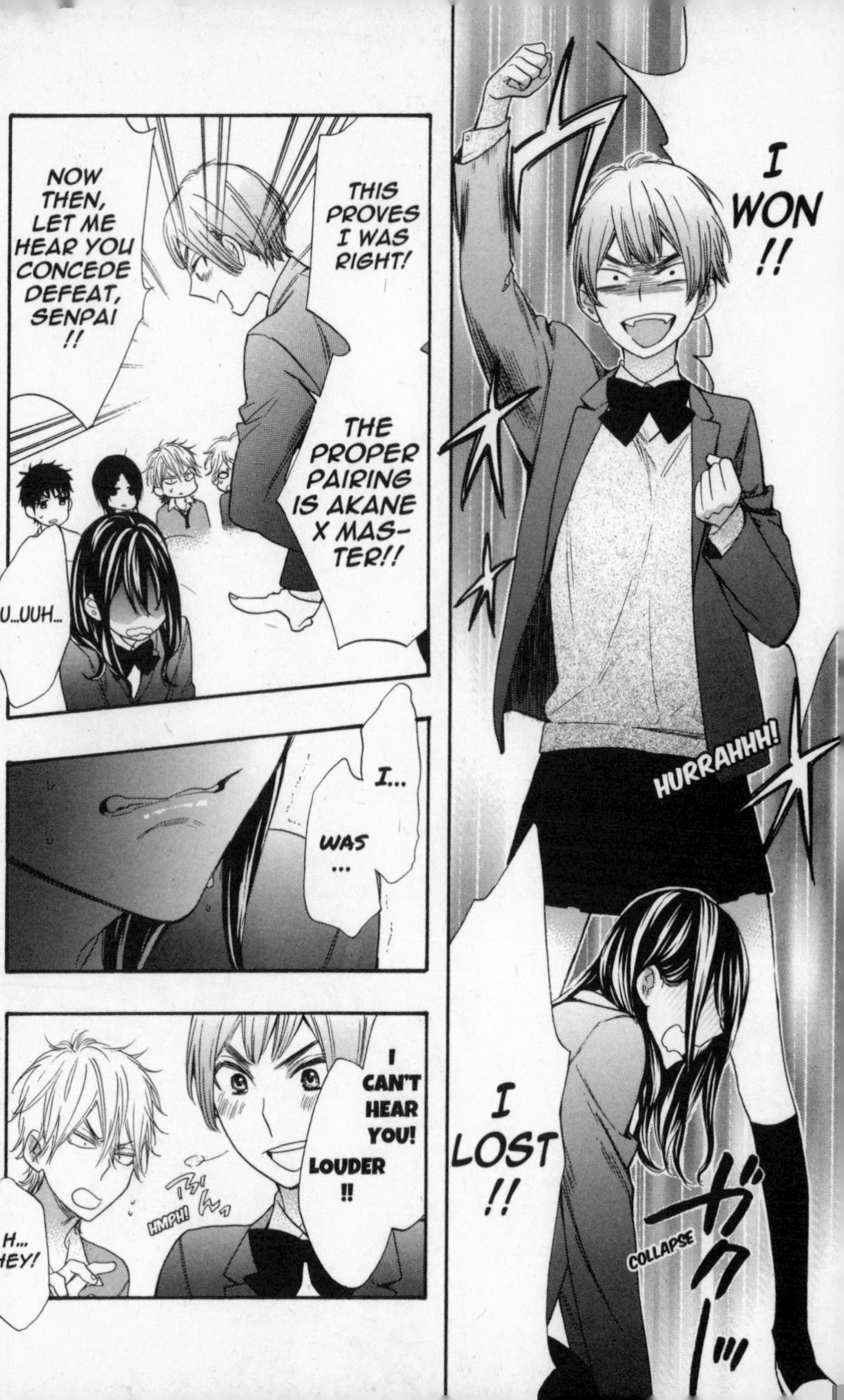
I WON!!
HURRAHHH!
I LOST!!
COLLAPSE
THIS PROVES I WAS RIGHT!
THE PROPER PAIRING IS AKANE X MASTER!!
NOW THEN, LET ME HEAR YOU CONCEDE DEFEAT, SENPAI!!
U...UUH...
I...
WAS...
I CAN'T HEAR YOU!
LOUDER!!
HMPH!
H... HEY!

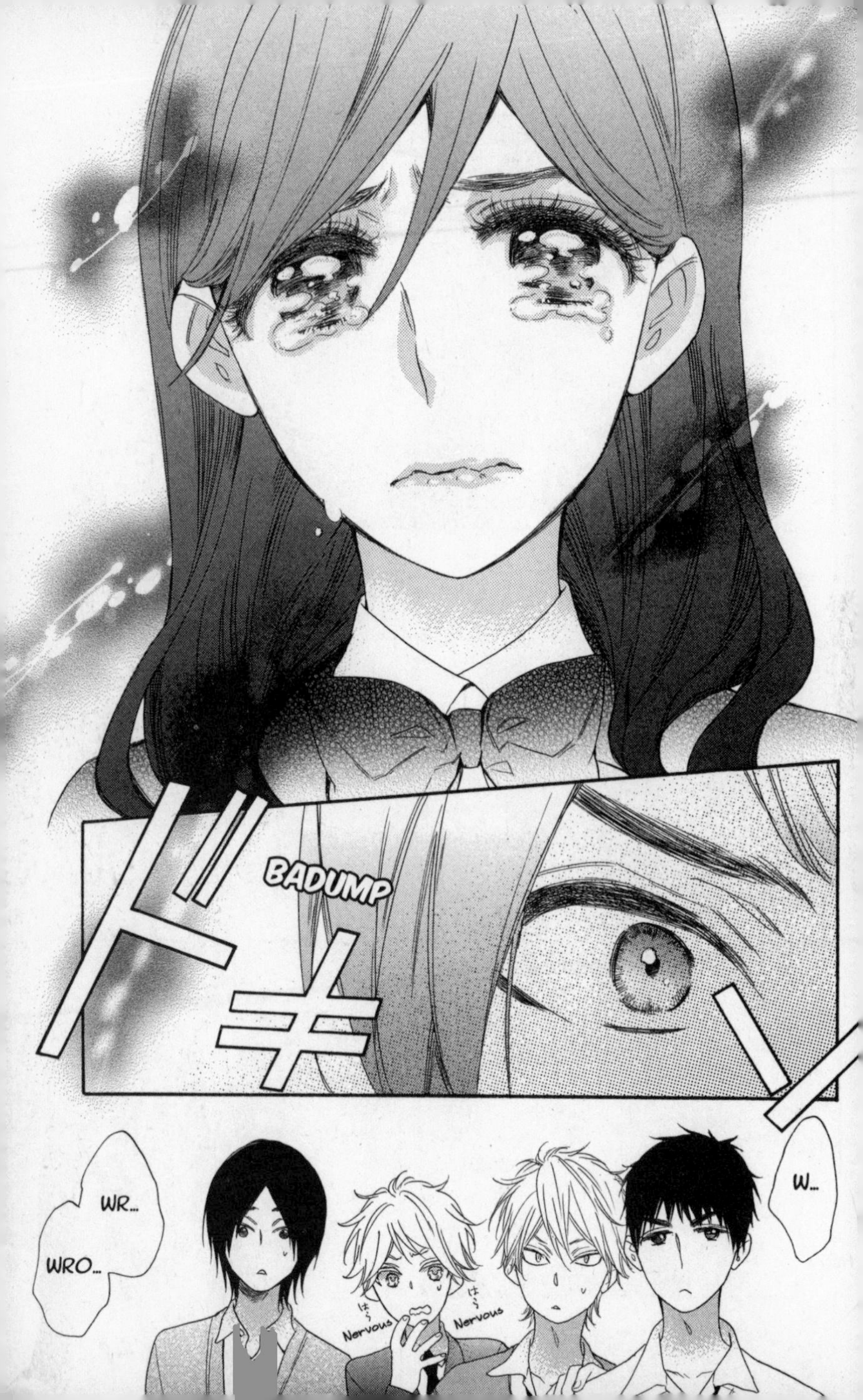
BADUMP
ドキン
W...
Nervous
Nervous
WR...
WRO...

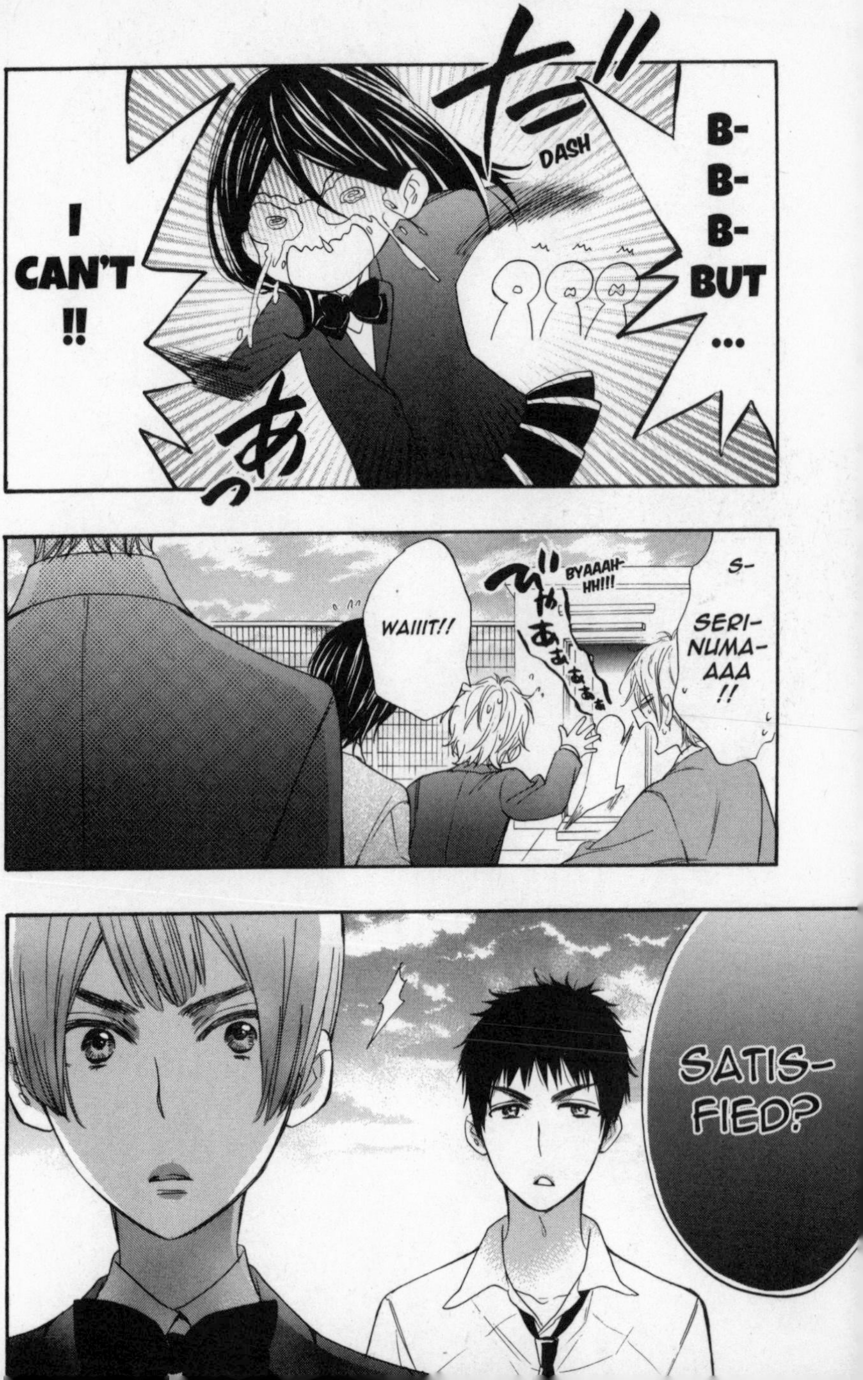
ダ
DASH
B-B-B-BUT...
I CAN'T!!
あっ
S- SERI-NUMA-AAA!!
びゃあああ
BYAAAH-HH!!!
WAIIIT!!
SATIS-FIED?

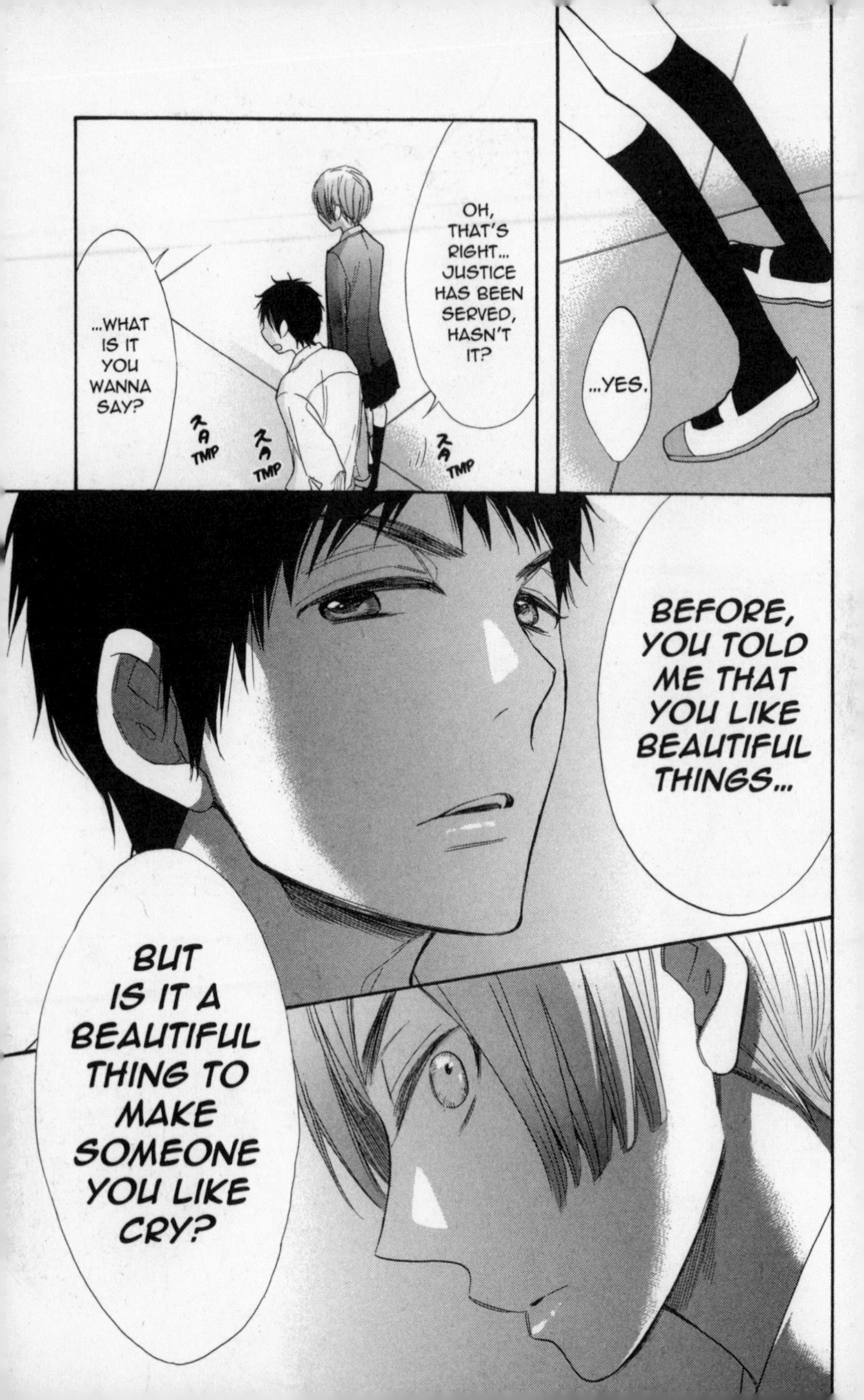
...YES.
OH, THAT'S RIGHT... JUSTICE HAS BEEN SERVED, HASN'T IT?
...WHAT IS IT YOU WANNA SAY?
TMP
TMP
TMP
BEFORE, YOU TOLD ME THAT YOU LIKE BEAUTIFUL THINGS...
BUT IS IT A BEAUTIFUL THING TO MAKE SOMEONE YOU LIKE CRY?

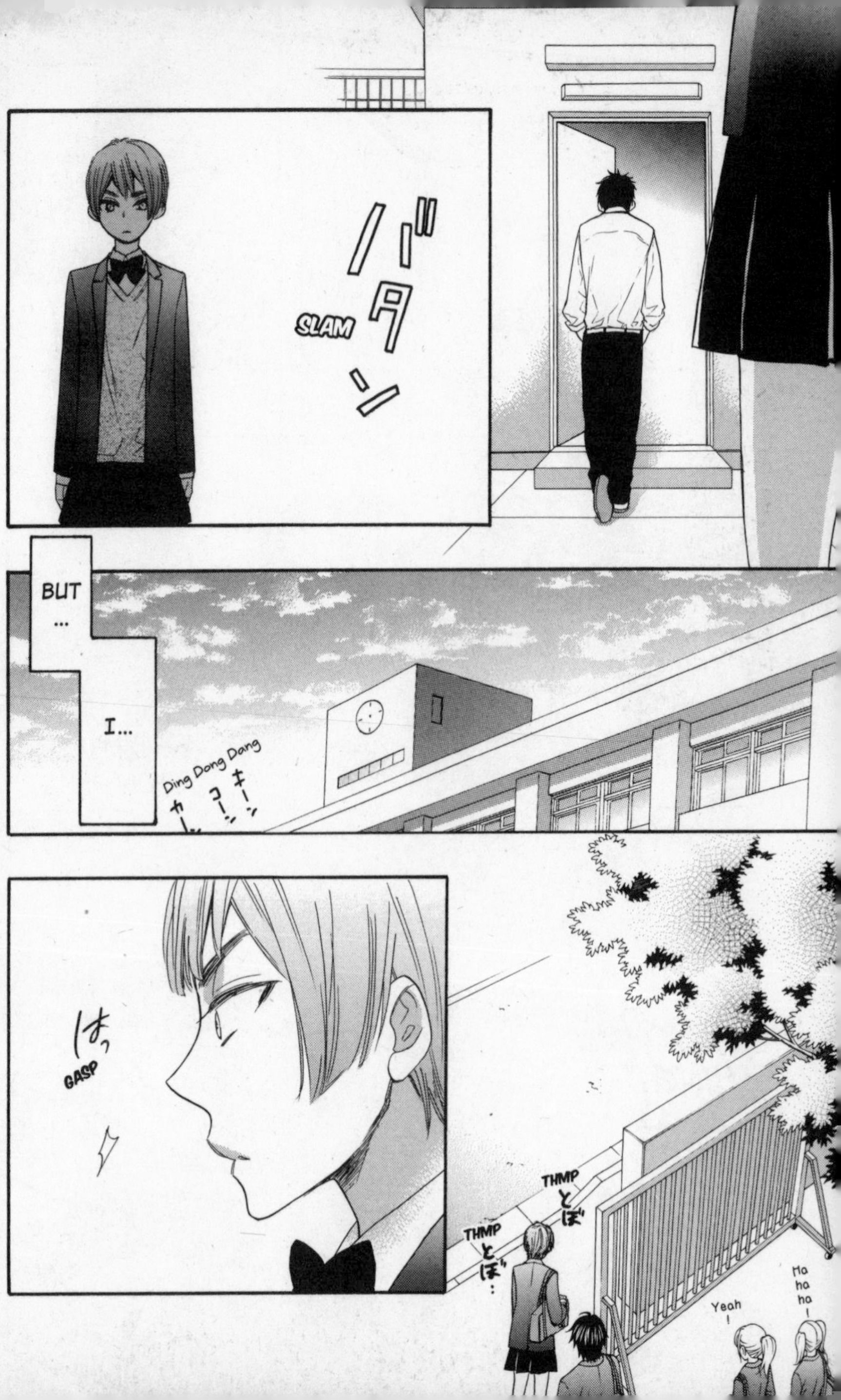

バタン
SLAM
BUT ...
I...
キーンコーンカーン
Ding Dong Dang
とぼ
THMP
とぼ…
THMP
Ha ha ha!
Yeah!
はっ
GASP

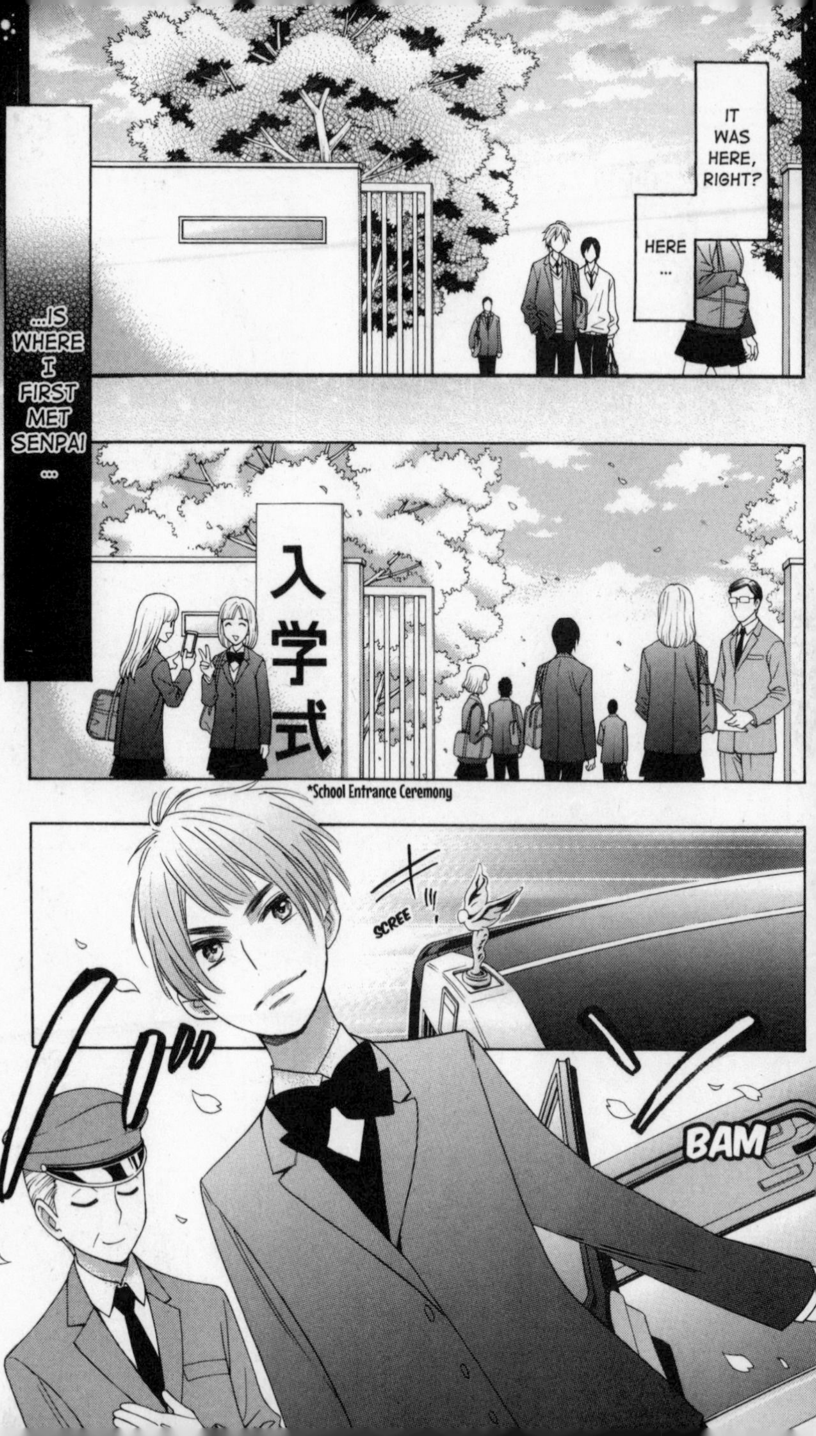
IT WAS HERE, RIGHT?
HERE...
...IS WHERE I FIRST MET SENPAI...
入学式
*School Entrance Ceremony
SCREE
BAM

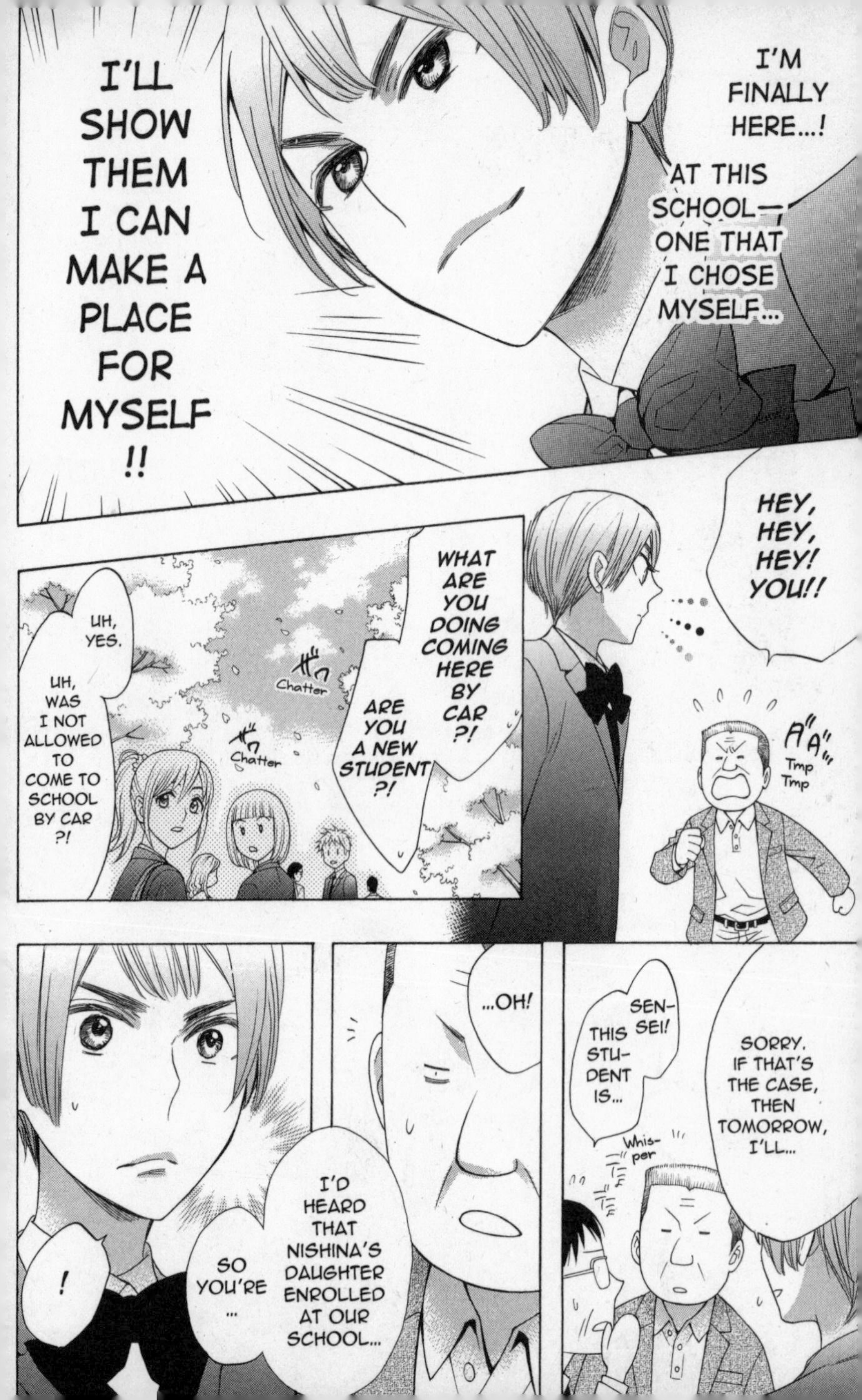
I'M FINALLY HERE...!
AT THIS SCHOOL— ONE THAT I CHOSE MYSELF...
I'LL SHOW THEM I CAN MAKE A PLACE FOR MYSELF !!
HEY, HEY, HEY! YOU!!
Tmp Tmp
WHAT ARE YOU DOING COMING HERE BY CAR ?!
ARE YOU A NEW STUDENT ?!
Chatter
Chatter
UH, YES.
UH, WAS I NOT ALLOWED TO COME TO SCHOOL BY CAR ?!
SORRY. IF THAT'S THE CASE, THEN TOMORROW, I'LL...
SEN-SEI!
THIS STU-DENT IS...
Whis-per
...OH!
I'D HEARD THAT NISHINA'S DAUGHTER ENROLLED AT OUR SCHOOL...
SO YOU'RE ...
!

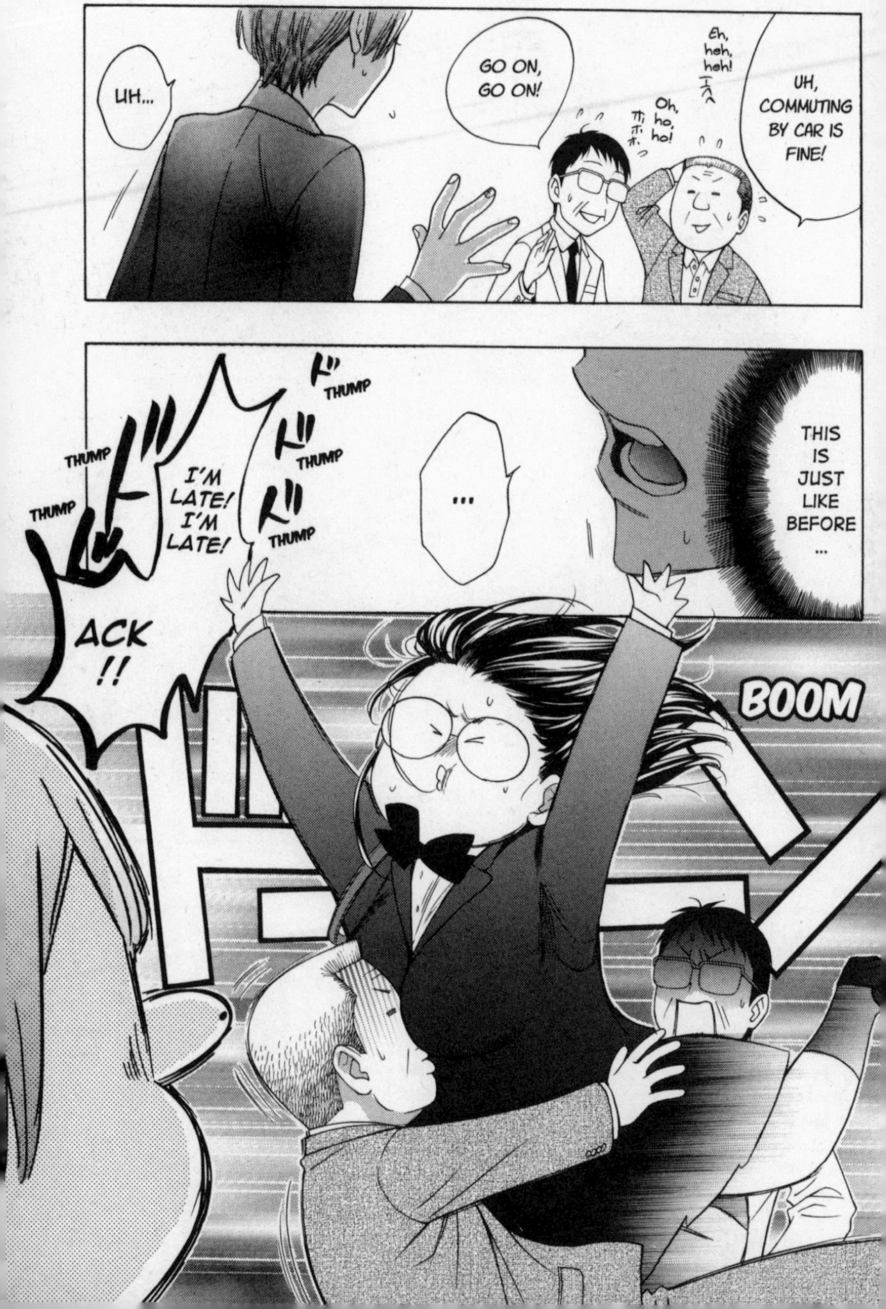
UH, COMMUTING BY CAR IS FINE!
Eh, heh, heh!
Oh, ho, ho!
GO ON, GO ON!
UH...
THIS IS JUST LIKE BEFORE ...
...
THUMP
THUMP
THUMP
THUMP
THUMP
I'M LATE! I'M LATE!
ACK !!
BOOM

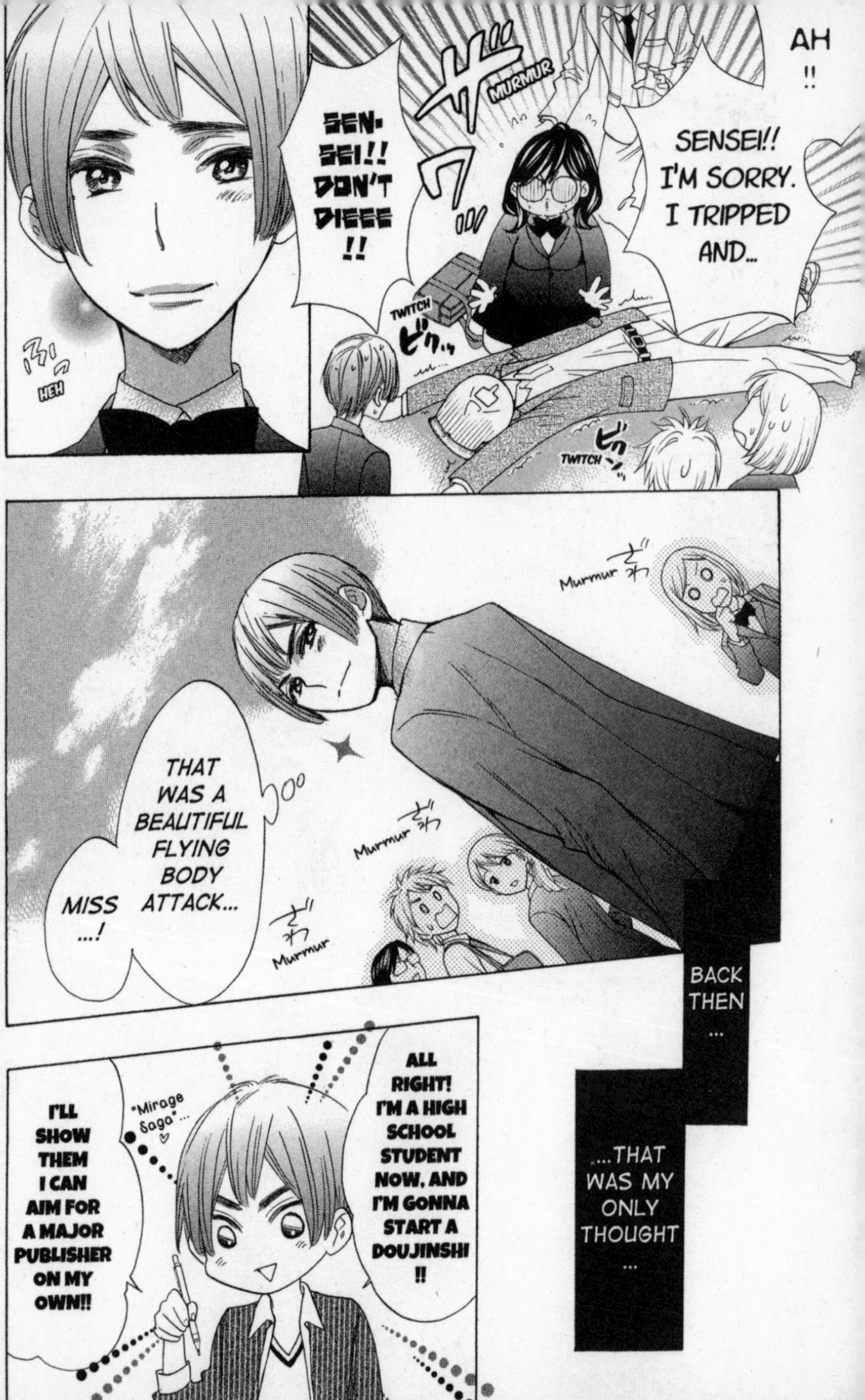
AH!!
SENSEI!! I'M SORRY. I TRIPPED AND...
MURMUR
SEN-SEI!! DON'T DIEEE!!
TWITCH
TWITCH
HEH
Murmur
THAT WAS A BEAUTIFUL FLYING BODY ATTACK... MISS ...!
Murmur
Murmur
BACK THEN...
...THAT WAS MY ONLY THOUGHT...
ALL RIGHT! I'M A HIGH SCHOOL STUDENT NOW, AND I'M GONNA START A DOUJINSHI!!
"Mirage Saga"...
I'LL SHOW THEM I CAN AIM FOR A MAJOR PUBLISHER ON MY OWN!!

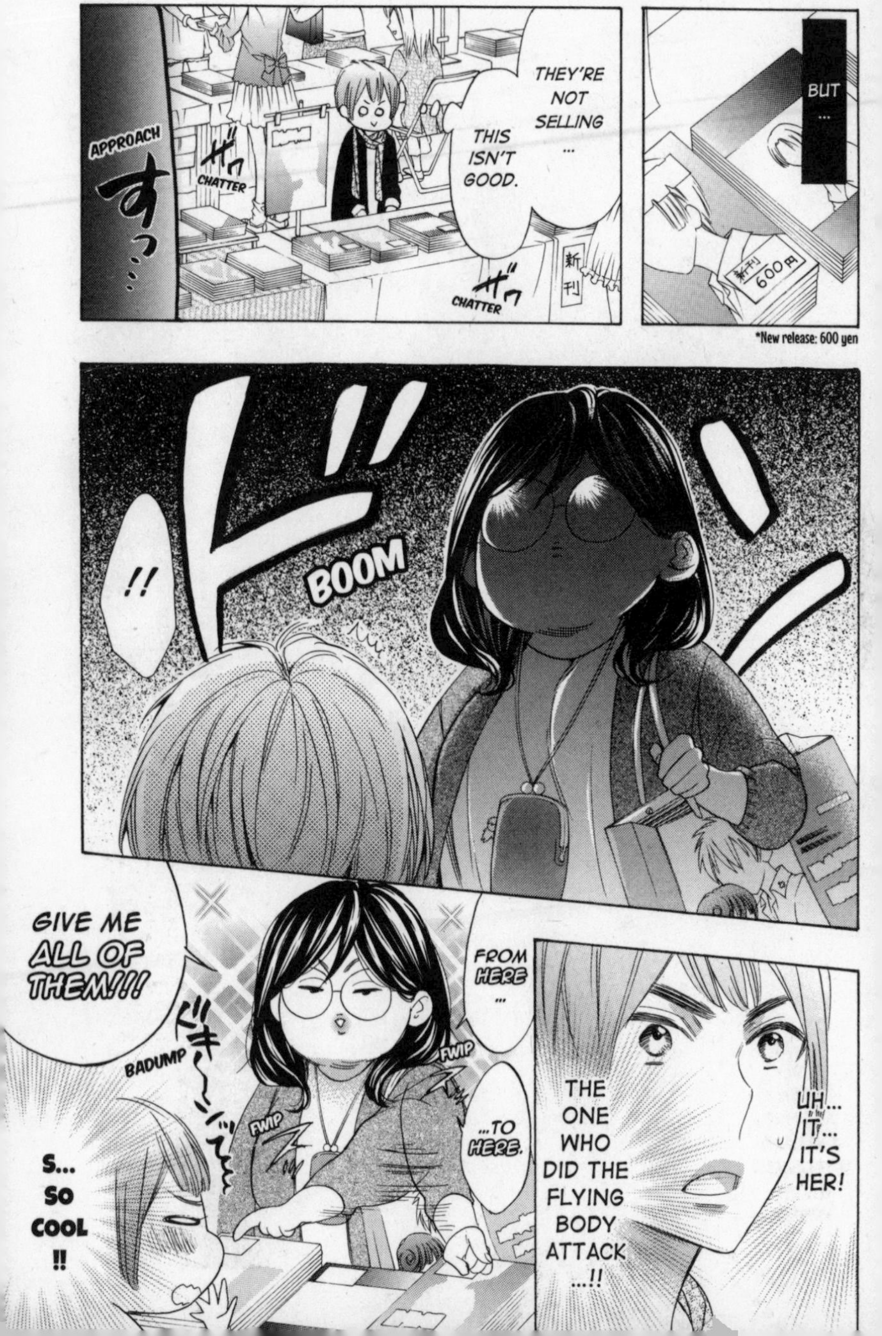
BUT ...
THEY'RE NOT SELLING ...
THIS ISN'T GOOD.
CHATTER
APPROACH
CHATTER
新刊 600円
!!
BOOM
UH... IT... IT'S HER!
THE ONE WHO DID THE FLYING BODY ATTACK ...!!
FROM HERE ...
...TO HERE.
FWIP
FWIP
GIVE ME ALL OF THEM!!!
BADUMP
S... SO COOL !!
*New release: 600 yen

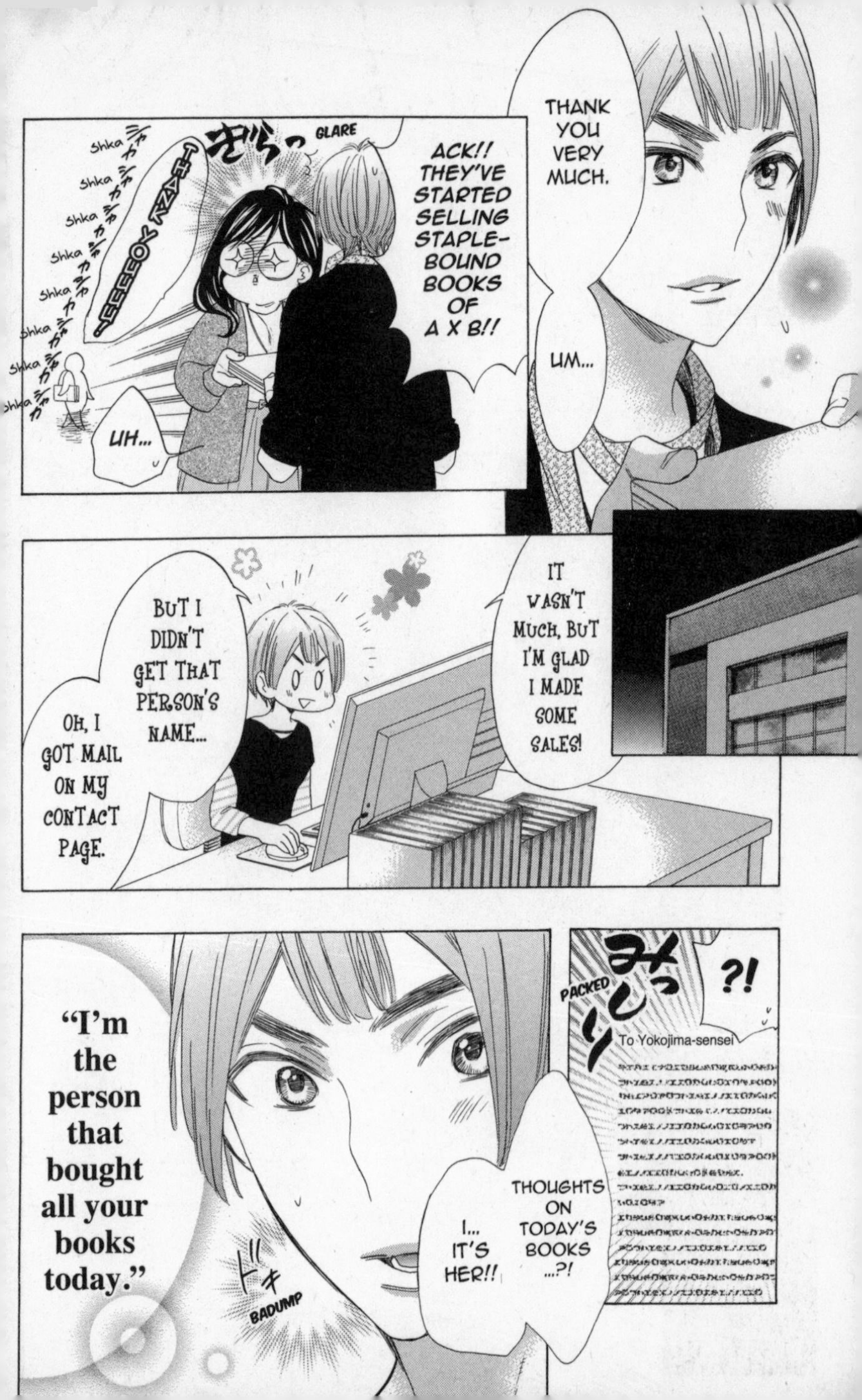

THANK YOU VERY MUCH.
UM...
ACK!! THEY'VE STARTED SELLING STAPLE-BOUND BOOKS OF A X B!!
GLARE
Shka Shka Shka Shka Shka Shka Shka Shka
UH...
IT WASN'T MUCH, BUT I'M GLAD I MADE SOME SALES!
BUT I DIDN'T GET THAT PERSON'S NAME...
OH, I GOT MAIL ON MY CONTACT PAGE.
PACKED
?!
To Yokojima-sensei
THOUGHTS ON TODAY'S BOOKS ...?!
I... IT'S HER!!
BADUMP
“I'm the person that bought all your books today.”

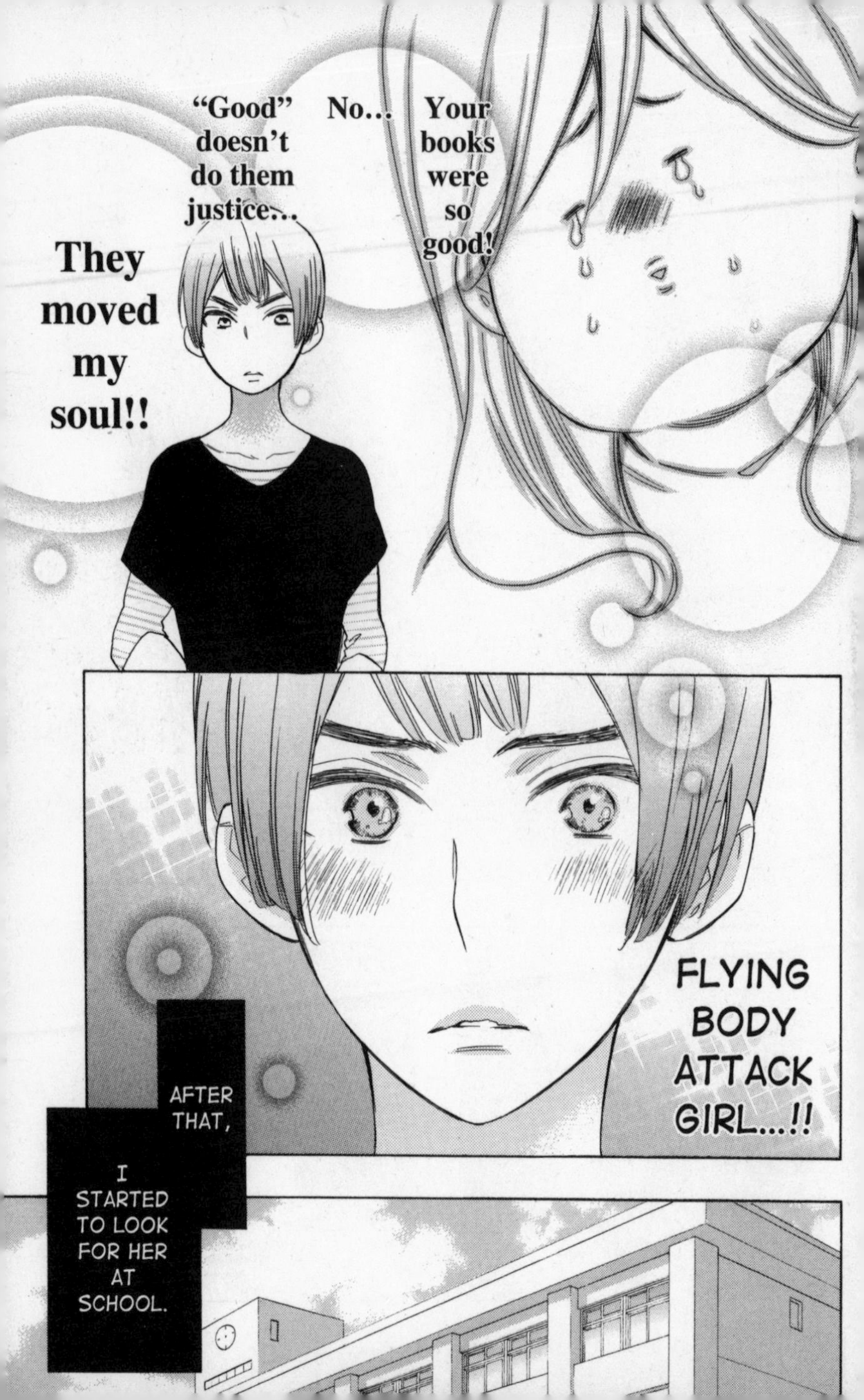
Your books were so good!
No…
"Good" doesn't do them justice…
They moved my soul!!
FLYING BODY ATTACK GIRL…!!
AFTER THAT,
I STARTED TO LOOK FOR HER AT SCHOOL.

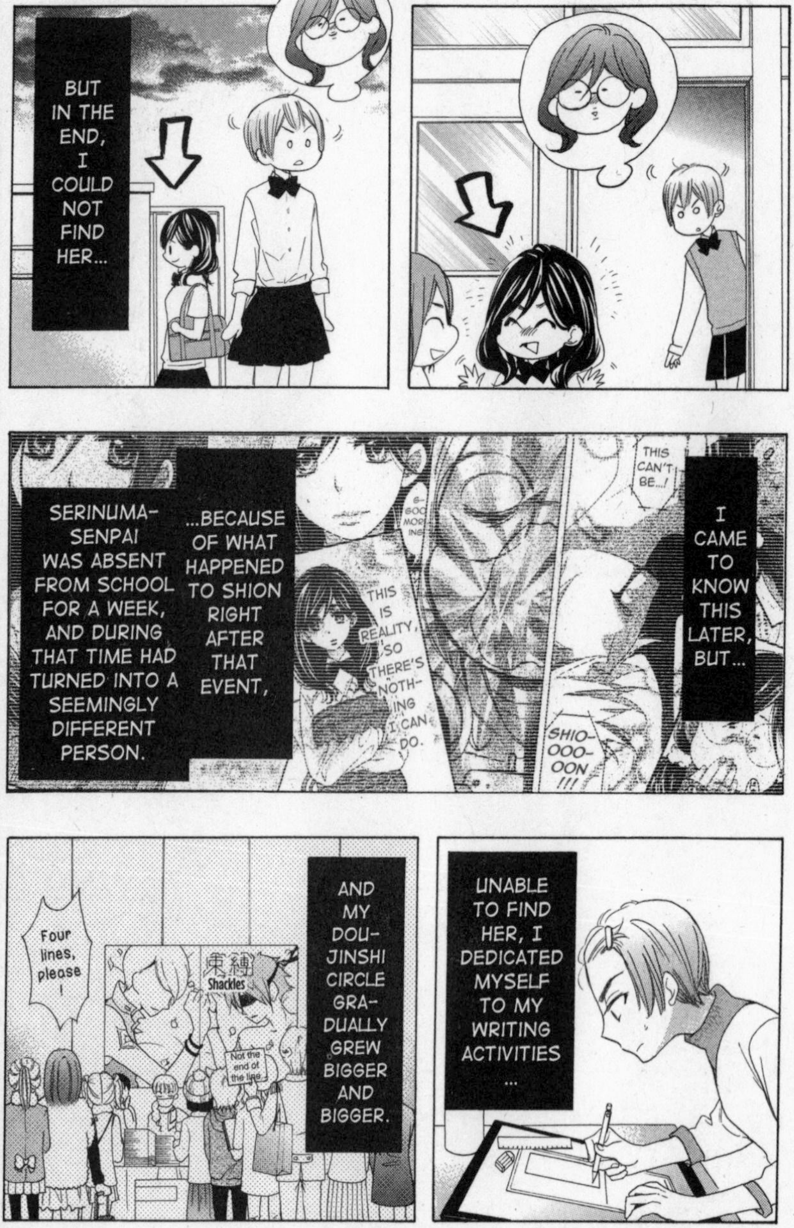
BUT IN THE END, I COULD NOT FIND HER...
I CAME TO KNOW THIS LATER, BUT...
THIS CAN'T BE...!
SHIO-OOO-OON!!!
THIS IS REALITY, SO THERE'S NOTHING I CAN DO.
...BECAUSE OF WHAT HAPPENED TO SHION RIGHT AFTER THAT EVENT,
SERINUMA-SENPAI WAS ABSENT FROM SCHOOL FOR A WEEK, AND DURING THAT TIME HAD TURNED INTO A SEEMINGLY DIFFERENT PERSON.
UNABLE TO FIND HER, I DEDICATED MYSELF TO MY WRITING ACTIVITIES ...
AND MY DOUJINSHI CIRCLE GRADUALLY GREW BIGGER AND BIGGER.
Four lines, please!
Shackles
Not the end of the line

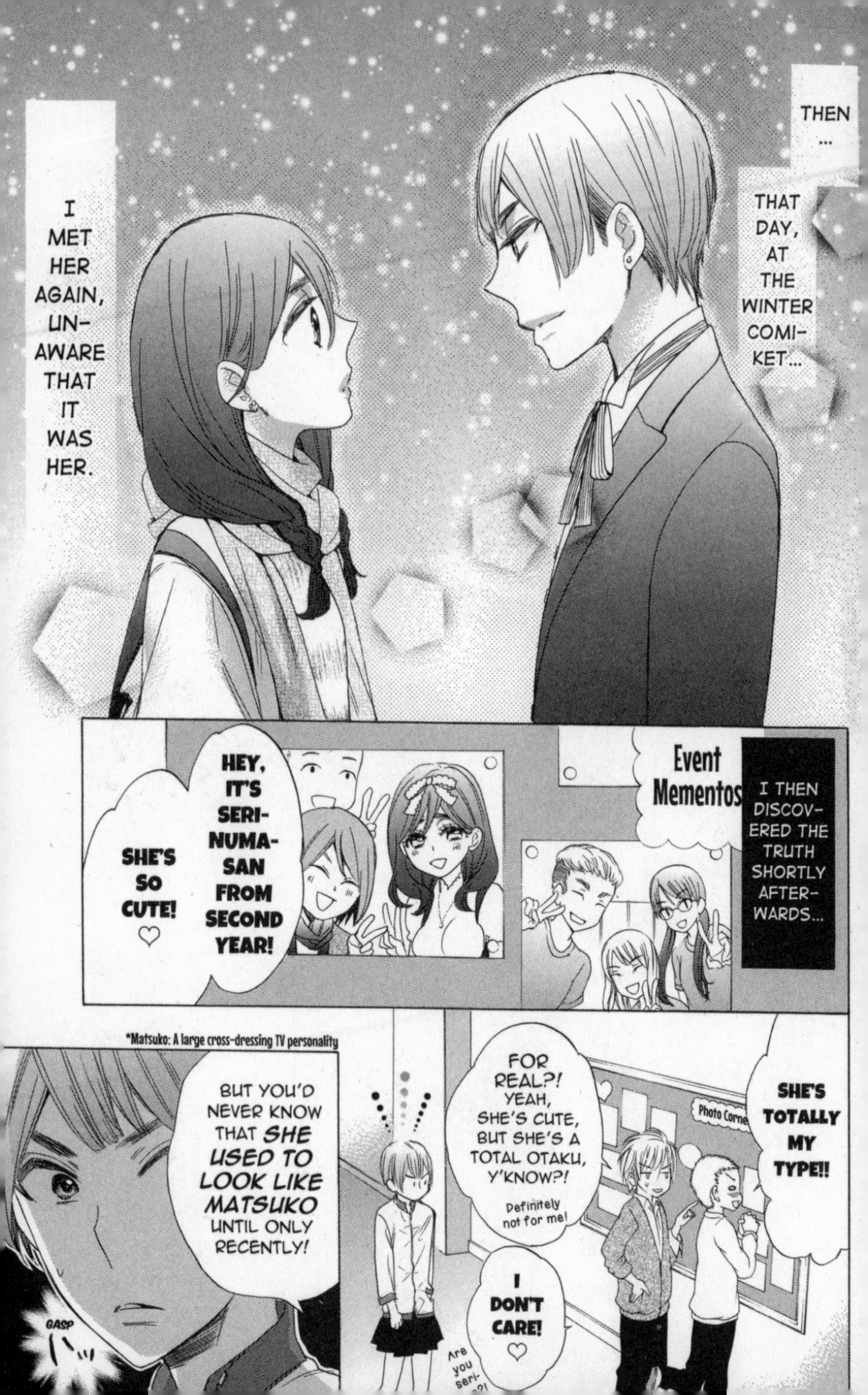
THEN ...
THAT DAY, AT THE WINTER COMI-KET...
I MET HER AGAIN, UN-AWARE THAT IT WAS HER.
I THEN DISCOVERED THE TRUTH SHORTLY AFTERWARDS...
Event Mementos
HEY, IT'S SERI-NUMA-SAN FROM SECOND YEAR!
SHE'S SO CUTE! ♡
SHE'S TOTALLY MY TYPE!!
FOR REAL?! YEAH, SHE'S CUTE, BUT SHE'S A TOTAL OTAKU, Y'KNOW?!
Definitely not for me!
I DON'T CARE! ♡
BUT YOU'D NEVER KNOW THAT *SHE USED TO LOOK LIKE MATSUKO* UNTIL ONLY RECENTLY!
GASP
*Matsuko: A large cross-dressing TV personality

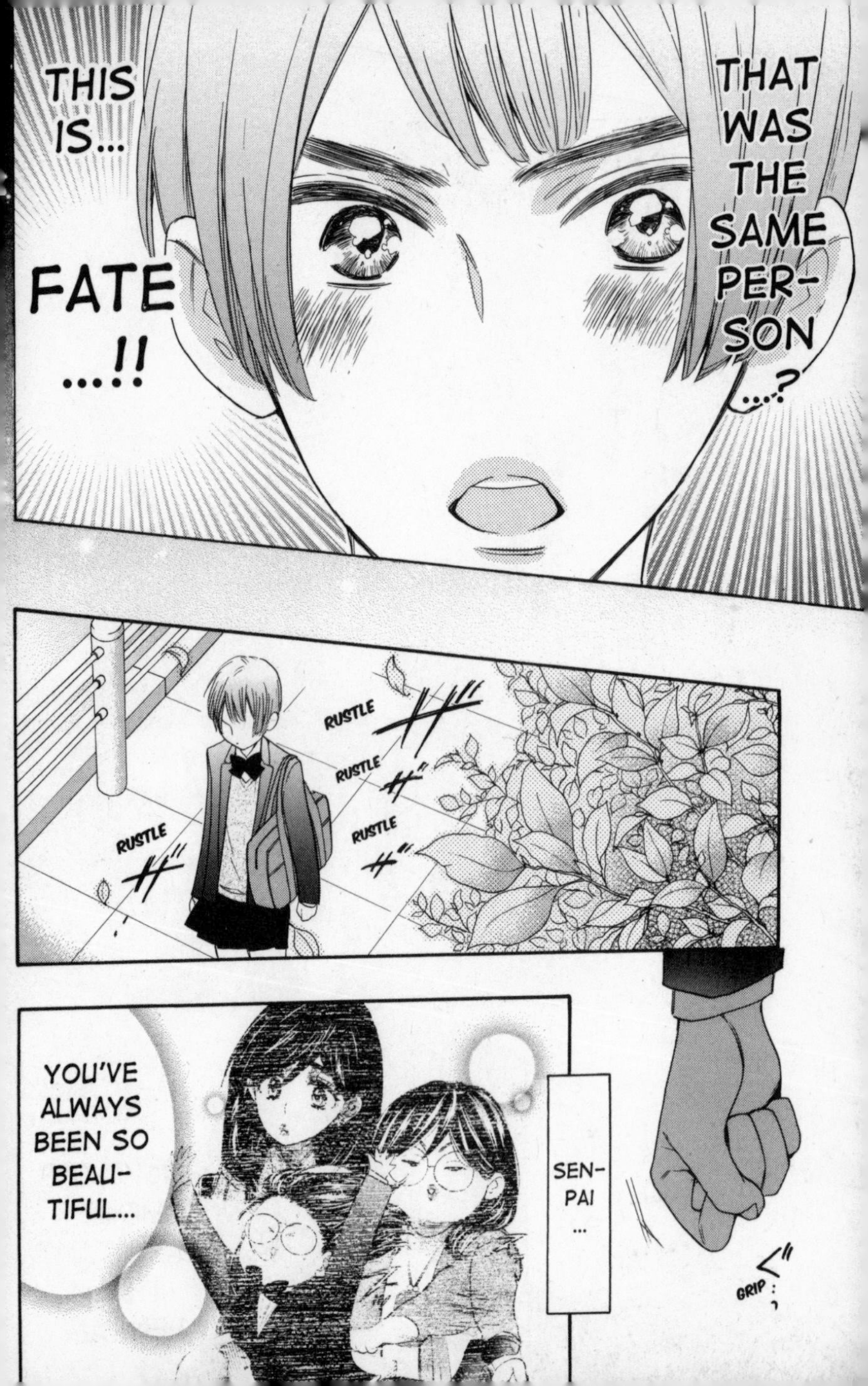
THAT WAS THE SAME PER-SON ...?
THIS IS...
FATE ...!!
RUSTLE
RUSTLE
RUSTLE
RUSTLE
GRIP
SEN-PAI ...
YOU'VE ALWAYS BEEN SO BEAU-TIFUL...

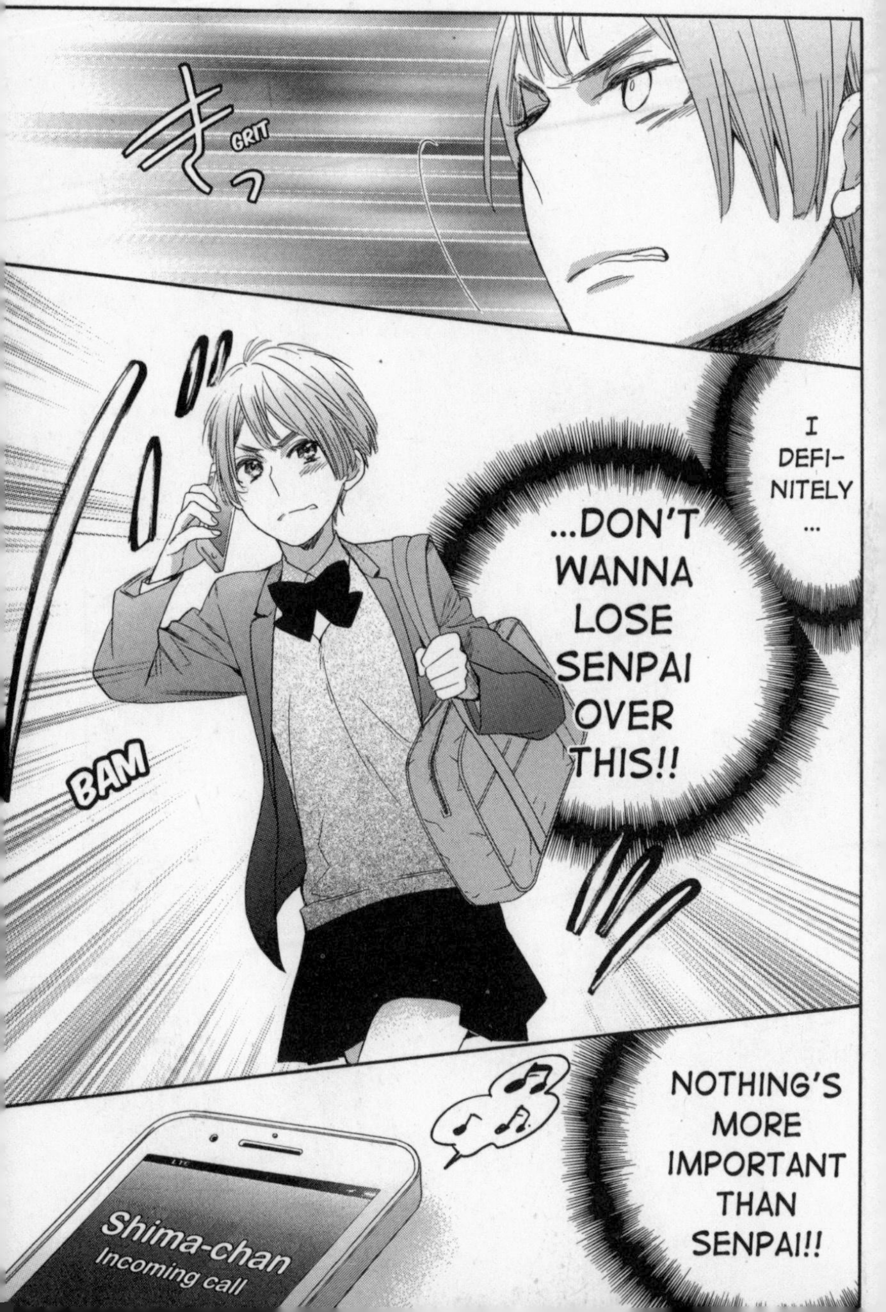
きっ
GRIT
I DEFI-NITELY ...
...DON'T WANNA LOSE SENPAI OVER THIS!!
ダッ
BAM
NOTHING'S MORE IMPORTANT THAN SENPAI!!
Shima-chan
Incoming call

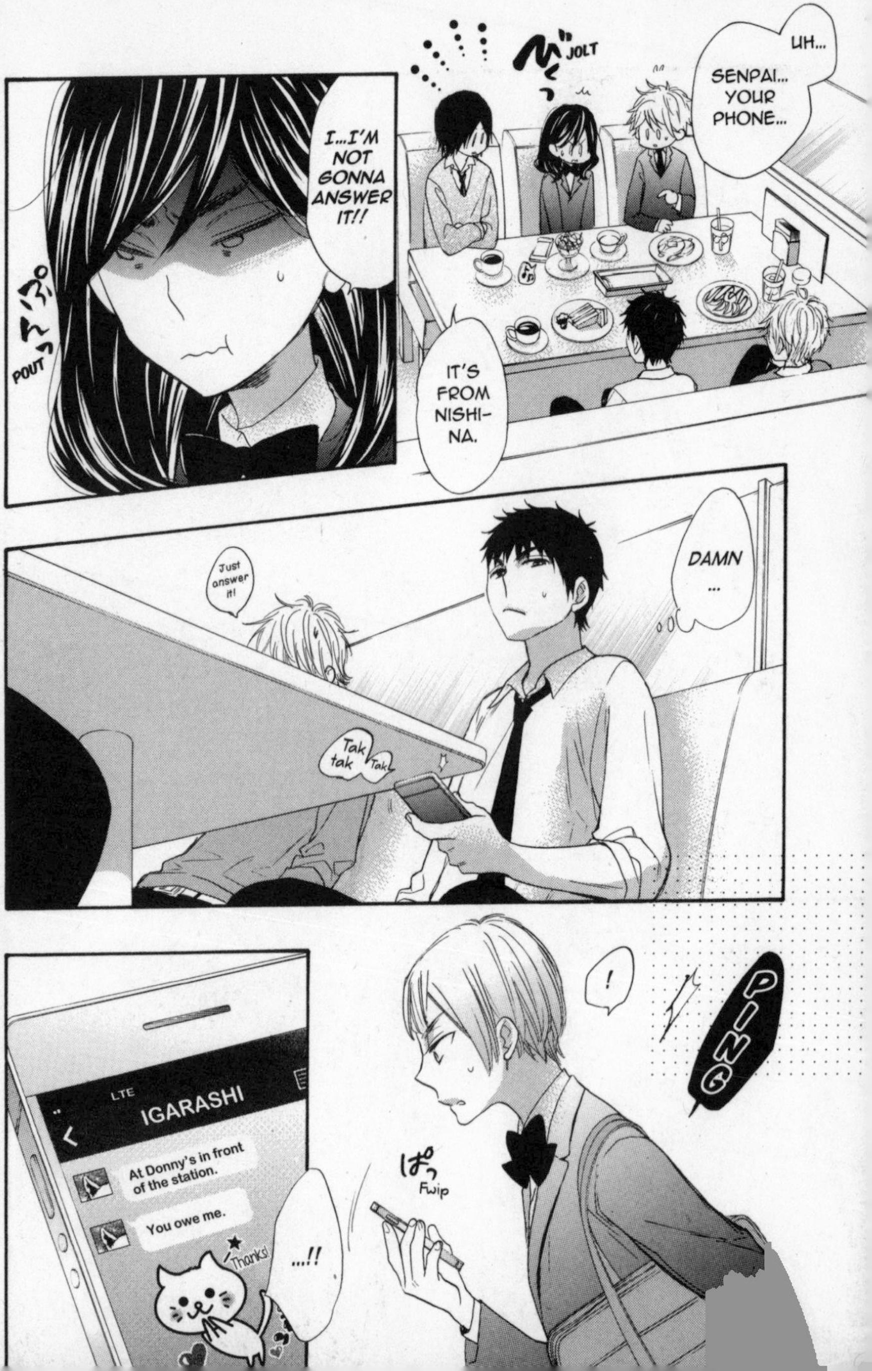
UH... SENPAI... YOUR PHONE...
JOLT
IT'S FROM NISHI-NA.
I...I'M NOT GONNA ANSWER IT!!
POUT
DAMN ...
Just answer it!
Tak tak Tak
PING
!
Fwip
...!!
LTE
IGARASHI
At Donny's in front of the station.
You owe me.
Thanks!

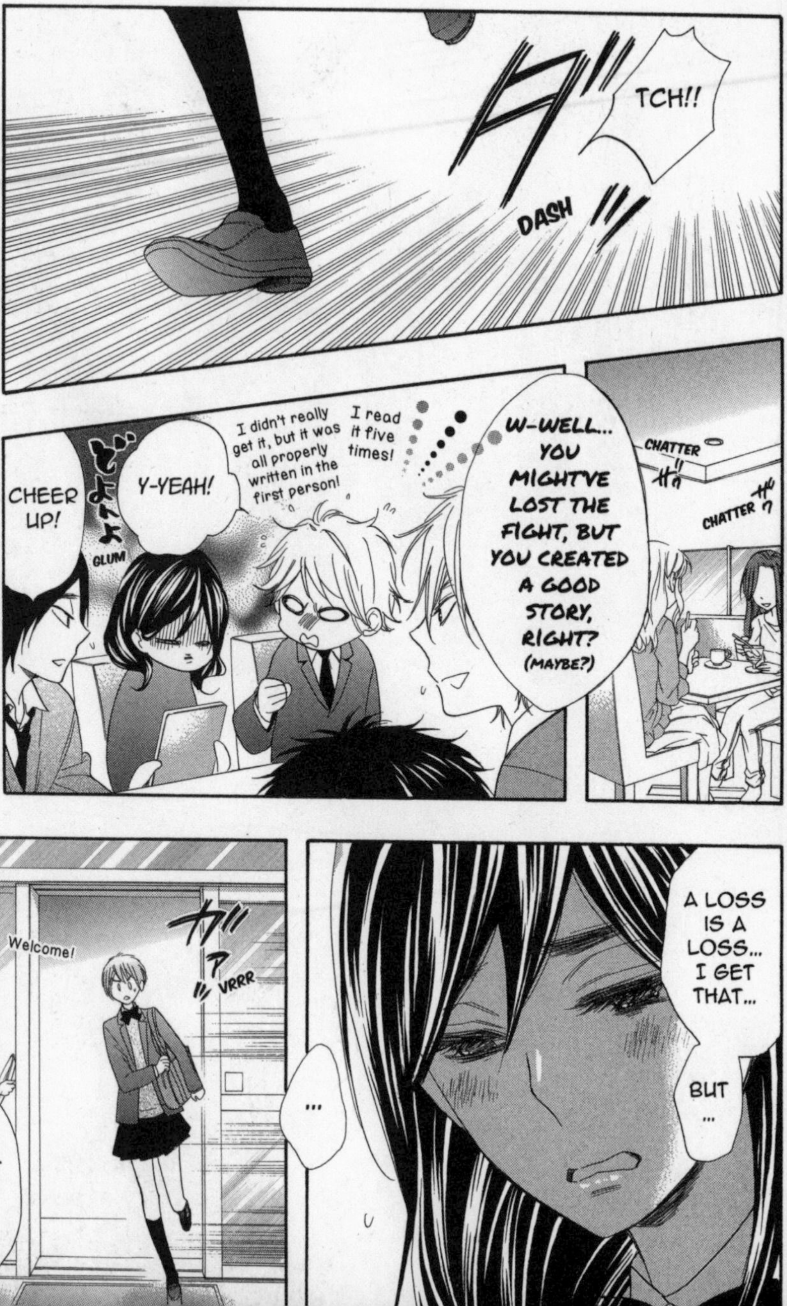
TCH!!
DASH
CHATTER
CHATTER
W-WELL... YOU MIGHT'VE LOST THE FIGHT, BUT YOU CREATED A GOOD STORY, RIGHT? (MAYBE?)
I read it five times!
I didn't really get it, but it was all properly written in the first person!
Y-YEAH!
どよんよ
GLUM
CHEER UP!
A LOSS IS A LOSS... I GET THAT...
BUT...
...
VRRR
Welcome!
BUT I...

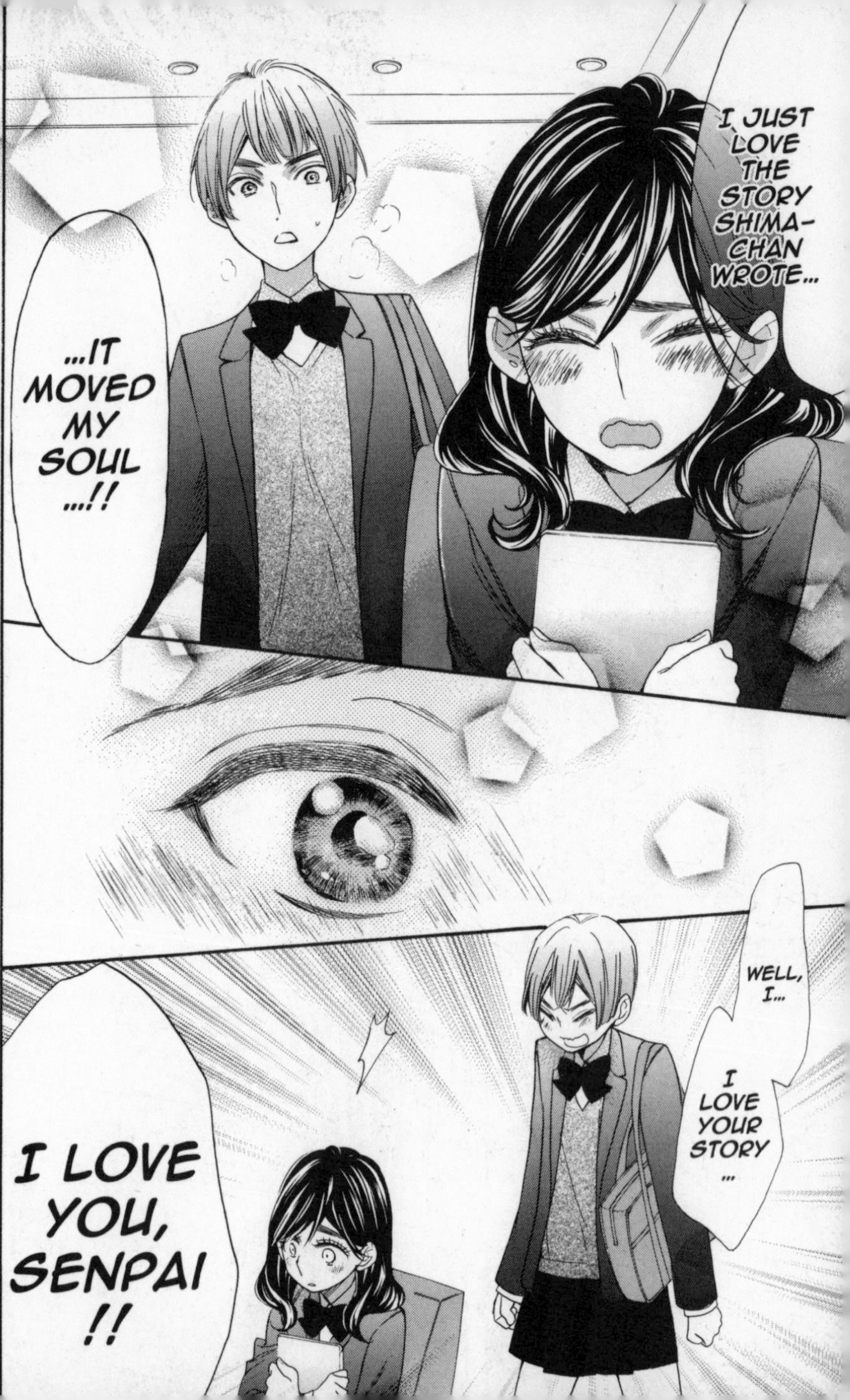
I JUST LOVE THE STORY SHIMA-CHAN WROTE...
...IT MOVED MY SOUL ...!!
WELL, I...
I LOVE YOUR STORY ...
I LOVE YOU, SENPAI !!

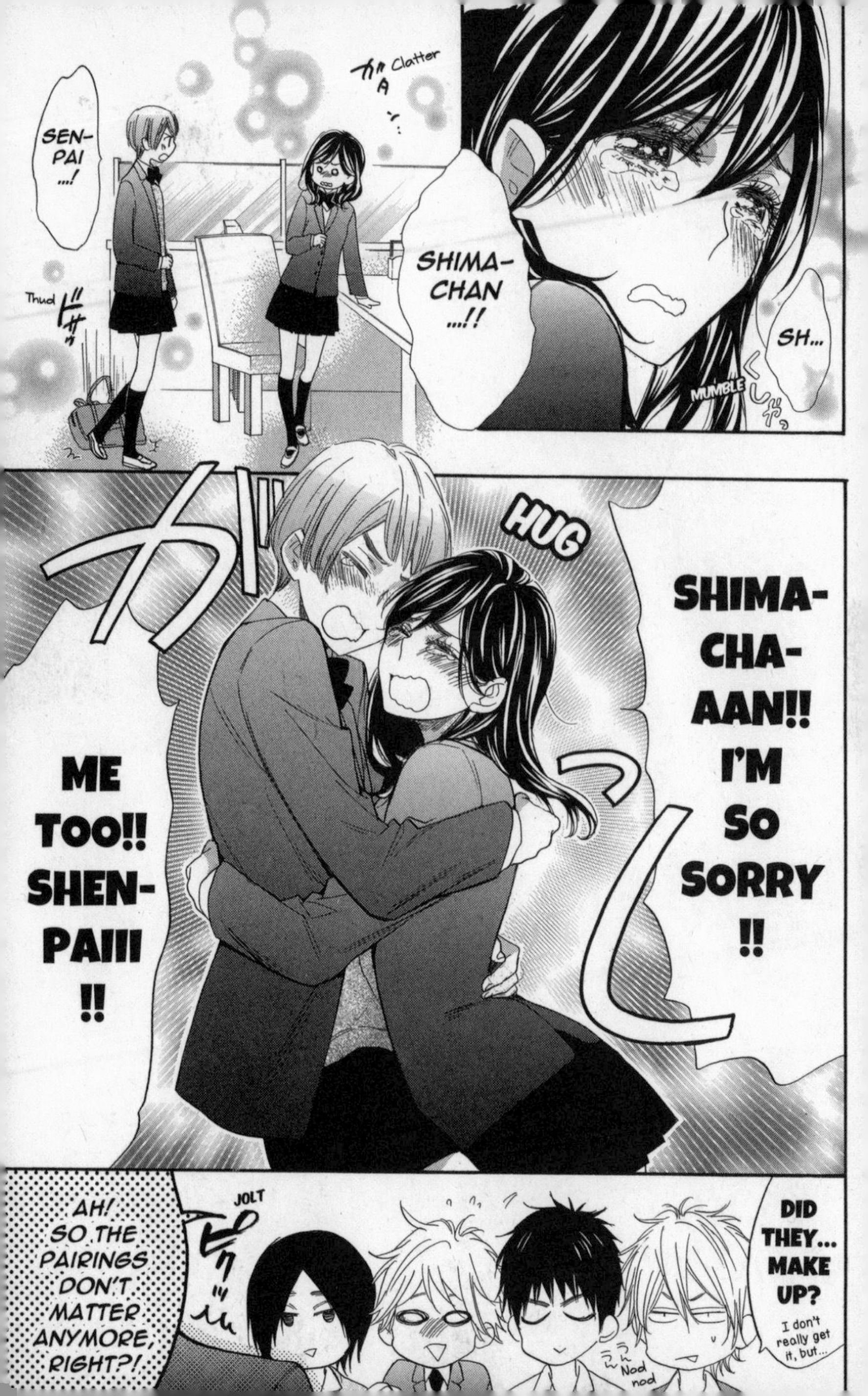
SHIMA-CHAN ...!!
SH...
MUMBLE
Clatter
SEN-PAI ...!
Thud
HUG
SHIMA-CHA-AAN!! I'M SO SORRY!!
ME TOO!! SHEN-PAIII!!
DID THEY... MAKE UP?
I don't really get it, but...
Nod nod
JOLT
AH! SO THE PAIRINGS DON'T MATTER ANYMORE, RIGHT?!

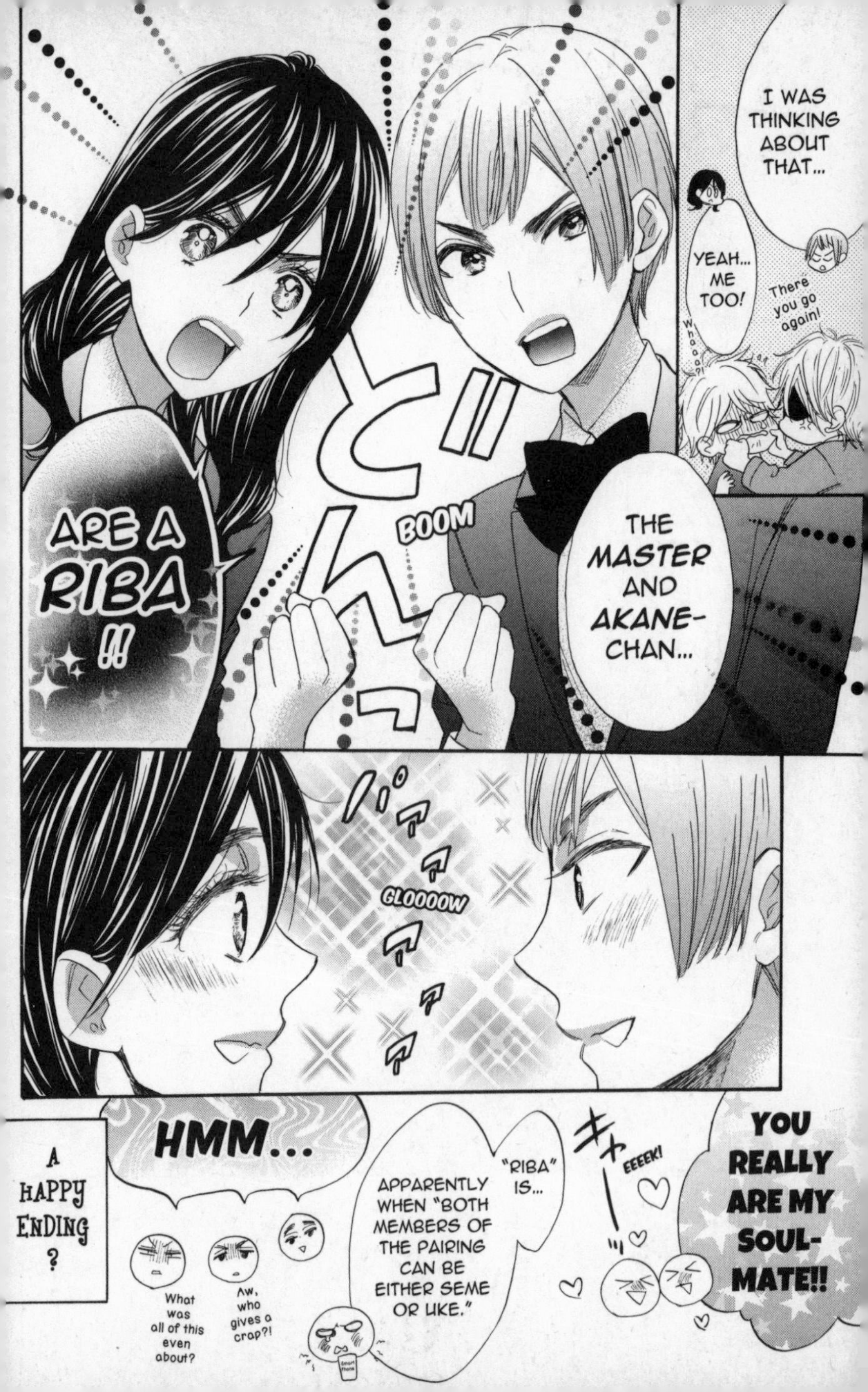

I WAS THINKING ABOUT THAT...
YEAH... ME TOO!
There you go again!
THE MASTER AND AKANE-CHAN...
BOOM
ARE A RIBA!!
GLOOOOW
YOU REALLY ARE MY SOUL-MATE!!
EEEEK!
"RIBA" IS...
APPARENTLY WHEN "BOTH MEMBERS OF THE PAIRING CAN BE EITHER SEME OR UKE."
HMM...
Aw, who gives a crap?!
What was all of this even about?
A HAPPY ENDING?

TO BE CONTINUED
IN VOLUME 7 OF

KiSS HiM,
NOT ME!

AFTERWORD

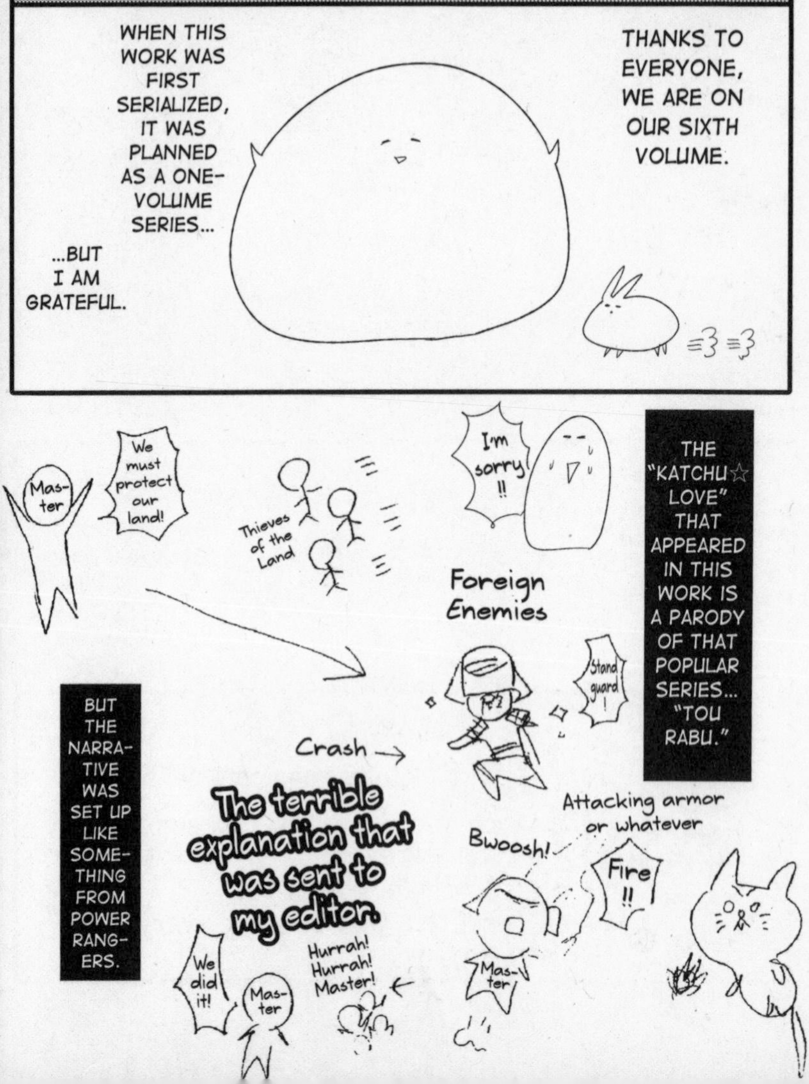

THANKS TO EVERYONE, WE ARE ON OUR SIXTH VOLUME.
WHEN THIS WORK WAS FIRST SERIALIZED, IT WAS PLANNED AS A ONE-VOLUME SERIES...
...BUT I AM GRATEFUL.
THE "KATCHU☆LOVE" THAT APPEARED IN THIS WORK IS A PARODY OF THAT POPULAR SERIES... "TOU RABU."
I'm sorry!!
Foreign Enemies
Thieves of the Land
We must protect our land!
Master
Stand guard!
Crash
BUT THE NARRATIVE WAS SET UP LIKE SOMETHING FROM POWER RANGERS.
Attacking armor or whatever
Fire!!
Bwoosh!
Master
The terrible explanation that was sent to my editor.
Hurrah! Hurrah! Master!
Master
We did it!

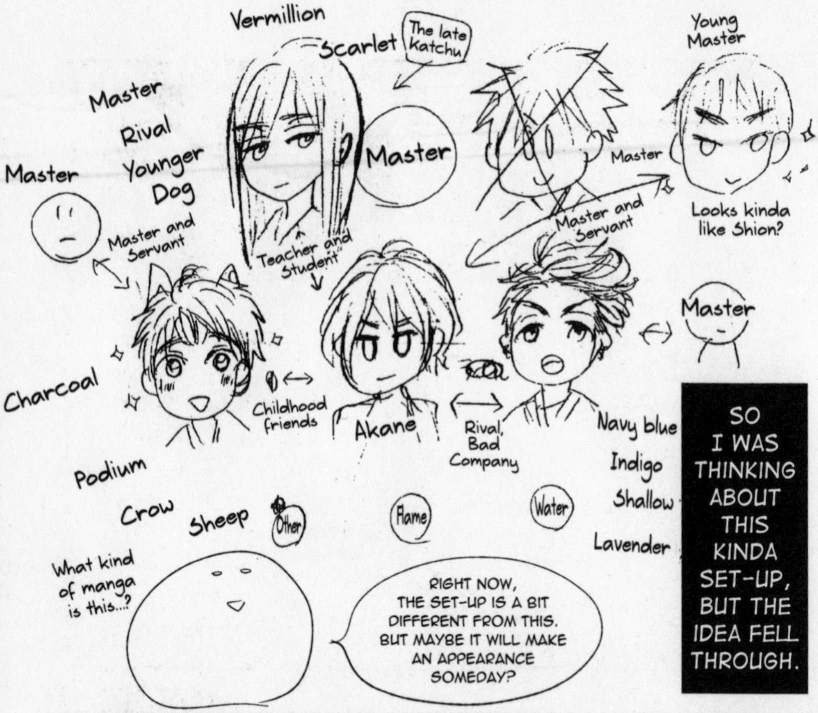
SO I WAS THINKING ABOUT THIS KINDA SET-UP, BUT THE IDEA FELL THROUGH.
Young Master
Looks kinda like Shion?
Master
Master and Servant
The late Katchu
Scarlet
Vermillion
Master
Master
Rival
Younger
Dog
Master
Master and Servant
Teacher and Student
Charcoal
Childhood friends
Akane
Rival, Bad Company
Navy blue
Indigo
Shallow
Lavender
Podium
Crow
Sheep
Other
Flame
Water
What kind of manga is this...?
RIGHT NOW, THE SET-UP IS A BIT DIFFERENT FROM THIS. BUT MAYBE IT WILL MAKE AN APPEARANCE SOMEDAY?

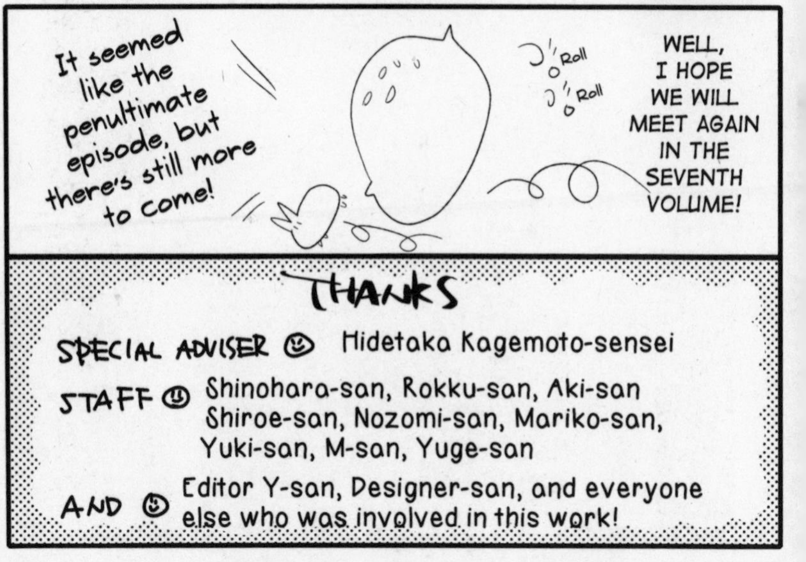
WELL, I HOPE WE WILL MEET AGAIN IN THE SEVENTH VOLUME!
Roll
Roll
It seemed like the penultimate episode, but there's still more to come!

THANKS

SPECIAL ADVISER Hidetaka Kagemoto-sensei

STAFF Shinohara-san, Rokku-san, Aki-san
Shiroe-san, Nozomi-san, Mariko-san,
Yuki-san, M-san, Yuge-san

AND Editor Y-san, Designer-san, and everyone else who was involved in this work!

AUTHOR'S NOTE

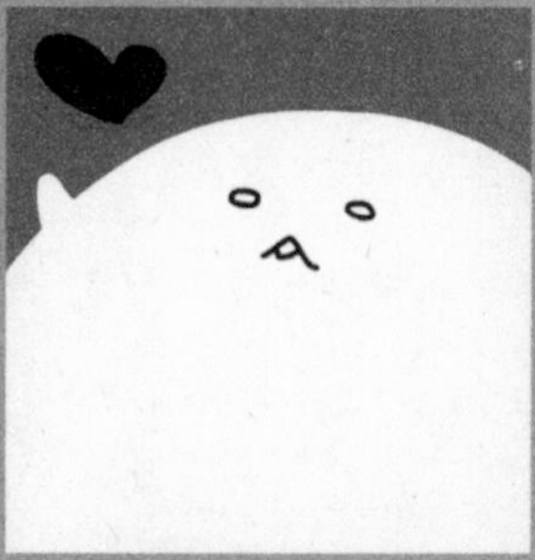

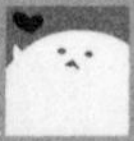

I DROPPED AND BROKE
MY SMARTPHONE THAT
I BOUGHT BARELY SIX
MONTHS AGO.
I DEFINITELY...SHOULD
HAVE HAD A COVER
ON IT... (TEARS)

-JUNKO

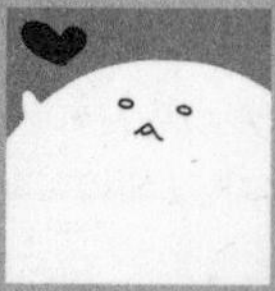

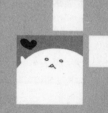

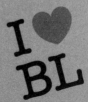

I ♥ BL

Translation Notes

Garigari-kun, page 9

Garigari-kun is the brandname and mascot for a line of popsicles produced by the ice cream maker, Akagi Nyugo Co., Ltd. Garigari-kun popsicles have been made since 1981 and because of their low price and large variety of flavors, they continue to be one of Japan's favorite cooled treats. The *garigari* of Garigari-kun is the crunching sound you would make when biting into one of their icy bars and the mascot is known by his huge mouth, which he uses to chow down on popsicles.

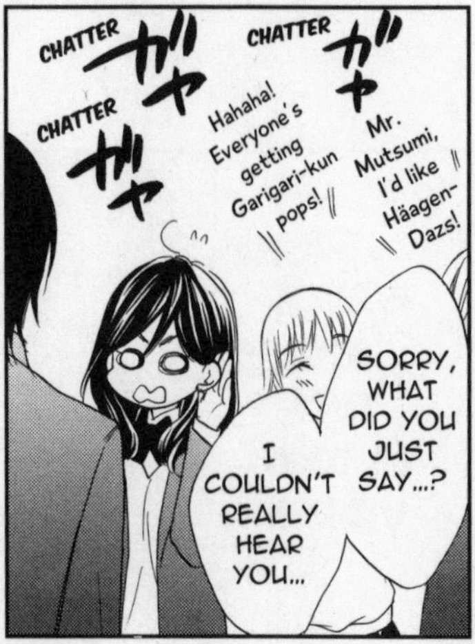
CHATTER
ガヤ
Mr. Mutsumi, I'd like Häagen-Dazs!
CHATTER
ガヤ
Hahaha! Everyone's getting Garigari-kun pops!
CHATTER
ガヤ
SORRY, WHAT DID YOU JUST SAY...?
I COULDN'T REALLY HEAR YOU...

Ono no Imoko and Soga no Umako, page 22

Ono no Imoko was a famous Japanese diplomat during Japan's Asuka period (538-710 AD). Soga no Umako was an individual who was active in politics and the promotion of Buddhism also during the same Asuka period.

Otome-game, page 49

Otome games (literally "maiden games") are video games, usually with visual novel style gameplay on computers, phones, and handheld consoles, that are targeted to female consumers. These games almost always have a female protagonist and multiple male characters with which the player can develop a romantic relationship through different story "routes." Otome games often have historical settings or involve supernatural elements such as vampires or werewolves.

Sakana-kun, page 53

Sakana-kun (real name: Masayuki Miyazawa) is a famous ichthyologist (fish researcher/expert) and television personality. He is easily identified by his fish hat, which resembles a blue-spotted boxfish. Sakana-kun has an extreme love of fish and is often featured on various talk, variety, and quiz shows as the resident fish expert.

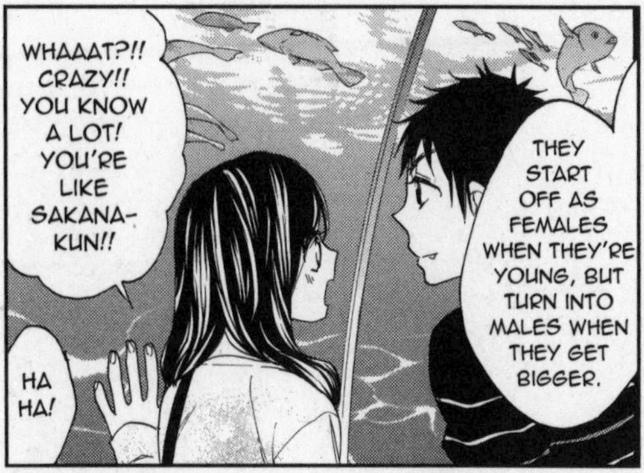
THEY START OFF AS FEMALES WHEN THEY'RE YOUNG, BUT TURN INTO MALES WHEN THEY GET BIGGER.
WHAAAT?!! CRAZY!! YOU KNOW A LOT! YOU'RE LIKE SAKANA-KUN!!
HA HA!

Sengoku Period, page 87

The Sengoku period, which is sometimes called the Warring States Period, took place between 1467 and 1603. During this time, the Emperor of Japan was largely a figurehead and true power rested with the Shogunate (military dictatorship). Despite the Shogun, many feudal lords (Daimyo) refused to unify under a central government and fought amongst themselves over land, political influence, and control over trade. The Warring States Period ended when Japan was unified under the warlord Tokugawa Ieyasu and the nominal Tokugawa Shogunate. Because of the political intrigue and famous historical figures that existed during this time, the Sengoku Period is a very popular and romanticized era in fiction, including gaming and anime.

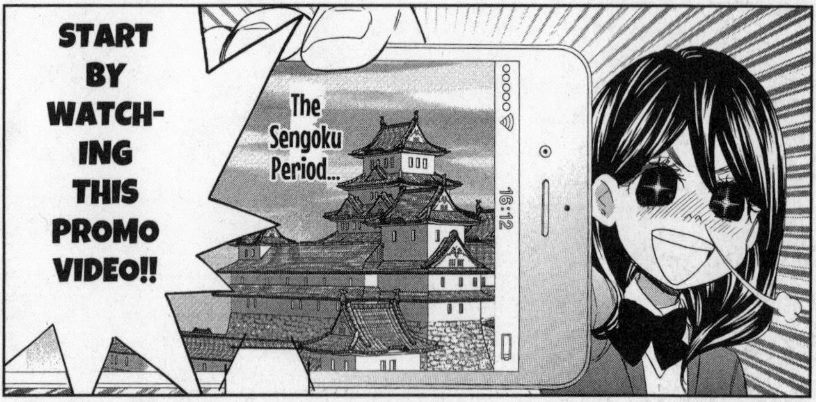

START BY WATCHING THIS PROMO VIDEO!!
The Sengoku Period...
16:12

Tou Rabu, page 154

Tou Rabu is an abbreviated version of the free-to-play collectible card game and upcoming anime, *Touken Ranbu* (EN: Wild Dance of Swords). The gameplay of *Tou Rabu* is simple and based on collecting cards that represent anthropomorphized versions of legendary swords, depicted as attractive young men. The game became extremely popular with female players, thanks in part not only to fujoshi who latched onto the character designs, but to a subculture of female history buffs, called *reki-jo* (short for *rekishi-josei* or "history women").

A Kodansha Comics Trade Paperback Original.

Kiss Him, Not Me volume 6 copyright © 2015 Junko
English translation copyright © 2016 Junko

Published in the United States by Kodansha Comics,
an imprint of Kodansha USA Publishing, LLC, New York.

Publication rights for this English edition arranged through Kodansha Ltd.,
Tokyo.

First published in Japan in 2015 by Kodansha Ltd., Tokyo, as *Watashi Ga
Motete Dousunda* volume 6.

ISBN 978-1-63236-265-0

Printed in the United States of America.

www.kodanshacomics.com

9 8 7 6 5 4 3 2 1

Translation: David Rhie
Lettering: Hiroko Mizuno
Editing: Ajani Oloye
Kodansha Comics edition cover design: Phil Balsman